George F. Root,
Civil War Songwriter

George F. Root, Civil War Songwriter

A Biography

P.H. Carder

McFarland & Company, Inc., Publishers
Jefferson, North Carolina, and London

LIBRARY OF CONGRESS CATALOGUING-IN-PUBLICATION DATA

Carder, Polly.
George F. Root, Civil War songwriter : a biography / P.H. Carder.
    p.   cm.
Includes bibliographical references and index.

ISBN 978-0-7864-3374-2
softcover : 50# alkaline paper ∞

1. Root, George F. (George Frederick), 1820–1895.
2. Composers—United States—Biography. I. Title.
ML410.R68C37   2008
782.0092—dc22   2008017579
[B]

British Library cataloguing data are available

©2008 P. H. Carder. All rights reserved

No part of this book may be reproduced or transmitted in any form or by any means, electronic or mechanical, including photocopying or recording, or by any information storage and retrieval system, without permission in writing from the publisher.

On the cover: This photograph of George Root is attributed to John Carbutt and dated 1868 (Hanzel Galleries, Chicago).

Manufactured in the United States of America

McFarland & Company, Inc., Publishers
  Box 611, Jefferson, North Carolina 28640
  www.mcfarlandpub.com

Acknowledgments

Grateful acknowledgment is offered to the following:

Dena J. Epstein, past president of the Music Library Association, for helping me to "leave no stone unturned," Mary Rubenstein of North Reading, Massachusetts, for sharing her genealogical research on the Root family and on the history of Willow Farm; Charles Woodman Root, a great-grandson of George Root, for access to the journal of Frederick F. Root and to several letters, and for his reminiscences about the family; Lief H. Carter, a great-great-grandson of George Root, for access to some of the photographs, to "A Little History of a Large Family," to George Root's letter to his sister Helen, and to his copy of *The Trumpet of Reform;* William C. Davis for reading the manuscript and for his constructive and greatly valued comments; Mary Elizabeth Lindon for her expertise and patience in correcting the style of the manuscript; Spencer Hall for digitizing many of the illustrations; my husband, A. W. Carder, for his continuing interest and support in researching Root's life and collecting his works; New York Public Library at Lincoln Center for use of *The New York Musical Review and Gazette* (with its various title changes); the staff of the Chicago History Museum Research Center; the staff of the Newberry Library, Chicago; the Music Division of the Library of Congress; the British Library for microfilm copies of some of Root's British publications; and the Interlibrary Loan Department, Virginia Tech.

Table of Contents

Acknowledgments v
Introduction 1

1. Sheffield, Willow Farm and Boston 1820–1844 — 5
2. New York and Paris 1844–1851 — 22
3. Public Taste at Mid-Century 1851–1855 — 37
4. Music for the Popular Market 1855–1861 — 67
5. The First Gun Is Fired 1861–1863 — 101
6. Rally Once Again 1863–1865 — 129
7. A Future Full of Promise 1865–1871 — 165
8. Music for the People 1871–1895 — 185

Appendix: Songs 199
Chapter Notes 211
Bibliography 227
Index 233

Introduction

In the summer of 1862 the Civil War was not going well for the Union. The people had responded to the calls for volunteers; they had flocked to war rallies; they had supported the war effort with men and money. Still the army was not winning as many battles as expected. President Lincoln called for more volunteers to fill the ranks that had been thinned by casualties. George Root's answer to Lincoln's call was "The Battle Cry of Freedom." People referred to it by its most memorable words, "Rally Round the Flag."

President Lincoln heard the song again and again, most memorably on an evening in March 1864, when he took his son Tad to Grover's Theater. The place was crowded with fashionably dressed women, congressmen, visitors, and newcomers to Washington. Throughout the audience the predominant color was army blue. Coming to the theater this evening was Tad's idea. He had seen tonight's play, *The Seven Sisters*, more than once. He was well acquainted with Mr. Grover and the people who worked in the theater. Grover said that during the long rehearsals Tad spent more time on stage than in a seat, and sometimes he helped the stagehands.[1]

The Seven Sisters, billed as a "spectacular extravaganza," was a play that called for added scenes depicting current events and accompanied by current popular songs. On this evening a leading male soloist, surrounded by a chorus of men in uniform and women in beautiful costumes, was to sing George F. Root's "The Battle Cry of Freedom." The chorus would sing the refrains and the audience would join in.

Lincoln didn't notice that Tad had slipped out of the presidential box. Familiar with the backstage area, Tad went to a wardrobe and found an army blouse, much too large for him, and a cap. The cast took their place, and the soloist, John McDonough, sang the first verse.

> Yes, we'll rally round the flag, boys,
> We'll rally once again....

McDonough noticed an extra singer at the end of the front line; he saw that it was Tad and handed him a flag. After the second verse[2] McDonough brought Tad to the center of the stage and in recognition of the president, repeated the refrain of the song with the first line of another popular song thrown in.

> We are coming, Father Abraham, three hundred thousand more,
> Shouting the battle-cry of freedom,
> While we rally round the flag, boys, rally once again,
> Shouting the battle-cry of freedom.

Whispers swept across the audience. Someone had recognized the president's son on stage. Lincoln leaned forward, rocking with laughter. The flag in ten-year-old Tad's hands was large and heavy, and as the song went on McDonough had to help him wave it. The huge crowd stood and joined the singing. As the song ended an army officer led three cheers for "Father Abraham and his boy."[3] Lincoln stood and, with utmost dignity, bowed. The curtain came down.

On an October morning in 1838, George Root left his farm home to work and study in Boston, where fortunes were about to be made in music books, in sheet music, in music as a business. He started as a teacher's assistant, tending the fires and keeping the studio in order, and he began to teach singing classes. In 1853 he found that he could write a hit song. In the same year he wrote a musical play that was a huge success. He came to realize that, in his words, "Mine must be the people's" music.[4]

By the spring of 1861 Root was nationally known as a songwriter, a composer of hymn tunes, a compiler of music books, and a teacher. He was a partner in Root & Cady, the most promising music business of the northwest, selling sheet music and musical instruments from fifes to pianos and publishing songs and music books. He had taught hundreds of people in music classes across the country. His knowledge of people and their preferences was the best preparation he could have for his wartime role. In his words, "When anything happened that could be voiced in a song, or when the heart of the Nation was moved by particular circumstances or conditions caused by the war, I wrote what I thought would then express the emotions of the soldiers or the people."[5]

After the war Root's music reflected the era's values, its quirks, its trends, its people and events. Today it illustrates the roles of religion and morals in education; it reflects what people were reading: reformers like Harriet Beecher Stowe, poets like Bret Harte, novelists like Fanny Fern. It documents historic events: the Chicago Fire, the golden spike that joined railroads east and west, election campaigns, and the assassination of President Lincoln. It documents reform movements: temperance, social causes, and the organization of farm labor. Root described his role in American life as making music for the people. As the *Chicago Tribune* claimed when he died in 1895, "His life work is part of the history of the American people."[6]

1

Sheffield, Willow Farm and Boston, 1820–1844

From his earliest days George Root seemed to be sensitive to music. Other babies fell asleep to the sound of a lullaby; this infant listened wide-eyed to his mother's singing.[1] His love for music was inherited from both sides of his family through several generations. But music was a demanding art, as seen in the experience of Josiah Flynt, who was very probably a distant relative of George's mother, Sarah Flint Root. In 1661, when he was a freshman at Harvard, Josiah wrote his uncle Leonard Hoar, later president of Harvard, asking for a fiddle from London. Uncle Leonard refused the request and counseled Josiah against taking too strong an interest in music. If you are not an excellent musician, he warned, it will be worthless; if you are excellent, it will take so much of your time, and occupy your mind to such an extent that you will achieve little else. There would be no profit in it unless Josiah made fiddling his trade or profession.[2] Uncle Leonard did not need to mention the questionable respectability of music as a lifework. It was still questionable when George Root chose it.

Sarah Flint Root was born in North Reading, Massachusetts, April 27, 1797, one of six daughters, all considered good singers. A shy girl with light hair and large gray eyes, she was remembered for her pleasant disposition.[3] She attended school in Andover, Massachusetts, five miles from her home. When Sarah was 18 her father suggested that she put her schooling to use, and she began as a teacher in Andover.

Sarah's sister Hannah married Samuel Train,[4] a Boston merchant. On her visits to their home Sarah heard the Boston Handel and Haydn Society's renowned choral performances and sampled other fine musical offerings in the city. She enjoyed the social life of the Train family and attended the prominent Park Street Church, where Samuel Train was a deacon. Sometimes Sarah went with her sister's stepson Elijah and his friend Nat Willis when they drove cows to the pasture on Boston Common.[5]

George Root's maternal grandfather, Daniel Flint, built and operated a tavern on the road to Boston, one of three taverns in North Reading, and lived there with his family. He was a farmer, a dealer in cattle, a member of the Constitutional Convention of 1820, a representative to the legislature in Boston and a selectman of the town of North Reading. Selectmen were chosen annually to manage the concerns of the town, which included providing for the poor. Music was an ongoing part of Daniel Flint's life. He led the choir of his church and taught singing schools. Sarah Flint enjoyed the winter evenings when students from the Andover seminary came to the Flint home to sing with the family in front of the fireplace.[6] Sarah's mother, Priscilla Flint, played a small bass viol, used in church to accompany the singing, and she sang well.[7]

Sarah Flint visited her sister Margaret Bradford in Sheffield, Massachusetts, and there she met Frederick Ferdinand Root. He was the squire's son, one of his daughters wrote later, and he lived in the finest house in the village. Like Sarah's father, he taught singing schools and led the choir in his church. Sarah's singing charmed Frederick; he proposed marriage to her more than once. They were married in North Reading on November 3, 1819. It was a cloudy day except for a burst of sunlight just as they were pronounced man and wife. Sarah wore a dress of dotted Swiss muslin; Frederick wore newly fashionable long pants instead of the traditional knee breeches. After the wedding they went on a sight-seeing trip to Boston with two other couples. Then Sarah and Frederick went home to Sheffield, 160 miles away. As a wedding gift, Frederick's father gave them a new house near his own home. Sarah's trousseau contained fine linen from Boston and coarser linen made of flax grown in her father's field, spun and woven at home. A blue and gold carpet for the parlor was made of wool from Sarah's father's sheep.[8]

George was their first child, a blue-eyed, sandy-haired boy born in Sheffield on August 30, 1820. Sarah wanted to name him Frederick Handel Root after the imminent composer best known for the oratorio *Messiah*. Her husband disliked the thought of two Fredericks in the house, and so the baby became George Frederick Root. Sarah engaged ten-year-old Hannah Rogers, a Native American on her mother's side, to care for the baby. Hannah worked for Sarah and her family for twenty years.[9]

In addition to a strong instinct for music, George Root inherited a strain of patriotism, an awareness of heritage, a respect for New Englanders and their achievements. The immigrant John Root had come to New England with a company of Puritans about 1640. A Sergeant George Flint had built a blockhouse in the early 1650s for defense against the Indians.[10] It had stood about a half-mile from the site of the farm where George Root would later grow up. George's father Frederick was a captain in the militia company at Sheffield, a service his family considered part of a young man's education. His mother was related to Israel Putnam, an officer in Washington's army.[11]

Another son, Ebenezer Towner Root, was born in 1822 to Sarah and Frederick Root. Towner, as he was called, had black hair and brown eyes. Unlike his brother George, the infant Towner slept peacefully during his mother's lullabies.[12]

In 1827 George's grandfather Azariah Root lost all his property. The house that had been his wedding gift to Frederick and Sarah had to be included in the sale of the estate. Such an economic mishap had nearly happened to Sarah's father, Daniel Flint. He was a prosperous farmer; occasionally he signed papers as security for neighbors. On one occasion the debtor failed to pay, and Flint's farm was to be sold to cover the indebtedness. Two men came from Boston to seize the property, but they came on Sunday. Flint knew it was illegal to seize property on the Sabbath. He did not lose the farm, and his granddaughter Mary, who described the incident in a memoir, could not say how the matter was settled. These incidents may have come to George Root's mind in later years when he faced decisions on business and legal matters.

When he heard of the loss of Sarah's and Frederick's house, Sarah's father, Daniel Flint, suggested that they come to North Reading and live on what he called the old Pratt place. It was on a tract of land that was settled before 1691.[13] Sarah would deeply miss the social life of Sheffield and particularly the company of the Bradfords, her sister and brother-in-law. It was difficult for Frederick Root, as well, to leave Sheffield—the social life, the church and community of which he had been a very active part. Adjusting to the new circumstances in North Reading would be particularly hard for him.

On the 160-mile journey from Sheffield, a friend drove the team with a wagonload of household goods while Frederick Root drove the carriage that held his family. They made the journey in September, staying in taverns along the way and stopping briefly at Sarah's parents' home. When they arrived at the old red house where they were to live, Sarah heated the brick oven and served her family baked apples and milk.[14]

In the eighteenth century Ephraim Pratt had built a tannery on this farm; it had long since fallen into disuse. Traces and partial foundations of the tannery — the vats, the dam and the sluiceway — remained. Sometime before 1790 Ephraim had built a narrow lane from the red house to the main road. A tan-bark base was laid with waste from the tanning process. This material dried, packed down and became a solid, all-weather surface.[15] Lined with willow trees, the narrow roadway was called the Willow Lane. In time the farm became known as Willow Farm. Frederick Root rebuilt the tannery and brought it back into production, forming a partnership with Putnam Flint, Sarah's brother. Frederick produced harnesses and other leather goods and Putnam sold them. Leather products were in demand, and Massachusetts was a center for their production. The tannery made this farm an interesting place to grow up. A horse walked in circles, grinding tanbark in a mill. Underneath, powered by water falling over a dam, two huge upright beams swung back and forth, washing the hides. The hides were moved from vat to vat, soaked and scraped and beaten.[16]

As soon as George Root was old enough, his father taught him to play an old-fashioned four-keyed flute. When he was eight, George played the flute at church. Frederick enjoyed taking him to a music store in Boston, where he was allowed to try playing different instruments. After he became a well-known teacher, George liked to say that by the time he was thirteen years old he could "play a tune" on as many as thirteen different instruments.[17] This did not include piano or organ.

Years later George's sister Mary described the parlor of the old red house at Willow Farm. She remembered the chintz-covered sofa and the attractive rush-bottomed chairs Frederick had made, the Franklin stove, and a table with twisted legs. There was a bookcase with green silk curtains inside its glass doors. The family's bass viol, used to accompany singing at church as well as at home, stood in the corner. George's flutes were kept on a table that stood under an old looking-glass.[18]

In late 1837 an economic panic closed factories all across the east.

The leather industry seemed to die. Frederick Root suffered the same loss that most of the New England leather industry did. The tannery had to be closed, and as George's sister recalled, "poverty came" to the family. Frederick's partner, Putnam Flint, took his family to Argentina and began raising sheep. In 1836 George's younger brother Towner was fourteen and

In January 1896, *New England Magazine* published Lydia Avery Coonley's article "George F. Root and His Songs." In it this drawing was captioned "Dr. Root's Home at North Reading." The family moved to Willow Farm in 1826. George Root's parents lived there year — round; each summer his brothers and sisters, with their families, gathered there. Root often commented about their love for this home. In his autobiography he wrote, "No palace ever gave kingly occupants greater pleasure."

Detail from a pen and ink drawing of Willow Farm. The artist and the date are unknown (courtesy North Reading Historical and Antiquarian Society, North Reading, Massachusetts).

not in the best of health. He was advised that an ocean voyage might be helpful, and so he went by ship to Argentina, joined uncle Putnam Flint and began tending sheep. With the tannery closed, Frederick Root decided to follow his partner and join his son Towner in Argentina.[19] While it was still dark one morning in the fall of 1837, Frederick said goodbye to his family and made his way to Boston. From there he sailed for Buenos Aires.

That New England businessmen would sail from Boston to Buenos Aires in search of economic opportunity was not entirely strange in the 1830s. New Englanders of this period are associated in memory with entrepreneurship and determination. One of them was the man George Root and his brothers and sisters called Uncle Train. He had made his fortune in hides and leather. His merchant ships sailed the seas over, Root's sister Mary wrote.[20]

George Root at 17 worked the farm in the spring of 1838 with the advice of his grandfather Daniel Flint. George was now the mainstay of his mother and his younger siblings. The family had moved to North

Reading with three children: George, Towner and Helen. Five more were born in North Reading: Mary in 1827, Sarah in 1829, Cynthia in 1833, William in 1835, and Frances in 1838.

In April 1838, George wrote his father in Buenos Aires about the family, the farm work and shoemaking in a poor economic year. The weather had been unusually mild; the family had gotten along comfortably through the past winter. George had made shoes until the spring planting season began. Shoemaking had not brought in any cash because of the hard times. In all likelihood the principle reason for the letter was to announce the birth of another daughter to Frederick and Sarah; George named her Frances Amelia. George reported on each of his siblings; they were all well, the younger ones growing fast. He described himself as almost six feet tall and weighing 160 pounds. Music was on his mind. He had improved "largely" on the flute; now he thought he was "a decent sort of a player."[21]

Duty weighed more heavily on him after his grandfather Daniel Flint died on June 5, 1838. Yet he felt compelled to pursue music as his life's work. He described the circumstances that led to this conclusion: "How many times I have walked, after the day's work was over, through dreary forest roads, to neighboring towns to exercise my musical powers with some embryo performer like myself...." Years later, looking back on his life, he wrote, "The dream of my life was to be a musician." He considered looking for work in a theater orchestra, playing second flute. This would not be reputable, according to public opinion of the time, so family and friends opposed the idea. "I knew I should have to fight my way," he recalled.[22] Only his mother, Sarah, encouraged him.

During the summer of 1838, Sarah Root's friend Annette Goodwin came from Boston to spend a few weeks in North Reading. Goodwin's brother, a friend and co-worker of Towner's, had been murdered in Argentina by thieves. Annette described some of the musical offerings she enjoyed in Boston and Harmony Hall, where the Musical Education Society met under the direction of A. N. Johnson. Root thought "it would be heaven on earth to be in the midst of such opportunities." Soon after she left he went to western Massachusetts with a friend. He hadn't meant to stop in Boston on the return trip, but he missed a connection in Worcester, and Worcester had a music store. Instruments, instruction books, sheet music filled the place. Root stepped inside, and as he said, by the time he came to himself the train had gone. As a result he spent some time in

Boston on the way home. He decided to go to Harmony Hall and ask A. N. Johnson if there were any possibility of an opening for him there. He would always remember climbing those stairs, knocking at that door. Most memorable was the "somewhat astonished" look on Johnson's face. "What he said afterward of that interview, not being very complimentary either to my personal appearance or my modesty, I omit," Root confessed in writing later. Johnson asked him whether he could sing or play the piano. He could not. Johnson advised him to learn to play the piano first. Root could practice while Johnson was out of the studio, which would be most of the time. Johnson needed someone to stay in the room, to take care of the fires and the general order of the place, to answer questions about his engagements and to make himself generally useful. Root could board at Johnson's house; his pay would be three dollars a week. Root considered that "a great deal of money" at the time. He planned from the beginning to send money to the family at Willow Farm. Through the years Root was grateful to A. N. Johnson. "I have thought many times since how extraordinary it was in Mr. Johnson to take me as he did, for, from his own representation, I could not have been a very promising subject," he wrote.[23]

Normally reserved in his speech and in his writing, Root described the sheer joy he felt on the way home in the old stagecoach from Boston after his successful interview. "I was in another world," he wrote. "The ride in the wonderful [railroad] cars was nothing to this. That was on iron rails, this was in the golden air. The dusty old towns through which we passed were beautiful as never before ... I was going where the air was filled with music, and pent-up desires and ambitions could have unlimited freedom." He was leaving his mother with six younger children to care for; certainly there would be hard times. Grandfather Daniel Flint had feared that the company of other musicians might lead a young man astray. But George's mother knew what going to Boston meant to him; she wanted him to have his chance. She advised him to go, and she asked him to learn a tune for her, the words of which kept running through her mind: "Why will ye waste on trifling cares the life that God's compassion spares?"[24]

Root was to begin work October 1, 1838. On the appropriate day he wheeled his trunk down to the end of the Willow Lane, about a quarter of a mile, and waited an hour for the stagecoach that ran every morning. On this, of all days, the stage did not come. Finally a neighbor drove him the six miles to a new railroad stop, where he boarded a train. Arriving at

A. N. Johnson's home in Boston's North End, Root was ready to begin what he called "the duties and pleasures" of his "new vocation."[25]

A. N. Johnson's music studio, called Harmony Hall, was a light, cheerful room with a piano at one end and an office desk at the other. Piano lessons were a priority and they began immediately. Thinking back on it later, Root explained that a piano in a country town was a rarity in 1838. Even in Boston, a person who could play as well then as hundreds of young people all across the country played by mid-century would have attracted a great deal of attention. Beginning piano lessons at the age of eighteen was impractical. Root described himself as being in a chronic state of astonishment that his hands would not do what he clearly saw must be done. Each succession of chords must be gone over a great many times before it would go smoothly. Still, he found making musical sounds on the keyboard delightful. Using Johnson's published method of instruction for piano, Root practiced the hymn tunes that had so impressed him as part of the current church music reform. He wrote later that these hymn tunes moved him as no music had done before. Fairly soon, Johnson insisted that Root accompany the singing of hymns at evening church services. After about six weeks a young man came to the studio inquiring about piano lessons. Much to Root's amazement, Johnson assigned the young man to him for his introductory lessons. "What I lacked in experience I made up in good will and attention," Root commented later.[26]

Some six or seven weeks after Root began his work in Boston, his employer proposed a new one-year agreement at what Root called a very considerable increase in pay. News of this event went to Willow Farm with all possible speed. Root's first visit to the farm that Thanksgiving was indeed a happy one. At about the same time Lowell Mason, the leading figure in church music in Boston, advertised that new members would be admitted to the chorus of the Boston Academy of Music. Johnson advised Root to audition; singing in Boston's most prestigious chorus would be excellent training. Root had sung the bass part in hymns, but as he said, family members usually suggested that he play along on his flute instead. He passed the audition, and afterward Mason asked him to join his Bowdoin Street Church choir as well. The Bowdoin Street choir was virtually without equal in Root's opinion. He was already committed to Johnson's church choir, but the invitation made up his mind about the issue of his voice. Mason's invitation must mean that he could succeed as a singer.[27]

Not long afterward Johnson advised Root to study voice with George

James Webb. He explained that private voice teaching was very profitable, and he thought Root could do that kind of work. In Root's opinion, George James Webb was the best voice teacher in Boston and an accomplished organist. At their first lesson Webb gave Root's voice a thorough test and assigned some exercises for practice. At the second lesson Webb, pleasantly surprised, said "I believe you *will* learn to sing." Root fully intended to do so, he told Webb. Webb admitted that at their first lesson he had been extremely doubtful that Root could become a vocalist.[28]

After he came to be regarded as a promising singer, Root sang in a performance of Neukomm's oratorio *David*. It was a performance he remembered as especially entertaining, though unintentionally so. He sang the role of Goliath, written for bass voice, in a duet with a tenor who sang the role of David. Colburn, the tenor, was more than six feet tall and weighed, by Root's estimate, almost three hundred pounds. In the course of their duet Root had to sing, in his most ponderous tone, "I can not war with boys." Both the audience and Colburn, who had a most infectious laugh, broke up. The singers finished their duet, but Root said it could not be called an unqualified success.[29]

For George Root, Boston was a place where the air did seem to be what he called "filled with music." Some of the most interesting concert artists came from Europe. The violinist Herwig amazed his audiences by playing harmonics — unusually high sounds — that made the violin sound like a fine wind instrument. The eccentric Norwegian violinist and composer Ole Bull and the English pianist and songwriter Jane Sloman also had great success, and in the years that followed the quality of concert performances rose steadily. He heard the elderly John Braham, who, as Root explained, had been the greatest English tenor for a generation. His voice was expansive and at the same time intense.[30] The grand choral music of the Boston Handel and Haydn Society, which Sarah Root had enjoyed so much, was readily available. Haydn's oratorio *The Creation* and Handel's *Messiah* were performed fairly often.

In 1839 Root heard what were for him the most important public performances of those days, the concerts of Henry Russell. Russell's songs, and the way he sang them, shaped Root's views on popular songs and on the relationship between singer and audience. Unlike most of the concert artists of the time, Russell composed virtually all the songs he sang and played his own accompaniments. He set to music the words of a poem called "A Life on the Ocean Wave," which became one of the most popular songs in the country by 1839. Russell decided to write descriptive songs after he heard the compelling orator Henry Clay, who had a remarkable ability to move an audience.[31] Russell appealed to his audience's affection for home and familiar surroundings with songs like "The Old Arm Chair," "My Mother's Bible," and "Woodman, Spare That Tree." Some of his songs were melodramatic or theatrical, like "The Ship on Fire." He addressed relevant issues, such as the condition of Native Americans and enslaved people. He wrote about what was on the public mind, addressing social conditions that would hardly seem to be the material of popular music. Among musically sophisticated listeners, his songs were controversial. But hearing Russell's beautiful baritone voice and the accompaniments he played himself made an indelible impression on Root. He recalled that songs like "The Maniac" and "The Gambler's Wife" made people cry when Russell sang them. Root was disappointed when he heard that Russell was amused by his audience's weeping; he commented that a singer should treat the hearer's emotions with respect. A man might sing convincingly, in a heartfelt manner, about the delights of being a farmer (a personal example), when in fact that was not his preference at all. But a scornful attitude was not acceptable in an artist. Root admitted that he worked harder than ever before to be able to play and sing Russell's songs as well as Russell did. In the first few months of hearing them, Root said, they filled him with delight. They were just what he needed as a step in the process of learning and relating to more sophisticated music. In less than a year, in his words, he "craved something higher." At the time, "higher" music meant more classical, more advanced in harmony, rhythm and melody. Schubert's songs came next. Root felt that no amount of simpler music would have kept him from studying and enjoying the songs of Schubert, because they met his musical needs. He came to the conclusion that "emotional or aesthetic benefit by music can come to a person only through music that he likes. By that alone can he grow musically."[32]

The quality of immediacy in Root's Civil War songs, picturing events and capturing feelings, can be traced at least partly to Henry Russell's "descriptive" songs. Russell wrote and sang about what he saw around him. "The Maniac" was a response to cruel conditions in mental hospitals. "The Gambler's Wife" spelled out the misery of a deserted mother and child. Russell romanticized daily experience in a way that influenced American popular music and lasted at least through the Civil War years.

Root had arrived in Boston in the midst of a reform movement in church music. The long-term outcomes would be new hymns and new ways of teaching people to sing them. Root remembered well the traditional singing schools, local classes taught by local singers like his father and grandfather. In all likelihood his grandfather Flint taught the old-fashioned syllable names, only four of them completing the scale: faw, so, law, faw, so, law, mi, faw. While Root was still at home, a new system from Boston came into use. Each scale tone had its own name: do, re, mi, fa, so, la, si, do.* Lowell Mason was credited for instituting the reforms in church music.[33] Together with George James Webb, Mason had opened the Boston Academy of Music in 1833. Their purpose was to teach the fundamentals of vocal music to the general public and by doing so, raise the standards of church music. In a comparatively short time Root became an associate of Webb and Mason in teaching vocal music.

The flute had been Root's first musical instrument. While he was in Boston he took flute lessons and taught them. He decided to organize a flute club. Ten flutists played pieces arranged in six parts. They played popular marches, quicksteps, and waltzes. More a novelty than a serious performing group, the flute club played in nearby towns and once in a concert at the Odeon, where, to Root's satisfaction, they were encored.[34]

Looking back, Root tried to remember when he taught his first singing-school. He decided it must have been during his first winter in Boston, 1838–39. The class was held in A. N. Johnson's Harmony Hall; the students were young people who wanted to sing in the Musical Education Society chorus. Root had watched Johnson teach a few times, but he had no orderly method of his own. He called this first attempt experimental, and he felt it must have been crude. In spite of his doubts he taught a large class in Boston's North End the following autumn that lasted almost all winter.[35]

Music classes in public schools were unheard-of until the late 1830s. Lowell Mason began to experiment with such classes in 1837, teaching the first year without pay in order to prove his point. The second year Mason and one assistant taught in all the elementary schools of Boston. The third year Root taught in five of the schools, each school offering two half-hour lessons per week.[36]

Looking back on his beginning, Root felt he should explain his "getting on so fast in a city like Boston." Church music was emerging from

---

*At the time, and for years afterward, the seventh tone was si; "ti" is a later usage.

what he called the "florid but crude melodies and the imperfect harmonies" of earlier years. Lowell Mason had begun what Root called a revolution in hymns and hymn-singing. In Root's words, "Our choirs produced the new kind of simple, sweet music that went to the hearts of the people." At the same time Mason had begun to use new methods of teaching, adapted from European methods, that Root believed were far better and more attractive than anything previously seen. Those who began using the new methods early had a great advantage, he thought. In his words, "We had no competition and were sought for on every hand."[37]

While Root's work was going so well, his father's work in Argentina was not. On March 15, 1839, his father wrote an anguished letter and addressed it simply to "Mr. George F. Root, N. Reading, Mass — U. S. A." Frederick was hanging on in South America in the hope of earning money, in his words "running the risk of worse times in hopes that better will follow." He felt isolated, he had gotten only a handful of letters, and he was in a dangerous place. Ports were blockaded and there were rumors of a revolution. George's younger brother Towner had been seriously ill, and their father had decided to send him home. Towner had lost all his personal property — his clothes, his flute, the "pistol knife" his father had given him, and the "Church Harmony" book he cherished — probably in the robbery during which his friend Daniel was killed. Deeply discouraged, Frederick could not say when he would see his son George again. He asked George to care for his mother and to see that the younger children were educated. He urged him to write immediately, and said that he was known in the northern part of Buenos Aires as "the Americano."[38]

One of George Root's strongest incentives in his early career was the realization that his father might return from South America and find that his experiment with a musical career in Boston had been a failure. He had left his mother and the children at Willow Farm after his father's departure, and now music required all his time and effort. In the second year of his employment, 1839–40, his father returned and George was relieved that no fault was found.[39] While her husband and both her older sons were away at work, Sarah Root found ways to manage Willow Farm. Several neighbors planted and harvested crops on her land in exchange for a share of the produce. The upper floor of the tannery building was finished and rented as dwelling space. One of the tenants supervised the farming. At some point the schoolmaster boarded at Sarah's home. Towner came home from South America, and George found work for him in a Boston carpet store. Both brothers returned home occasionally. Their sister Mary remembered that on these visits their mother had "a quiet discussion of finances" with George, and that "singing and good cheer" followed.[40]

Mary Root described the way their father's two-year stay in South America ended. Frederick Root knew the ports of Buenos Aires and Montevideo were blockaded by the French. He decided to risk running the blockade as a passenger on a privateer. The ship was captured, and everyone on it taken to France and put in prison. Three months later his being a Freemason led him to a friend who obtained his release. He had lost his money and his clothes. He worked his passage to New York and borrowed money from an uncle there to buy clothes and pay his fare home.[41]

George Root had begun playing the organ fairly early in his association with A. N. Johnson. At first he played only the final hymn, always chosen for its simplicity and familiarity, in the Congregational service where Johnson was the regular organist. For an organ student, this was an ideal way to begin. His first independent engagement as organist was in Charlestown, just across the river from Boston, where he played for six months.[42] For a while he and Johnson shared the work of organist, each of them playing for what Root called a half-day.

According to Root's memory, it was during his second year at Harmony Hall (1839–40) that a fine-looking old gentleman knocked at the door unexpectedly and explained that, although it might seem strange for a man of his age, he wished to learn to play the organ. He would be in Boston only for a short time, but while he was there Root began his lessons. His name was Abbott; meeting him would make a difference in Root's life within a very few years. Root described him as a typical New Englander of the best kind in those days, practicing all the virtues of the Puritans without their hardness.[43] Mr. Abbott's oldest son, Jacob, wrote a number of books, fiction and non-fiction, for young people. His *Rollo* series of 28 books taught young readers geography and history through the fictitious adventures of a boy called Rollo, whose "Uncle George" infused the lessons with examples of honesty, hard work and self-improvement. After Root became a member of a boat club, he invited Jacob Abbott for a boat ride. Both the boat and the club to which it belonged were called the "Shawmut," after what Root said was the traditional Indian name for Boston. Jacob Abbott was greatly interested in the way the boat worked and in the nautical terms used to direct the ten oarsmen. Root and the rest of the crew went through all the boating maneuvers they knew for Abbott's benefit. All this became part of a book in Abbott's *Rollo* series.[44]

The work arrangements between George Root and A. N. Johnson were modeled on business principles rather than a teacher-student relationship. Johnson had received rigorous business training in a large hardware store in Boston before he made music a full-time occupation. Root was his apprentice at first; near the end of 1838 Johnson suggested a new agreement for one year, during which Root was his confidential clerk. As Root remembered it, he became Johnson's partner in 1840. For the next five years Johnson was to have two-thirds of their combined earnings and Root one-third. Johnson was to spend a year studying in Germany, the monetary arrangement staying the same while he was out of the country. Soon after the partnership agreement of 1840 Johnson became organist and choir director at Park Street Church, the largest and most important Congregational church in Boston. This was the church Root's mother had visited with her sister and brother-in-law, Hannah and Samuel Train. Johnson continued as organist at another large Congregational church as well, and now as Root explained it, Johnson was to play half a day at each church and Root was to play the other half. Evidently the organist also served as choir director in each case. Soon after he assumed responsibility for the music at Park Street Church, Johnson decided to give up the studio at Harmony Hall and take three rooms in the church's fine basement that looked out on Boston Common. Root reminded him that this would cost quite a bit of money, but Johnson's plan included hanging out an attractive sign, raising fees, and taking a few new students. This would increase business more than enough pay the added expense. The view, looking out under the large trees on the historic Boston Common, was picturesque and beautiful.[45]

As Root remembered it, it was in 1841 that A. N. Johnson went to Germany, and Root took charge of the two choirs they had shared, and one of their students played, in Root's words, "the other half-day." Root changed his residence to the Marlboro Hotel. He described it as a temperance and religious house where the landlord conducted family prayers in the public parlor every morning.[46]

Root's training as a church musician was a combination of apprenticeship, study at the Boston Academy of Music Teacher's Class, private lessons, personal experience, and criticism. In one case, the criticism was both uncomfortable and helpful. On a Sunday afternoon he was in the parlor of the Marlboro when a visitor began to ask questions about the churches in the neighborhood, about the organs and the music. He had been at Park Street Church that afternoon, he said, and the organist had played so loudly that the voices of the choir were almost drowned. Root explained that in summer, some of the leading singers were away and the organist played louder in order to give added support to the remaining singers. The visitor did not seem to think this was an adequate explanation, and he asked the question Root dreaded most. "Do you know who the organist is at Park Street Church?" Root's fellow boarders, looking mischievous, crowded around to listen. If they had not been there, Root thought he might have found some way to avoid embarrassment, but he had to admit that he was the organist. After quite a lot of discussion, Root and the visitor, who was a lawyer and an amateur organist, reached an accord. The following day the two of them visited Boston churches and saw several fine pipe organs. Several years later this gentleman offered cordial assistance when Root, Mason and Webb held a musical convention in his hometown, Troy, New York.[47]

At one point in Root's Boston experience, criticism of his work as director of a church choir proved valuable, though stressful, and left him feeling appreciative. Lowell Mason left the position of music director at the Bowdoin Street Church to move to the Winter Street Church.[48] Root was left in what had been Mason's place at the Bowdoin Street church while most of Mason's well-trained singers followed him to Winter Street. Johnson remained at the Park Street Church. One of Mason's best bass singers, a Mr. Benson, stayed in the choir that was now Root's. Benson was a prosperous businessman, prominent in the church and in the Sunday school, opinionated and outspoken. Root felt that Benson had denied himself the pleasure of membership in the finest choir in the country to help him in his difficult undertaking. With considerable trepidation Root went to his first rehearsal as Mason's successor. He was a bit late in starting. When Root asked Benson a question about the music, or about the customs of another choir, the answer was invariably quiet and modest. Root was frankly astonished. This was the gentleman who had previously treated him more like a boy. Before the rehearsal was over, Root began to surmise what the purpose was. When everyone had gone, there was no longer any doubt. First checking to make sure that no one could see or hear, Benson listed Root's mistakes methodically. In the first place, he should begin on time; else how could he expect the choir members to be prompt? Then, there had been errors in the singing that Root had not corrected. And making the members laugh would probably not wear well in the end. Root said all the suggestions were helpful, even the ones he did not follow. But Mr. Benson's personal example Root called "invaluable" in the new choir work.[49]

Root seemed to have a strong aptitude for teaching. While he was still a student at the Boston Academy of Music, he adapted the techniques of private voice lessons to a class setting. He noticed that some of his fellow-students' voices had a harsh, constricted sound. He called some of the men together during a lunch break to experiment with individual instruction in a group setting. Some of the students requested that this kind of instruction be given on a regular basis. Lowell Mason, as principal, agreed. Root believed there was no previous work of the kind for comparison. It became a permanent part of classes like the Academy's.

In 1844 the prominent educator Jacob Abbott needed a music teacher for a school he and his brothers were starting in New York City. Abbott knew how to persuade a young man to follow his advice. "There is a great field in New York," he told Root. Nothing like Mason's work (and Root's) had been done there. In Boston, Mason and Webb were the leading teachers: Root must for a long time occupy a subordinate place, Abbott cautioned. In New York he would "have a clear field." Root visited New York, gave a demonstration of his teaching, and interviewed for a position in church music. He sang his repertoire of songs from Russell's "Ivy Green" to Schubert's "Wanderer." The next day matters were settled for both church and school. Root made plans to begin his work in what he called "the great city of New York."[50]

2

New York and Paris 1844–1851

New York was what Jacob Abbott said it would be, "a clear field" in teaching. "Within six weeks after the commencement of my work in New York I was fully occupied," Root recalled. He was soon involved in the several kinds of work that his musical contemporaries were doing: teaching vocal music classes, working as a church musician, authoring his first music books, and writing songs and articles for a music periodical. His teaching was enriched by the variety of his classes: privileged young women in private academies, young men who were studying theology, and resident students at New York's State Institution for the Blind. At first he filled what he called his "spare time" by teaching privately. When classes filled his schedule he turned the private lessons over to other teachers. Years later he remembered how rural parts of Manhattan had been. Walking from one of the schools where he taught to the next, he crossed corn and potato fields. He was disgusted when his clean shoes were muddied as he crossed a ditch at what later became Madison Square.[1]

Root's work at Mercer Street Church began almost as soon as he arrived in New York. Upstairs in the chapel there was a study for the minister, Dr. Skinner. Since Skinner preferred to use the study in his home, the chapel room became what Root called his "pleasant musical home during my entire New York life."[2]

Jacob Abbott's school for young ladies was in a row of white marble houses on Lafayette Place in New York. Root called it "spacious and convenient beyond anything I had before seen," and he added "I found the work delightful." The instructional methods were new, as Abbott had told Root they would be; there was no tedium or lack of interest in the lessons. Here he taught a forty-five-minute lesson each weekday rather than the two half-hour lessons per week he had taught in the Boston public schools. Root was astonished that the students sang in parts so soon. Visitors came frequently to see the new methods in use and to hear the part-singing. A few weeks into the term Root received a surprise visit during class. Dr. Isaac Ferris, minister of Rutgers Street Church and president of the board of trustees of Rutgers Female Institute, and Charles E. West, principal of Rutgers Female Institute, had come "to see if the new Yankee music teacher would do for their celebrated old Knickerbocker institution," Root commented later. For the next ten years Root taught daily classes for the four hundred girls and young ladies at Rutgers.[3] Among the course offerings during those years were French, needlework, calisthenics, and art (using oil, watercolors, and pencil). Chapel services were held every weekday morning. At public "exercises" on Friday afternoons, students sang "select pieces of music" and read their essays. In 1850 Cynthia E. Root, a sister of George's, was a student in the Collegiate Department; in later years she was a member of the faculty. At the 1850 commencement, several pieces of music, with words by students and music by Professor Root, were presented. Near the end of each academic year, an invited committee of examiners heard the students in the Collegiate department sing prior to the commencement. The examiners' reports were read during commencement ceremonies. Among the distinguished musicians invited to chair the examining committees were Theodore Eisfeld, Emile Girac, and William Henry Fry. The students' singing of unaccompanied two-octave scales, diatonic and chromatic, brought praise from the examiners and the comment that the singers' ending tone was remarkably in tune with their beginning one.[4]

While George Root's teaching career was steadily moving ahead, his father Frederick was starting over in the leather business. George's sister Mary described her father, as well as her uncles Warren and Putnam, as "born to" the leather business.[5] Warren and Putnam Flint had worked for their wealthy uncle Samuel Train. On November 8, 1844, Frederick Root sailed for New Orleans to join Warren Flint in the leather business there. For companionship on the voyage Frederick had books to read and visits with the captain of the ship. He kept a journal, which he called "The Old

Man's Log—and no great affair." In it he confessed a profound love of the sea, an abiding interest in everything about it, and a wistful thought—"Were I a young man I would follow it." On the first Sunday at sea he prayed for the children in the Sabbath school at home. On election day he wrote that he was deeply concerned for "our Federal Union." On November 14, recovering from a bout of sea-sickness, he observed his fifty-fourth birthday. On one occasion a gale blew all night; the next day the ship seemed to leap from the top of one wave to the next, strong and steady and graceful, and he wrote again about how he loved the sea and sailing. November 28 was Thanksgiving Day in Massachusetts; Frederick's thoughts were with his family. Reaching the Gulf of Mexico, he was thankful for his safe journey thus far, having been in what he called "as dangerous waters as there are in the known world." As the ship sailed up the river to New Orleans, Frederick saw "splendid plantations" and fields of sugar cane. He landed in New Orleans on Saturday, November 30.[6]

George Root's brother Towner (E. T.) "decided to make music his business."[7] In the winter of 1844 the brothers sent a piano to Willow Farm so that Towner could be at home, practicing and giving lessons to his sisters. The music of the brilliant pianist and composer Sigismond Thalberg "was the rage then," their sister Mary wrote, and Towner practiced Thalberg's twelve waltzes faithfully.[8]

One of the New York schools in which Root taught was Miss Haines's School for Young Ladies. In 1846 one of the new students was Kate Chase, whose father would be secretary of the treasury under President Lincoln. A teacher at Miss Haines's School described an average day among these privileged young women: prayers after breakfast; a morning walk with their teachers; classes from 9:00 to 2:00 with a brief recess. Lunch was at 2:00 P.M. with time for study and practice afterward. At 4:00 there was another walk for exercise, then dinner at 6:00. During and after dinner Miss Haines read aloud to the students. They were allowed to study until 8:00 P.M. After a "light tea" they were expected to be in bed early. Miss Haines's pupils attended the best public concerts and lectures available.[9]

In Root's choir at Mercer Street Church there were students from Union Theological Seminary. This acquaintance led to his adding two lessons a week at the seminary to his teaching schedule. Subsequently he began classes at the New York State Institution for the Blind, where he taught adults and children, both male and female, in approximately equal numbers.[10] In due time these blind students won the admiration of what

Root called the city's "best musical people" for their performances of classical music.[11] One of the students there was Fanny Crosby, the prolific writer of verses, who would become a highly effective lyricist for some of Root's compositions as well.

Early in 1845 Jacob Abbott gave Root valuable advice about keeping a diary. Asked whether he had ever kept one, Root replied that he had begun at least half a dozen diaries. Abbott guessed correctly that Root had burned each one after a few months at most. He also guessed correctly that the reason had been too much personal feeling. He advised Root to write concise, factual entries about pupils, classes, concerts, the people he met, letters, journeys — matters of any importance in connection with work or home. He cautioned him not to "give an opinion or admit a word of sentiment" in diary entries. In Root's new blank book Jacob Abbott wrote an opening entry. He described the room where Root worked — octagonal in shape, with oak woodwork and an octagonal table in the center. There were bookcases with glass doors and there were several "easy chairs." There was a piano and a lounge. Writing his autobiography decades later, Root remembered details about the room even though the diary had burned in 1871.[12]

Root's New York schools had longer summer vacations than those in Boston, and so he was able to go back to the Teachers' Classes of the Boston Academy of Music. In addition, he attended similar classes taught by Mason and Webb in other places in 1845 and afterward. Root called it "a great delight" to go with Mason to Day School Teachers' Institutes when Horace Mann and some of the other leading educators taught. He believed "the principles of teaching as an art were more clearly set forth [there] than they were in our musical work."[13] *The Boston Musical Gazette,* published from 1846 through 1850, listed Root's lectures on "Cultivation of the Voice" in some of the descriptions of the day's work at the Boston Academy of Music.

The home and family George Root had left at Willow Farm in 1838 were never far from his mind. His concern showed in a letter he wrote to his mother in June 1845. He folded the letter and wrote the address on the back, to make its own envelope. In the upper left corner of the improvised envelope he wrote "Money Enclosed" and in the upper right "$30.00." His letter needed only the simplest address: "Mrs. Sarah F. Root / North Reading, Mass[tts]." She had not been feeling well; he urged her to hire more help and take better care of herself. He asked her to let him know what he could do to help. "You may depend upon it," he reminded her, "I shall do everything that I am able, and with the greatest pleasure." He ended the letter "in haste, your affectionate son," and he signed it, but he wasn't through. Mary Woodman had gone with him to a music class at Rutgers Institute yesterday, he added. With "much love to all" he ended the letter a second time. Finally he announced, "I expect to be married on my next birthday."[14]

George Root met Mary Olive Woodman in Boston, while she was a member of Lowell Mason's choir. The Woodmans were a musical family; Mary Olive had a lovely singing voice. The wedding took place in

Mary Olive Woodman and George F. Root were married August 28, 1845. This picture shows them "in early married life." *New England Magazine,* January 1896.

Charlestown, Massachusetts, on August 28, 1845.[15] George's brother Towner was best man and his sister Helen one of the bridesmaids. Their sister Mary remembered the wedding as a "tableau of pretty white dresses and pretty young faces."[16]

George and Mary Olive each received advice from caring relatives on their marriage. In a letter, Mary Olive's brother George Woodman gave her level-headed, fair-minded counsel. He wrote in the flowery language of 1845, illustrating that charming American quality of solid good sense mixed with blatant sentimentalism, about "the romance of your real life." He told her that he had already written to Root, expressing a brother's concern and fondness for her. "I regard him as a worthy object of your love," he told her. He hinted at an earlier friendship between Root and a young lady and reassured his sister that she need have no doubts about Root.[17]

Married and living in New York City, Root began bringing one after another of his family members to study and enjoy the music there. His father had written him from South America six years earlier asking him to "see to" the education of his sisters and brothers. "I do not expect you to do anything more than to see they have the privileges of the Public Schools, and what you may be able to teach them yourself," their father wrote then.[18] Now George could give them more than a basic education. In return they usually sang in his church choir.

Root's successful beginning in New York gave particular pleasure to his mother. It was probably in the winter of 1845 that Sarah Flint Root visited her son and his large household in New York. George brought one after another of his sisters to New York to study.[19] At one time eight members of his family and his former student Henry T. Lincoln sang in his Mercer Street Church choir. "Those were delightful days," Root's sister Mary wrote.[20] After a time Root's youngest brother, William A. Root, joined the others in New York, attended a commercial school, and found work in a business office.[21]

Almost as soon as he began to teach, Root began to write tunes. At first he wrote a few notes on the blackboard, off the top of his head. In Root's words, "Up to this time I had not written anything to speak of" though he had "put together some simple tunes while in Boston."[22] The earliest known piece of sheet music by George Root, "See the Sky Is Darkling," was published in 1845.[23] (Words by "H. D.") The words tell the story of an alcoholic revel and its consequences. The beginning was to be sung in a lively tempo and "joyfully." The piano accompaniment dramatized the death scene with arpeggios and tremolos. Abstinence from alcoholic beverages had been a vigorous cause even before the founding of a temperance organization in Boston in 1826. After 1840 temperance meetings took on a more fervent tone and temperance poems and songs followed naturally. Thinking back on what he called his "first efforts at composition and book-making," Root either forgot "See the Sky Is Darkling" or considered it unimportant.

Root's students needed a steady supply of new music for daily lessons, for religious programs, and all the special occasions of the school year. New music was expensive; finding appropriate songs took time. Fellow teachers W. B. Bradbury and I. B. Woodbury asked Root "Why don't you make books? We are doing well in that line." At first he resisted, looking somewhat contemptuously on what he called "their grade of work." His students were singing what he called "higher" music—that of acknowledged master composers. In the Institution for the Blind he conducted a choir of sixty select voices; among the pieces they sang were Romberg's "Song of the Bell," several part songs by Mendelssohn, and several choruses from oratorios by Mendelssohn and other composers. In 1846 Root put together a book he titled *The Young Ladies' Choir*. It was a collection of sacred pieces in one, two and three parts for ladies' voices. In the preface he credited the Reverend Gorham D. Abbott with the selection and arrangement of the words for most of the songs. He had it printed privately, only enough copies for his classes. The religious pieces in it were used for two or three years, he said, but the secular music lasted only a few months.[24] Root would write and compile more than seventy books in his long career.[25]

While they lived in New York, George and Mary Olive became the parents of a son, Frederick Woodman Root, born June 13, 1846. In 1848 they welcomed their second child, a boy they named William Flint Root. Tragically like so many babies of his time, "Willie" Root died before his first birthday.[26] Their son Charles Towner Root was born November 9, 1849.[27] According to George Root, if their children inherited musical abilities they "got quite as much" from Mary Olive's "side of the house" as from his.[28]

Root's sister Mary recalled that he planned to "fill his house with musical helpers as well as kindred," and in the winter of 1846 the house must have been full. A former student, Henry T. Lincoln, sang in Root's choir and, along with Towner Root, assisted in George's teaching. The Roots' sisters Helen, Mary, and Cynthia were there to study as well as to sing in the church choir; Mary Olive's brother George Woodman and sister Abby were there as well. George's mother Sarah came to New York to meet her husband Frederick on his return from New Orleans; then George went with his parents to Sheffield for a visit with relatives and friends.[29]

By 1847 Root was doing remarkably well as a teacher and as a church musician, but one ambition was not satisfied. He wanted recognition from the musicians in New York who advocated only the best music. He felt he must make what he called "a musical demonstration" to the people who condemned simple music and the New England way of teaching it. His sister Cynthia had an excellent contralto voice. Root, his wife Mary Olive, his brother Towner, and his sister Cynthia made a well-balanced quartet.[30] Henry T. Lincoln joined them when they sang quintets. They found Mendelssohn's part songs delightful — the songs were comparatively new at the time — and they enjoyed practicing old madrigals and glees. After a while the quartet's balance and blend were excellent; better, Root thought, than most quartets who sang classical music. This encouraged him, he said, "to strive for the highest perfection" in every detail of quartet performance. During a summer vacation the singers went home to Willow Farm in North Reading, and practiced daily for six weeks. Finally they sang together so precisely that in loudness and in tempo, and in "sudden attack or delicate shading" they seemed to have one mind. As soloists they would be regarded as mediocre, Root believed. As a quartet, with their polished ensemble performance, they were ready to demonstrate what he called their "musical competency." Fortunately Theodore Eisfeld, conductor of the New York Philharmonic Society, had been an examiner at one of Root's schools. Root asked him to listen to the quartet; Eisfeld invited them to sing at the next Philharmonic concert and they did. At the end of the quartet's first song, the musicians in the orchestra joined the audience in hearty applause; Root felt they had passed the test at what he called "the highest musical tribunal." The newspapers gave them good reviews. From that time on he enjoyed the friendship and good will of some of the finest musicians in the city, he recalled.[31] When Root lectured on "Cultivation of the Voice" at the Boston Academy of Music, the family quartet, together with Henry T. Lincoln, demonstrated the musical styles he described by singing various pieces, including opera excerpts. They also sang in some of the academy's evening concerts.[32]

A new school for young ladies was built in 1847 on Union Square in New York City, on land that had been a part of the Spingler family's dairy farm. Root described the Spingler Institute as "an elegant structure, fitted in a costly manner for its purposes, and filled with young ladies of culture and refinement."[33] Gorham Abbot, a brother of Jacob Abbott, was director of the school.

One of the cultural distinctions of the school was a series of four important original paintings by Thomas Cole called "The Voyage of Life," which Gorham Abbott purchased and hung in the chapel.[34]

Root was teaching the best music he could find for his classes, attending concerts by some of the best performers New York offered, and associating with men who believed in a high standard of aesthetic quality. In the midst of all this, he set to music a poem by W. L. Rede called "The Voice of Love."[35] The sheet music cover claimed the song had been "Sung with Enthusiastic Applause by Mrs. Jameson at the Concerts of the Teachers' Institute of the Boston Academy of Music." Root's composition brings to mind a gifted lady singing in well-trained tones to a select audience. Runs and ornamented passages would show the skill of the singer and the quality of her training.

In 1848 a song by George Root appeared in *The Columbian Lady's and Gentleman's Magazine*.[36] "The Lay of the Wounded Heart" was not as difficult or elaborate as "The Voice of Love." Representative of mid–nineteenth-century taste and style, it had a more free-flowing, lyrical quality than some of Root's later songs, with larger intervals and more chromatic tones in the melody. Here Root was not thinking about the musical limitations of students. The poem by Francis C. Woodworth began, "O, chide me not for weeping, She's still the same to me, though she has long been sleeping beneath the willow tree." The death of a lovely young woman was a prevailing theme in the arts for a number of years.

New York was rich in musical offerings, from symphony concerts to minstrel shows. Root heard a number of star performers, including Jenny Lind in her first New York performance. He described her coming to New York as "the great musical sensation of 1849" with the relish of a man telling one of his best stories. P. T. Barnum had signed Lind for a number of concerts in the United States at what then seemed a huge amount of money. "With consummate skill" Barnum "seized upon the fine reputation which she had among musicians and extended it among all the people." Since no hall in New York was large enough to hold the crowds that wanted to hear her, Castle Garden was made ready for an audience estimated at about ten thousand. Even the lowest-priced seats were quite expensive, and the choice of seats was sold at auction. A "breathless hush" held the audience when the time came for Lind's entrance. Root watched every move, fascinated. Lind swept onto the stage dressed simply in white and stood calmly waiting for the orchestra to finish the prelude to "Casta Diva." Root was amazed that she dared "risk a first impression" on the long, soft tone that began that aria. Yet her first note was so penetrating that it went to the farthest corner of the hall. The concert was a historic success.[37]

Root gave a lecture on "Styles of Music" at a "Teacher's Institute and Musical Convention" in Livingston County, New York, in September 1850. His explanation of the characteristics of Italian music focused on opera excerpts. His family quartet, together with Henry T. Lincoln, sang the excerpts that illustrated his lecture. He and his singers presented pieces from *Ernani, Don Pasquale, Linda di Chamonix, Lucretia Borgia, Lucia di Lammermoor,* and other operas. That evening his group sang glees and other pieces in a public concert and closed their part of the program with some of the Italian works they had sung during the lecture. The following evening, "Mr. Root and company" presented one of his illustrated lectures in a nearby town. On September 5 in a program at the Teachers' Institute they sang, among other pieces, "A Hundred Years Ago" and "Call Me From These Tempestuous Scenes." George Root sang "The Gravedigger."[38]

The large successful music publishers produced their own magazines. The best of these magazines carried announcements of forthcoming performances and classes, musical news and letters from correspondents in major cities, articles on composers and their works, advertisements, and a few songs as samples of the firms' publications. In June 1850 a new magazine, *The Choral Advocate and Singing-Class Journal,* appeared in New York City. It carried news of musical events such as the crowded concerts of the Hutchinson Family singers. For a while Root was a contributing editor and the magazine published articles and songs he wrote. His ideas on teaching and singing began to reach people who could not attend his classes. Letters to the editor acquainted him, as they did Mason Brothers, the publishers, with people's musical opinions.

By 1850 Root was tired, suffering from what he called "the usual trouble of overworked people — dyspepsia." Jacob Abbott, the teacher who had suggested he come to New York, made the startling suggestion that he go to Paris. The travel would be good for him; Paris would be an interesting place to see and a good place to study French as well as music. "The best teachers in the world congregate there," Abbott told him. It was not entirely unusual for the nineteenth-century American teachers, church musicians, and book compilers like Root to go to Europe for musical study. Lowell Mason, the patriarch of their profession, had first gone to Europe in 1837. Root's early mentor A. N. Johnson studied in Germany, as did Root's fellow-teacher William B. Bradbury. I. B. Woodbury studied in Paris and London. In December 1850 the *Choral Advocate* announced that Root was leaving for Paris, planning to study music, primarily "vocal culture," for the coming year.[39] Those who were seriously interested in a musical career were advised to go to Europe, not only to study but to listen, since the only way to become thoroughly acquainted with good music was to hear a great deal of it.

"My wife was considerably astonished when I told her," Root said, but she agreed that he should go if substitutes could be found to direct the choir and play the organ at Mercer Street church. With some of his family and friends, Root gave a farewell concert November 25th, 1850, at the church. His wife Mary Olive sang "Come Unto Me" and he sang "Why Do the Nations," both from Handel's *Messiah*.[40] Fanny Crosby, since 1847 a teacher at the New York State Institute for the Blind where Root taught music, wrote a "farewell song" for him.[41]

"I took my passage for the fifth of December, 1850, on the Franklin, a new steamer of a new line just established between New York and Havre," Root recalled. The *Franklin* "bowed and rolled as gracefully as she could at every wave of that wintry sea, and made nearly all of us very seasick," he wrote, but "she carried us safely across and landed us in due time (thirteen days, I think)."[42] Root described his daily routine in Paris. Mornings were spent in lessons and recitations, voice and piano practice, and in studying French. In the afternoons he visited "picture galleries, museums, libraries, palaces, cathedrals, parks, gardens"— there seemed to be no end to the places of interest. After dinner Root and his fellow boarders gathered in the parlor for conversation and occasionally for music.[43]

On one occasion in Paris, Root's religious beliefs conflicted with his studies. Americans had mixed feelings about the theater and its music. They loved the popular songs that had originated in the theater and the ones that were adapted from operas. At the same time, a sizeable number of church members and respectable people avoided the theater and the opera because actors might be lowlifes or because a lady did not present herself to the public to be looked at in a theatrical setting or because drama was by nature fiction and therefore threatening to a conforming religious public.

In Paris, Root studied with Giulio Alary, said to be the best voice teacher outside the Conservatoire. At the close of the lesson one day, Alary invited Root to the final rehearsal of an opera he had composed. "I was in trouble," Root realized. "I determined when I left home that I would do nothing in Paris that I would not do in New York." The church to which he belonged at the time held that going to the opera or to "theatrical representations" was immoral. Giulio Alary could not possibly understand that. He seemed to think Root's view was fanatical. Root said he began to agree with that opinion a few years later. For the rest of his stay in Paris he studied voice with Jacques Potharst, a tenor at the Paris Opera.[44]

The concerts in Paris were an education in themselves. Root heard Henriette Sontag and Pauline Viardot-Garcia, who were celebrities in Europe and the United States, and Luigi Lablache, whom he called the greatest basso in the world. In Paris Root became acquainted with Louis Moreau Gottschalk. Years later, when his own position on classical versus popular music had solidified, Root called Gottschalk a great pianist. Critics agreed that he was the most successful pianist who had played in America to that time, an "exquisite" pianist, but not a great one. In his popular concerts he usually played his own compositions, which the public loved. Root claimed those who knew Gottschalk well knew he had "a wonderful repertoire of classic music," that he could play Beethoven's piano works from memory, and that he "delighted in Bach." Root heard Hector Berlioz conduct his own works, and he wrote, "That pale, wild face, surmounted by shaggy locks, black as night, haunted me for months. He was a disappointed man." Berlioz's works "did not find much recognition in his lifetime."[45]

An incident in Paris illustrated the power of a song. Root and five other Americans celebrated the Fourth of July, 1851, in a suburb a few miles from Paris and returned home for dinner at five o'clock. After dinner they went to the parlor for what Root called "a grand wind-up." They made speeches and sang songs — "The Star-Spangled Banner," "America," and other appropriate songs. Finally Root began to sing "'The Marseillaise'" ("Ye sons of freedom, wake to glory"). Their landlady ran into the room urging the men to stop and slamming the windows shut. She told them a crowd was gathering in the streets; she was afraid the *gendarmes* would come. One of the Americans explained that they were only celebrating their independence. "We are not independent enough yet to sing "The Marseillaise,"' she answered. The song had been banned some time before and the government was still "afraid of its effect," Root discovered. Writing about the incident years later, he recalled that his stay in Paris had been "just before the famous *coup d'etat* of Louis Napoleon." "A half-concealed anxiety" had pervaded Paris at that time.[46]

Soon after July 4 Root and his friend Levi P. Homer, who later became a professor of music at Harvard, left Paris on a Friday morning and arrived in London that afternoon. Still feeling some ill effects from the channel crossing, Root went to a performance of the *Messiah* that evening. The performance was uncut and lasted four hours. Six hundred singers were in the chorus, accompanied by a large orchestra and an organ. One of the soloists was Carl Formes, a renowned bass who was at his best then. A week later the same musicians presented the oratorio *Elijah*. In later years Root valued the memory of those two performances greatly. "They were authentic and authoritative, both for tempos and style," he felt. The traditional performance of the *Messiah* came down through time from Handel himself, and Mendelssohn had conducted his *Elijah* just a few years earlier in Birmingham, England. Root thoroughly enjoyed the Crystal Palace exhibition in Hyde Park, London. What was said to be the first sewing machine was being shown there by two brothers who had sung in the choir of Park Street Church in Boston. Another Boston acquaintance named Hobbs was exhibiting a lock. A Philadelphia man exhibited his adjustable reclining chair in which Queen Victoria had sat earlier in the day. Now the exhibitor planned to charge a fee for sitting there. The McCormick Reaper, a "rusty, weather-beaten machine that had been the butt of so many jokes at the expense of the Yankees," won praise when it was demonstrated in a grain field. About the same time the new yacht *America* won a race against the English yachts. Americans were proud of these achievements, Root recalled, but were a bit embarrassed that they had not had greater trust in "the ability of Uncle Sam to hold his own in this contest of nations."[47]

Root and his friend Levi Homer stayed in London about four weeks before going to Southampton to board the *Humboldt* for home. Their voyage was "remarkably smooth," Root recalled, except for one unforgettable incident. He had been a little seasick and a little apprehensive, "especially after hearing stories of running into icebergs or fishing craft" and about the density of fogbanks off Newfoundland. One night he went peacefully to bed. The moon was bright, the air clear, "and the ocean almost as calm as a mill-pond." He was awakened about midnight by shouted orders and the sound of running feet overhead, followed immediately by the feeling that the ship had hit something, "for she heeled over in a most perceptible and alarming way." Fearful that something worse was about to happen, he jumped out of his berth and shouted to Mr. Homer in the upper berth. Homer, only half awake, lost his balance and fell on Root's back while Root was bending over to put on his shoes. For a moment Root thought the ship had "gone to the bottom." As soon as he could, he hurried on deck and saw that the ship was about a hundred yards from the rocks at Cape Race, Newfoundland. If the crew had not acted as quickly as they did, the ship would have crashed on the rocks and "gone down like a broken eggshell," he thought. When the ship arrived in New York, it went into dry-dock and remained there for a period of weeks, so it seemed the damage had been considerable.[48]

Arriving home from Europe on "a hot August morning" in 1851, Root went back to his teaching and his church work. "The first need I felt was for something new for my classes to sing," he recalled. William Bradbury's "floral concerts" with children's choirs gave Root the idea of writing a musical play about flowers for his students to perform. He titled it *The Flower Queen*.[49] Fanny Crosby wrote the lyrics. Root would describe to her what he wanted the characters to say in a particular piece; the following day Crosby[50] would hand him the lyrics for that piece. He "thought out the music," he said, while going from one class to another. The distances between schools were so great that he "had to spend a good deal of time every day in omnibuses or streetcars." He took advantage of the first free moments to put the music on paper. Sometimes there was a half-hour before a meal, sometimes a break between lessons, sometimes an hour at night. This continued until the cantata was finished. Root dedicated *The Flower Queen* "most respectfully and affectionately" to his former voice teacher in Boston, George James Webb. Needing a considerable number of copies for his students, Root took the cantata to the Mason Brothers, Lowell Mason's sons, who were publishers, to be printed. The brothers offered to publish it, thinking others might want to use it, "and so it proved."[51]

The Flower Queen was subtitled "The Coronation of the Rose, a cantata...." The word cantata was used then to differentiate a wholesome, harmless stage presentation from opera or the music hall. For many people religious objections precluded attendance at a theatrical presentation. Operettas were not yet known and the Broadway musical was far in the future.

The Flower Queen illustrated nineteenth-century American romanticism. It told the story of various flowers meeting in a forest to choose a queen. A hermit, called in the cantata a recluse, came to the forest to escape the disappointments of life. The flowers sang about love and duty. The recluse learned from them that happiness was to be found in doing his best, whatever life's circumstances. The part of the Recluse could be sung by a baritone or a mezzo soprano, often the teacher. Apparently Root enjoyed singing the role of the Recluse himself. Some of the solo parts were Sunflower, Crocus, Dahlia, Heliotrope, Lily, Hollyhock, and so on. A flute soloist played the Nightingale's part. For Rose, the leading soprano role, there was a duet with the Nightingale. This first cantata showed Root's sense of the dramatic and his ways of giving personality to the characters and creating picturesque moments on the stage.

Root's "Directions" for performance suggested that the piano be visible only to the singers and that part of the stage be concealed from the audience by evergreen branches. The plot required that singers be out of sight at times.

The Flower Queen was tailored to its singers and its audiences. It was relatively easy to learn, the singing was distributed so that large groups of singers could take part (bringing parents, neighbors and friends to hear them), and there were some very charming moments. In the first four years after it was published, *The Flower Queen* was performed more than five hundred times.[52] Notices and reviews of its performances appeared in the musical news for years to come.

3

Public Taste at Mid-Century 1851–1855

The early 1850s were pivotal years in Root's career. He found that he could write highly successful popular songs. He assumed the management of his own musical conventions, and with Lowell Mason, he opened the first Normal school specifically for teachers of music.

As Stephen Foster's extraordinary songs appeared one after another and Christy's Minstrels popularized them, Root decided to try writing songs in the popular style. At first he signed them "G. Friederich Wurzel" (Wurzel is German for root). He had previously shared the opinion of his associates that popular songs were not musically valid. It was not until he traveled around the country meeting people, becoming acquainted with them and with their music, that his thinking changed. In his words, "I saw these things in a truer light, and respected myself, and was thankful when I could write something that all the people would sing."[1]

The concept of "people's music" was part of a recognition of the power of public consensus that Lincoln summarized as the will of the people. "The people's song" was a current term in periodicals like the *New York Musical Review and Choral Advocate* in the early 1850s. Advertisements in the *Musical Review* differentiated between classical and popular songs by listing them under the headings "Music for the Drawing Room" and "Music for the People." The *Boston Musical Gazette* quoted an article in *Blackwood's Magazine* calling popular music a "moral infection" and concluding that "it is music for a democracy."[2] A periodical called *The*

Message Bird stated in 1852 that music belonged to everyone who desired it and everyone who was moved by it.[3]

New songs were heard on the street, in people's homes, and in theaters. They sold well in the form of sheet music. Minstrel shows fueled the composition of tender, sentimental songs, and American songwriters produced a flood of them. Audiences heard songs based on the current popular themes such as Stephen Foster's "Old Folks At Home" and on the current novels such as Harriet Beecher Stowe's *Uncle Tom's Cabin*. In 1852 William Hall & Son published a song by Root called "The Hazel Dell." In the same year Root signed a three-year contract with the company. In his words, "I was to give them all my sheet music publications for three years."[4] In 1853 "The Hazel Dell" became one of the most popular songs in the country.[5] Success convinced Root that he should write music for the public, not just for choirs and music classes. As he described it, his cantata *The Flower Queen* "quickly became popular, and 'Hazel Dell' began the run which was not to end until the boys whistled it and the hand organs played it from Maine to Georgia, and no ambition for a songwriter could go higher than that."[6]

"The Hazel Dell"[7] was typical of a strange genre, songs about beautiful girls who died young. It told the story of Nelly, buried among the hazel-nut trees in the valley where she and the bereaved one had walked, where now "the silent stars" wept each night over her grave. The song seems too pleasant, too happy to be sung over the grave of a loved one. The melody is in major rather than minor, the rhythms almost bounce. If it were the only mid–nineteenth-century song with lyrics about death and a melody that seemed to skip merrily along, it would be an oddity. But there were many such songs, some even livelier than "The Hazel Dell." Fanny Crosby claimed to have written the words of "The Hazel Dell" and there is no evidence that she did not. At that time it was not unusual to omit the name of the lyricist from a song.

Edgar Allan Poe explained the "dead girl" theme as he saw it. According to Poe the death of a beautiful woman was "unquestionably the most poetical topic in the world" and the person who could best tell her story was the bereaved lover.[8] Americans bought song after song about beautiful young women who had died. Cheerful, sprightly melodies co-existed with words that were completely opposite. Stephen Foster's 1849 minstrel show song "Nelly Was a Lady" is upbeat, almost rollicking. The same lack of sadness is found in Septimus Winner's "Listen to the Mockingbird"

3. Public Taste at Mid-Century 1851–1855

When "'Hazel Dell' began the run which was not to end until the boys whistled it and the hand organs played it from Maine to Georgia," Root felt that "no ambition for a song-writer could go higher than that."

(still singing o'er the grave of sweet Hally), written in 1855. Foster's "Ah, May the Red Rose Live Alway" (1850) has a more contemplative melody and words that crystallize the theme: "Why should the beautiful ever weep?" "Why should the innocent die?" Foster's "Gentle Annie" (1856) is arguably the best song of this kind. H. S. Thompson's hit song "Lily Dale" was published in the year Root's "Hazel Dell" was written; Root composed more songs on this theme after the dramatic success of "Hazel Dell." People sang unselfconsciously about death. Recognition of the importance of the individual and his feelings came together with grief for the lost one.[9]

Root composed a song called "Pictures of Memory"[10] in the same year as his first hit song, "Hazel Dell." "Pictures of Memory" was an art song. The words evoked a mental image of a younger brother who had died in childhood. The publisher advertised this song cautiously, calling the title page, words and music, all "beautiful," describing the accompaniment as "simple," the melody as "elaborate but not really difficult," and adding, "We could hardly say more in its favor." [11] In time this song became one of Root's favorite examples in his argument that, as a composer, he must focus on the people's tastes and abilities.

While Root was finding his way as a songwriter, he was also one of the prominent teachers who advocated "better" music and taught the works of Handel, Schubert, Mendelssohn and other master composers. But successes on the scale of "Hazel Dell" and *The Flower Queen* would make a difference in the life of any composer. They would color his thinking about songwriting, about the functions of music in everyday life, and about the people who bought his music and enjoyed it. Writing almost four decades later, Root still felt the sting of criticism. In his autobiography there was an opportunity to explain. Friends had asked him why he did not write better music than "The Hazel Dell" and songs of that kind. He decided to answer with a question: Would musicians who wanted to use better songs choose his when they could get songs by Schubert, Abt, and Franz for the same price or less? The criticism persisted; as Root explained, he decided to publish one or two songs that were better than what was commonly called "the people's" music. He found it much easier to write "where the resources were greater"; there was no need to change a melodic interval that seemed too difficult or a chord that was uncommon. Then when friends asked why he did not write better music, he could ask them if they knew his "better" songs: "Gently, Ah, Gently" (The Voice of Love) and "Pictures of Memory." He was confident they would have to say, "No,"

Root had friends who advocated only the finest classical music. Asked why he did not write something better, he produced "Pictures of Memory" and "The Voice of Love." After that he answered the challenge by asking "Have you ever heard of these songs?" Virtually no one had. This gave him the opportunity to explain, "That is why I do not write something better" (courtesy of the Department of Special Collections, Cairns Collection of American Women Writers, Memorial Library, University of Wisconsin–Madison).

and he would explain: "That is why I do not write 'something better,' as you call it. Neither you nor any one else would know anything about my work on that grade, and I should be wasting my time in trying to supply the wants of a few people, who are already abundantly supplied by the best writers of Europe.'"12

PICTURES OF MEMORY.

3. *Public Taste at Mid-Century 1851–1855*   43

Root was convinced that he should write "the people's" music. "Still," in his words, "I am ashamed to say, I shared the feeling that was around me in regard to that grade of music."[13] Some of the musicians whom Root most admired called popular songs "trash." These popular songs were the financially successful ones, favorites of the public, hummed on the street

and played on the parlor piano. Root called them "simple" songs. The melodies were sparse, easy to learn and fairly predictable, as were the harmonies.

Root composed "Fare Thee Well, Kitty Dear"[14] specifically for the well-known Wood's Minstrels, dedicated it to Henry Wood, and signed

it a bit more formally than usual: "G. Friedrich Wurzel." Fanny Crosby wrote the words. She said the song "described the grief of a colored man on the death of his beloved."[15] An advertisement assured the public that this was a polite, harmless song, and that it had "all the charms of negro minstrelsy without any of its objectionable features."[16] "Mary of the Glen"[17] never became a hit song like "The Hazel Dell," but it was charming and

lyrical, a pleasant story-scene. Asked whether she was engaged, Mary of the Glen said she was not, but there *was* a young man named Willie. The ballad was made more romantic by Willie's being a poor farmer while his rival for Mary's affection owned land, gold, and cattle. "The Reaper on the Plain"[18] appealed to mid-century Americans' love of songs that cele-

brated the commonplace, the ordinary, the everyday experience. The sheet music cover romanticized farm life with the image of a haymaking scene. The words held a moment of nostalgia for all those who, like Root, had left their farm homes behind.

Root admired the songs of Stephen Foster because they spoke so directly to people. They had an immediacy that made them easy to remember and an inevitable quality, as though the melody and the rhythm could hardly have been other than what they were. To learn one of Foster's best songs was to feel that one had always known it. Foster left behind notebooks that showed how he revised songs. There is little or no evidence that Root revised a musical setting once written. He seems to have committed to paper his first conception of it.

Root composed "The Old Folks Are Gone,"[19] his own version of Stephen Foster's "Old Folks at Home." Foster's song was one of the most popular songs in America, if not the most popular. A number of other songwriters copied the "old folks" theme in songs of their own. Some editions of Root's "Old Folks" were marked "Authorized Edition" and "Christy's Old Folks Are Gone as sung by E. P. Christy at Christy's Opera House, N. Y." The word rhythms were those of Foster's "Old Folks at Home."

The words of Root's "Early Lost, Early Saved,"[20] illustrate one of the ideas underlying popular songs about beautiful girls who died young: an attempt to find comfort in a supposed reason for the death. The words described a scene in which angels, hovering over the cradle of a baby girl, competed with each other to bestow the richest blessing on her. By the time she grew into a young lady the angels had made her "too lovely" for earthly life. Root's musical setting owed something to Henry Russell and something to Stephen Foster. The *Review* called this "One of the most touching ballads ever written."[21]

"They Sleep in the Dust"[22] was advertised as "A beautiful tribute to parental worth" with a melody that would "endear itself to the heart like [Russell's] 'The Old Arm Chair.'"[23] Root dedicated it to Jacob Abbott, whose suggestion had brought him to New York City to live and work. The words illustrated the homespun idealism of the time. All or most of the usual symbols and themes were present: death, the cares of earthly life, the home, parents, the summons of the church bell, a wood fire on the hearth, old furniture, a symbolic clock, angels, a reunion in heaven. The melody owed more to popular light opera arias than to the songs of Henry Russell, whose work Root so admired. The words were unattributed.

Root dedicated "Gently, Gently Wake the Song" (a "Serenade for Male Voices") to his brother Towner, who, he wrote "was always the singer of the family." Towner (E. T.) Root, who had gone with their father to work in South America, composed several very creditable songs himself.

He taught music in Boston, then joined George as assistant teacher in New York in 1846. About 1849 he went to Alabama to teach; he returned to New York in 1851. Tired of teaching as "Mr. Root's brother," Towner had decided to make his own career in the music business and had gone to work in the William Hall & Son music company.[24]

"Mother" was a favorite subject in the songs of the nineteenth century. "My Mother's Bible," with music by Henry Russell and words by George Pope Morris, was copyrighted in 1841. The singing Hutchinson Family wrote "The Cottage of My Mother" in 1848. In 1851 Stephen Foster's "Mother, Thou'rt Faithful to Me" was published. The 1860s brought more songs with Mother as the subject. The trend culminated with an undated broadside by De Marsan titled "Mother on the Brain." Using the tune of "The Bonnie Blue Flag," its lyrics were made up of the titles of songs about Mother, strung together in a kind of list. Root contributed his share to the growing stacks of sheet music honoring Mother. Fanny Crosby wrote the words for his 1852 song, "Mother, Sweet Mother, Why Linger Away?"[25] In the 1850's four more of his songs on this theme appeared. In the Civil War years he produced another five songs that culminated in his "Just Before the Battle, Mother."

"The Father's Coming" combined what the nineteenth century called "sentiment" with dramatic tension. A small family "mended" the fire and opened the shutters so the light from inside could welcome the father, who was "stronger than the storm." The music was not very dramatic, but there were opportunities for the singer to interpret: tense anticipation, places for dramatic gestures, the charm of the baby and little Nell, warm words for the father, a happy ending. An advertisement called the song "a household gem." Root's melody was not unlike that of Henry Russell's song, "My Mother's Bible."[26]

The New York Musical Review and Choral Advocate published a temperance song, "Clear Cold Water," with words by C. M. Cady and music by George F. Root in its May 1, 1852, issue. Lowell Mason and Isaac B. Woodbury were listed as editors for that year. The paper mentioned that Root, since his return from Europe, had, in addition to his professional duties, given considerable attention to writing songs and ballads for William Hall & Son, and suggested that his contract with Hall would be a "high compliment" to anyone. The paper summed up his "merits" in two words — simplicity and originality — and claimed that these qualities were found in his accompaniments as well as his melodies. The paper defined simple songs as "natural, beautifully expressing the sentiment of the words, and not too difficult for the great mass of singers and performers."[27]

The Review held a contest for the best original compositions submitted anonymously for publication. The prizes were fifty dollars for the best four-part song and twenty-five dollars for the second best. Root, already a regular contributor to the magazine, submitted two songs and won both prizes. "The Song of Spring" was published in the July 1, 1852, issue and was reminiscent of *The Flower Queen*. His other winning song, "Old Friends," was published the following month. In it the melody moved around among the four voices.

In its August 1, 1852, issue, the *Review* claimed that the popularity of Root's "Clear Cold Water," published in May, and the demand for what the magazine called "more music of the same sort" had led to the publication of "The Noble Law of Maine," with words and music by Root. Maine had passed a law prohibiting the manufacture and sale of alcoholic beverages in 1851.

When Root's piano piece "The Topsy Polka"[28] (signed G. Friedrich Wurzel) was published in 1852, "Topsy" was a household word. "Topsy" was a character in Harriet Beecher Stowe's phenomenal novel, *Uncle Tom's Cabin*. The explosive popularity of the book created a market in which songs, stage productions, or products with ties to *Uncle Tom's Cabin* sold exceedingly well. Scenes and atmosphere from the book were set to music in such pieces as "The Ghost of Uncle Tom," "Eliza's Flight," and "Eva's Parting." John Greenleaf Whittier wrote a poem that was set to music and published as "Little Eva; Uncle Tom's Guardian Angel." The Hutchinson Family sang "Little Topsy's Song" and "The Fugitive."[29] Most people thought of Topsy as a comical character, dancing and whistling and turning somersaults. Root's piano piece reflected the comical stage Topsy. In Mrs. Stowe's book, she was portrayed as an amoral child, stealing and lying, then transformed by the death of Little Eva, who was portrayed as a saintly child who read the Bible to Uncle Tom.

Harriet Beecher Stowe was an experienced writer and a member of the famous Beecher family, with whom Root was acquainted. She had moved to Cincinnati in 1832 and had lived among fervent abolitionists. The stories of black women moved her profoundly. Once she saw a black husband and wife separated by a slave trader.[30] In 1836 she married Calvin Stowe, and in 1850 Calvin began teaching at Bowdoin College in

Brunswick, Maine. The inspiration for *Uncle Tom's Cabin* took shape as Mrs. Stowe sat in pew 23 of the First Parish Church in Brunswick, where incidentally Root's brother-in-law, the Reverend George Adams, served as minister.[31] The image of a slave being beaten to death came so strongly to Mrs. Stowe's mind that she hurried home after the service and wrote down the scene.

The Academy Vocalist (1852), a book Root compiled for his classes, showed that popular songs, and a lyricism coming from opera and other theatrical works, made their way into the music that was used for teaching. Root included "Home, Sweet Home" in his *Academy Vocalist*, as well as "The Last Rose of Summer," "Oft in the Stilly Night," and other similar songs. Also in *The Academy Vocalist* were several songs by Lowell Mason and two by George's brother Towner. Several pieces in the book were "arranged from" opera composers: Rossini, Bellini, and Donizetti.

For quite a few years opera made an impact on American popular music. Where songwriters heard free-flowing, lyrical, ornamented melodies, with grace and charm and some breathless moments, suggestions of these could be heard in the songs produced by those writers. Root, who for some years did not attend opera performances, was familiar with some of the best-known excerpts, and his family quartet had sung some of these excerpts in his lectures on the voice. To musical audiences in New York, "opera" didn't always mean the same thing. Balfe's *Bohemian Girl*, first heard in New York about the same time Root came to live there,[32] was a different kind of music from Bellini's *Norma* or Donizetti's *Lucia di Lammermoor*. Undoubtedly the best known of all the light opera melodies was "Home, Sweet Home," from *Clari, or the Maid of Milan* by Henry R. Bishop.

One of Root's minstrel show songs received an honor accorded the most successful of "the people's" songs: the words of "Poor Robin's Growing Old"[33] appeared in *The New York Clipper*, an entertainment periodical. In the *Clipper*, news of musical events appeared side by side with news of boxing, horse racing, and other sports events. The musical news ranged from the minstrel stage to the symphony orchestra concerts of the French conductor Jullien, who came to New York promising to "please the masses." The *Clipper* protested Jullien's popularity: "Stand fast, Americans! No more European artists. America can produce musical wonders as well as reaping machines."[34] Advertisements in the *Clipper* described current trends like the Daguerrotype hat — when the customer bought a hat, his picture would be put inside the crown. Other advertisements showed why theater and the entertainment business were often thought to be socially unacceptable. One ad invited the public to a contest between dogs, the winner being the one that killed the most rats in a given amount of time. Another described, as a cure for a long list of human ailments, a product named "Gonorrhea Lotion." In the upper left corner of page one of its July 9, 1853, issue *The Clipper* printed the words of Root's "Poor Robin's Growing Old." Under the title were the words "Sung with great applause by Wood's Minstrels." All three verses and the chorus were printed without attribution, as often happened in the *Clipper*. The song described a happier past when "massa" sent a favorite old horse named Robin to carry corn to the mill. Just a few issues earlier the words of Stephen Foster's "Old Folks at Home" had appeared in the same place on page one. Foster's "My Old Kentucky Home" appeared in the same place July 23, 1853, again with no mention of the composer.

His sheet music publisher at the time, William Hall & Son, called Root "one of the most popular ballad writers of the day" in an advertisement and cited the "easy and flowing style" of his songs. His "Fare Thee Well, Kitty Dear, Composed for and sung by Wood's Minstrels" (advertised a few months earlier) and "The Old Folks Are Gone, Composed for and sung by Christy's Minstrels" were sung "nightly" by these companies. The words of these songs were not in dialect; they could be sung "by any lady in the drawing room," the ad claimed. Under the heading "Dance Music," "The Topsey [sic] Polka" by G. F. Wurzel was listed.[35]

Death and mourning, which were persistent themes in art, literature and music, inspired yet another song. The sheet music cover of Root's "Greenwood Bell"[36] pictured a bell tower at the entrance to a cemetery. By the 1850s Greenwood Cemetery was a New York landmark. Half a million people per year came to stroll on the grounds and look at the monuments.[37] When a funeral procession passed the bell tower, the bell tolled the age of the deceased.[38] The song described this scene. Root wove into the piano accompaniment a soft sound that suggested a bell tolling.

Like many songs of the time, Root's 1853 song "They've Sold Me Down the River (The Negro Father's Lament)"[39] hinted at *Uncle Tom's Cabin*. Like Tom, the person in this song was sold and sent far away from his family. The words mentioned a cabin, a wife and children, a kind master, and a strong religious faith.

The success of "The Hazel Dell" and his first cantata, *The Flower*

Queen, gave Root what he called "a new inclination to write."[40] He composed the cantata *Daniel* for his choir at Mercer Street church. Both Chauncey M. Cady, then a student at Union Theological Seminary, and Fanny Crosby helped Root prepare the words. The cantata depicted the trial of three young Israelites and their delivery from the fiery furnace and Daniel's delivery from the den of lions.[41] Someone suggested that Root and William B. Bradbury compile a church music book together and publish the cantata *Daniel* in it. This was done in the first and perhaps the second edition of their book, called *The Shawm*. People wanted to buy the cantata alone; it was taken out of the book and printed separately.[42] The preface to *The Shawm,* which Root and Bradbury signed on July 6, 1853, explained that they had been careful to include hymns sung by the various religious denominations in the country and had prepared a special index to correlate with Methodist hymn books used in the North. In the section called "The Singing Class," students were taught the elements of music theory in the customary categories: rhythm, melody, and dynamics. Lowell Mason and almost all the other compilers and authors taught rhythm first. Bradbury had introduced melody first. The Mason Brothers' reviewer was dubious about that, but Mason Brothers had published the book, so he commented on Bradbury's skillful presentation and his pleasant exercises, mingling theory with practice, and he gave the "Singing Class" his "unqualified commendation." The reviewer was much more critical of the "sacred concert music" in the *Shawm*. The pieces were too easy; in his opinion there was not an anthem or chorus in the entire book that would challenge even a "common country choir." Such simple music would be poor preparation for the study of the great oratorio choruses, he wrote.[43] Root's family quartet sang in a "Classical Quartet Soiree" at the Apollo Rooms in New York City in the early spring of 1853. Their performance of Mendelssohn's "Hunting Song" received high praise from the *Review's* critic, who had "never heard their quartet performances surpassed, if equaled, in New York."[44] They sang next in a Philharmonic Concert at Niblo's Concert Saloon on March 5, 1853. This program began with Beethoven's *Symphony Number 5 in C Minor, Opus 67*. After hearing this concert, the critic praised their singing, not because their voices were better than others, but because they "merge(d) their individuality in the general effect" and because their chromatic intervals, changes in loudness and softness, and "delicate shadings of expression" approached perfection. Their performance of William Mason's "Serenade" was encored. In April the group sang in Newport, Rhode Island, together with Miss Anna Thomas and Henry T. Lincoln.[45]

It must have been in 1853 that Root decided to build a new house on Willow Farm in North Reading, Massachusetts, where he had grown up. The new house would accommodate the large family that gathered each summer and would make the parents, Sarah and Frederick, more comfortable. Thinking back on it, he commented that no palace had ever given its residents more pleasure.[46] Later builders commented that the new house was on the site of the original 1751 structure and evidently incorporated parts of the original house.[47] About this time George Root's aunts and uncles on his mother's side, together with their families, deeded any interests they might have had in Willow Farm to George. By buying parcels of land surrounding the farm he increased its size from fifty to one hundred fifty acres.[48] For many years the family returned to Willow Farm in the summers.

In a series of articles published in 1853, Root gave readers a virtual visit to the classes he was teaching in Union Theological Seminary, the Spingler Institute, Rutgers Female Institute, and the New York State Institution for the Blind.[49] He had taught for about six years in the State Institution for the Blind, and almost nine years in Abbott's School for Young Ladies and the Rutgers Female Institute. Now his fifty-member class at Union Theological Seminary met two mornings a week at 8:30 in the chapel. It was evident that Root liked this class. He said the students were not there to be amused or entertained. In his words, "Solid, thorough work is the order of the day." Each class began with a C scale and went on to other scales, ascending and descending, sung in various meters. The chromatic scale followed. He asked the class to sing melodic fragments, using numbers for the tones of the scale—1, 3, 5, 8, for example. He wrote an exercise on the blackboard and questioned the class about the notes until they could hardly fail to sing them correctly.

Less than fifteen minutes from Union Theological Seminary, in the Reverend Gorham Abbott's Spingler Institute, Root taught two classes. After their scales and exercises, these students sang pieces from his *Academy Vocalist* and other sources. Root was pleased with the accomplishments of these students. At 2:00 P.M. he taught a class of about three hundred at Rutgers Female Institute. After their scales they sang exercises from the board in any key, major or minor, and then songs, anthems, and choruses. Next Root traveled by omnibus to the Institution for the Blind, between three and four miles from Rutgers. Here he taught three classes, grouped by age, each class having male and female students. He was very gratified that the older students sang music by Mendelssohn, Schubert, Donizetti, Rossini, Bellini, and William Mason among others.[50] In teaching these blind students to recognize specific chords, he found that there was too much "eye harmony" in the writing of hymns and songs. This experience made a lasting change in the way he taught harmony.

In his teaching, Root had seen a problem that he believed he could solve. There were normal schools for the teachers of the standard curriculum; it was becoming apparent that music teachers should have specialized classes in the art of teaching as well as in harmony and what Root called "general musical culture." He decided that three months' study would be appropriate, in the summer when teachers were free to attend, and in New York where the rest of his work was. He went to Boston to explain his plan to Lowell Mason, who was still the leading authority in the country on music education. If Mason's name appeared in its announcements, the new class would be far more likely to succeed. At first Mason said it wouldn't work. Root had made a decision: He would have this class. "You are the proper person to appear at the head of it," he told Mason, but he would do "the work of getting it up" himself. He promised Mason a better opportunity than he'd ever had to make his "ideas of notation, teaching, and church music" really known. At Mason Brothers, the publishing company of Lowell Mason's sons, Root suggested that the institute would promote the sale of their father's books and asked them to publicize the institute throughout the country.[51] Mason Brothers agreed. The first term of the proposed Normal Musical Institute was set to begin April 15, 1852. The notice appeared over the names of Lowell Mason and George F. Root. It was almost time for the institute to begin when Mason Brothers had to retract the announcement. Lowell Mason was in Germany and could not get back in time. Root would not begin without the man he called "the master," and so the class was rescheduled for the spring of 1853.[52]

The first Normal Musical Institute opened in Dodworth's Hall on Broadway April 25, 1853. The term lasted three months. More than a hundred students came from distant places, and a sufficient number of New York City residents attended to make what Root called "a good chorus." Lowell Mason led the faculty; Thomas Hastings, William B. Bradbury and George Root taught classes. Mary Olive Root's brother, J. C. Woodman, was one of the assistant teachers.⁵³ At the close of the first term, students sang choruses from Handel's *Messiah* and Root's new cantata, *Daniel*.

The next teachers' term of the Normal Musical Institute was announced for May 1 through July 15, 1854. "A few young ladies" were to be "received into the family of Mr. Root, at No. 95 Clinton Place, and boarded at five dollars per week." Pianos would be provided for the students' practice. Gentlemen were to board in the neighborhood. Between this and the spring session there were to be three terms of vocal and instrumental study. For these students, who were not preparing to teach, private lessons were offered by Clare W. Beames, John Zundel, E. Howe, Jr., Allen Dodworth, U. C. Hill, Osborn Oxnard, and George F. Root. The class instructors, in addition to Mason, Root, and Bradbury, were R. Storrs Willis and Thomas Hastings.⁵⁴

The New York Normal Musical Institute announced a full schedule for 1854–55 under the direction of Mason, Root, and Bradbury at Dodworth's Hall, 806 Broadway. A capsule description told the public what to expect. The ten months of the academic year were divided into four terms of about eleven weeks each, to start September 15, December 1, February 15, and May 1. In the first three terms instrumental training, in small classes and private lessons, would be under Root's direction. The fourth, or Teacher's Term, would begin May 1 under the direction of Mason, Root, and Bradbury.⁵⁵

While the Normal Musical Institute was in session, George and Mary Olive Root welcomed their first daughter, born May 26, 1854. They named her Clara Louise. Her two older brothers were Frederick Woodman Root and Charles Towner Root. The family still lived in New York City, but like his associates Bradbury, Cady, and others who taught musical conventions, George Root looked to the west, where teachers held sessions in Ohio, Wisconsin, and Illinois.

Root was invited to teach in a three-week Western Musical Institute in Jacksonville, Illinois. One hour of each day was devoted to teachers and choir directors and those who wanted to become such. Instruction for beginners in music occupied the rest of the time. Approximately 150 people attended. They performed Root's cantata *The Pilgrim Fathers* and, a few days later, *The Flower Queen*. The ladies in the class presented Root with a silver cup. Illinois College, site of the institute, included copies of the advertising circular and the proceedings of the class, as well as a copy of *The Pilgrim Fathers,* among the documents placed under the cornerstone of a new building on the campus. Following this class Root taught another in Quincy, Illinois.[56]

Eighteen fifty-four was a fine year for popular songs. Stephen Foster led the way with "Ellen Bayne," "Hard Times Come Again No More," "Jeannie With the Light Brown Hair," and "Willie, We Have Missed You." Septimus Winner, whose pseudonym was Alice Hawthorne, produced a hit song, "What Is Home Without a Mother," and George Root's song "There's Music in the Air" became a hit. Root had agreed to supply some of the music for each issue of the Mason Brothers' *Musical Review*. One day when their messenger came to pick up Root's manuscript, he had none ready. A quick search of the manuscripts in his desk drawer revealed "There's Music in the Air," which he had written months earlier and tossed aside, thinking it was not particularly good. He sent it to the publisher and it became an example of his theory that a composer did not know which of his compositions would "touch the popular heart."[57]

Root's songs in the *Review* in 1854 illustrated the romanticism, the religious tendency, and the popular themes of the time. Among them were "It Is the Savior's Voice," with words by Thomas Hastings, "Summer's Farewell," "Mourner, Why This Fruitless Sorrow?" and "In the Silent Midnight Watches." The latter evoked the image of the Savior knocking at the door of the heart. In its January 19 issue the *Review* published Root's "O Come and Buy My Hot Corn." With a respectful nod to Henry Russell, this song painted a picture of a struggling street vendor on a cold, windy night.

While *Uncle Tom's Cabin* was being presented onstage and called an "opera," related to the book only through the names of some of the characters,[58] Root's "Old Josey" appeared in sheet music form. Its words began "Come, old Josey, strike a tune," and called for "the banjo and the bones." The piano accompaniment simulated banjo sounds.[59]

Like George Root, the Mason Brothers firm was subject to the pressures of public taste. Normally the firm published music books, but in 1854 they published a novel titled *Ruth Hall* by Fanny Fern. Mason Brothers' *Review* said Fanny Fern's name was "a household word" and commented that "Woman literature is all the rage, now."[60]

At a time when most women were totally dependent, *Ruth Hall* was the story of a woman whose husband died, leaving her with three little girls. Then one of the girls died in the mother's arms. The mother appealed to her parents and her influential, prosperous brother for financial help.

The blind poet Fanny Crosby wrote the words of "There's Music in the Air" and several of Root's other songs, including "Hazel Dell" and "Rosalie, the Prairie Flower." All three of these became hit songs. "There's Music in the Air" could still be found in songbooks in the 1930s.

Neither they nor the family of her late husband would help her, and she had only one marketable skill—she was a good writer. With great difficulty she found publishers for her work, and after a few years of struggle, supported herself and her remaining children quite well. The novel *Ruth Hall* was widely read, especially after the public discovered that it was basically autobiographical. Fanny Fern was a pseudonym for Sara (or Sarah) Willis, sister of N. P. Willis, editor of the *Home Journal*, and he was the object of her scathing criticism in fictional terms in the novel.[61] Root called N. P. Willis "an author of considerable celebrity."[62] Perhaps Root had heard the story of his own mother's going with her nephew and Nat Willis to Boston Common when she was a girl, driving cows to pasture there.[63]

Root set to music the scene in the novel where Ruth Hall's daughter Daisy died. Reading that scene would cause "a moistened eye and a swelling heart," Firth Pond, publisher of the song, said in an advertisement.[64] On the first page of the sheet music the publisher quoted the death scene from the novel. "Slowly the night waned and the stars paled. Up the gray east the golden sun slowly glided. One beam penetrated the little window, hovering like a halo over Daisy's sunny head. A quick, convulsive start, and with one wild cry (as the little throat filled to suffocation) the fair white arms were tossed aloft, then dropped powerless upon the bed of death [*Ruth Hall,* p. 84]." The song closed with a feeling of resignation: Daisy was "recalled to Heaven" and her family should not weep.[65] The sprightly melody was marked "not too fast" and had a lilting quality.

Root's 1854 cantata *The Pilgrim Fathers*[66] appeared at a time when critics and the public anticipated works that were distinctly American, yet were modeled on the works of the European master composers. *The Pilgrim Fathers* took a step in that direction. The opening scene was set in England in the autumn of 1620. A chorus of Puritans sang about " oppression's dark night." As the Mayflower moved slowly away, the Pilgrims on board sang a musical dialogue with the people on shore, ending with farewells that grew gradually softer so they seemed to recede in the distance. This kind of dialogue between two groups of singers became a favorite device in Root's cantatas. *The Pilgrim Fathers* ended with Indians and settlers celebrating the signing of a peace treaty.

In July 1854 Root sent a light-hearted letter to his sister Helen Adams and her husband in Brunswick, Maine, telling them about the cantata and its introduction in the Roots' hometown.

> To my dear Sister
> Mrs. Helen Maria Root Adams
> and
> My dear Brother The Rev. Dr. George Eliashib (?) Adams
>
> Greeting — When in the course of human events — no that isn't right — When one makes a promise he cannot keep, what must be done? That's the question — to be or not to be — able to go to Brunswick." Teasing his readers, he put in details about the farm work that was going on. "But that is not the reason I did not go to Brunswick to day — no — not that — but this — I am to have a musical convention in North Reading — in which the choirs of Woburn, Stoneham, South Reading, Lynfield and North Reading are to join — our

concerts will take place about the time you come—We are to bring out the Cantata of the Pilgrim Great Grand Fathers.

Family visitors were expected and George must be there to help entertain them. The short letter ended playfully.

This is the 31st of July 1854 and I don't think of any think [sic] more.[67]

More than two hundred singers from North Reading and the nearby towns sang *The Pilgrim Fathers* on two consecutive evenings.[68] Root conducted his choir at Mercer Street Church in the first New York performance of *The Pilgrim Fathers* on April 18, 1855. The *Review's* critic praised the singers, gave the composer a mixed review, pointed out Root's potential, told him how to improve, and said, in effect, "We'll see." He called *The Pilgrim Fathers* Root's best composition thus far, "admirably adapted" to the needs of choirs and musical associations all across the country, easy, and for the most part, effective. "It is really quite massive and Handelian," he wrote. The work as a whole, "from an artistic stand-point," he called "common-place" in its "musical ideas and its forms of expression." He objected to the repeated arpeggios at the beginning of one piece and the "common chord frivolities" in another. He said Root had certainly demonstrated in this cantata a kind of talent that "should encourage him to adopt for himself a higher standard of artistic excellence." Now he should break away from the hymn-tune style and focus on larger musical ideas. "Whether he has the stamina to do this, remains to be seen," he concluded.[69]

By January 5, 1855 Root had already been in Unionville, New York, to conduct a four-day musical convention.[70] In mid–January the seventh term of the New York Normal Musical Institute was in full swing at 258 Greene Street with Root as director. Like the Boston Academy of Music before it, this institute had four twelve-week terms.[71] Unlike the better-known summer term, the others did not produce reports in print about daily classes, teachers or special events. The summer term for teachers was the one most people recognized as "the normal."

In March 1855 Root taught in what was said to be Virginia's first musical convention, a four-day session in Richmond. The Richmond *Daily Dispatch* announced a "Grand Concert" for the evening of March 20 with three hundred singers in a program of solos, duets, trios, quartets, and choruses under the direction of Root and William C. Van Meter in the First Baptist Church on Broad Street.[72] A committee recommended that a four-week session to be called Southern Musical Institute be held in

3. *Public Taste at Mid-Century 1851–1855* 61

December 1855 specifically for teachers and choir directors and that Lowell Mason and George Root be invited to teach. In the meantime, Richmond's musicians and teachers were advised to become familiar with the work of Lowell Mason and to read the *Review,* each issue of which contained a lesson he had written.[73] While he was in Richmond, Root visited an African-American church where most of the congregation were slaves. He had been told that the choir would sing before the service began. He asked an elderly member of the church about the choir and was surprised to hear that the man much preferred the singing of the congregation, who sang "the solemn old tunes fit to do your soul good." Another elderly man who sat near Root began singing "My God, the spring of all my joys" to what Root characterized as a slow, quaint melody. Other singers joined him. This was genuine congregational singing, Root thought. He described the sound as strong and mellow, even though the singers added odd turns and embellishments to the tune. The teacher in him made Root notice that the singers did not always keep together. Still there was such genuine devotion and what Root called "soul" in their singing, such solemnity and humility in their manner, that he was more affected by their music than he had been by any comparable experience he could remember. The pastor called on one after another to lead in prayer. Root observed that they became so emotional the speaking voice seemed inadequate, so they chanted their heartfelt prayers, invariably on a minor third. During the service Root observed that the choir sang very well indeed, but their singing was more like a performance than an act of devotion. The elderly gentleman with whom Root had spoken before the service seemed pleased to see that Root agreed with his own assessment and that he appreciated the congregation's singing more than that of the choir.[74]

On Tuesday April 17, 1855, Root's family quartet appeared in a public rehearsal for one of Theodore Eisfeld's "classical entertainments." When the time came for the evening performance, Root's sister Cynthia, the contralto, was unable to sing and the program went on without the quartet. On another occasion members of the quartet sang in Jersey City, New Jersey. Three of them sang "Lift Thine Eyes" from the oratorio *Elijah;* Mary Olive sang "Come Unto Him" from the *Messiah;* and George sang one of his favorite solos, "Rocked in the Cradle of the Deep."[75]

The market for popular songs like Root's was strong. Musical styles were much the same as they had been when Root's first hit song, "The Hazel Dell" appeared. In 1855 at least eighteen of Root's pieces appeared as sheet music. Published by Firth, Pond and Company, one of Stephen Foster's publishers, "Bye and Bye" showed the influence of Foster's work on Root's songwriting in its free-flowing melody and graceful octave intervals. The chorus, in keeping with a practice of the day, could be repeated very softly after the last verse.

Published in the year the Western Union Telegraph Company was founded, "Come to Me Quickly"[76] was based on a "telegraphic dispatch recently sent from the South." The lyricist was not identified. Death was still a popular topic, but this time the song was in the first person: "Come to me quickly! Lov'd ones dear, in a distant land I'm dying." The four-part chorus allowed for dramatic interpretation: "Quickly they sped to the loved and lone, but the gentle soul had gone." A song called "My Weary Heart Is All Alone"[77] expressed a dark, romanticized loneliness both in a silent forest and on a crowded street.

Americans were fascinated by what they heard about the great unsettled territories to the west. There was a rash of "prairie" songs. Henry Russell, whose music played a role in Root's career, wrote a song titled "To the West, To the West." William B. Bradbury's "O, Come to the West" appeared in the *Review* when several of the musical convention teachers were conducting classes in Ohio, Illinois and Wisconsin.[78] In 1855 Root's "Rosalie, the Prairie Flower" became one of the most popular songs in America.[79] Others among the most popular songs that year were Stephen Foster's "Come, Where My Love Lies Dreaming" and Septimus Winner's " Listen to the Mocking Bird."[80] After Root's "Rosalie, the Prairie Flower" became so well known, William Vincent Wallace wrote a ballad called "My Prairie Flower" and dedicated it to "his friend, Geo. F. Root."

Looking back on the success of "Rosalie, the Prairie Flower," Root liked to tell a story that vindicated his writing popular songs. His friend Nathan Richardson had lived for some years in Germany, and when he returned, he had started a music publishing house in Boston with a sincere desire to improve the musical tastes of the American people. His music store became a favorite place for teachers and advanced amateur musicians to spend time. As Root remembered it, there was no American composer then whose music Richardson would have published, even if the composer had given it to him as a gift. After a few months Richardson had to face the fact that his business was not making enough money. Most people were not buying the music that, as Root said, they could neither understand nor perform. Richardson would have to change, at least briefly, from what

3. Public Taste at Mid-Century 1851–1855

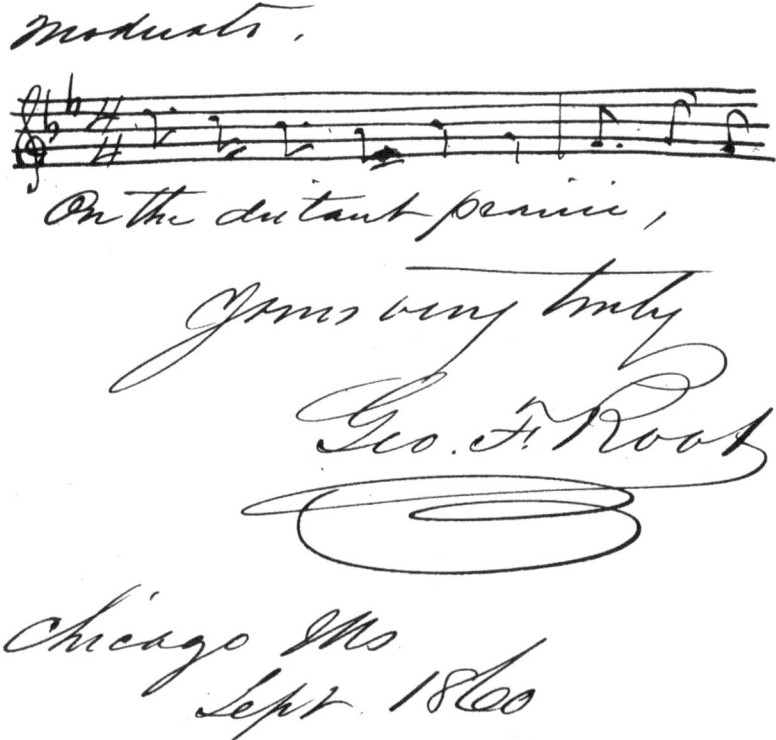

When asked for an autograph, songwriters and teachers often included a few notes that would have particular meaning for the person receiving it. This autograph, written in September 1860, includes the beginning of Root's highly successful 1855 song "Rosalie the Prairie Flower." Purchased from Hanzel Galleries, Chicago.

the public should have to what they would buy. Root was beginning to be recognized as a successful songwriter, so Richardson asked him to write a set of six songs, which Root was happy to do. He finished the songs during his summer vacation at Willow Farm. As he and some of his family members sang through them for the first time, he decided to ask each member in turn, from the oldest to the youngest, to choose the song he or she thought would become the most popular. The last person to choose was his sister Fanny, and the song that was left was "Rosalie, the Prairie Flower." Richardson offered to buy the six songs outright, and asked Root how much he would take for "the lot." There was a tinge of sarcasm in the question. Root told him that, since this was to be a wholesale rather

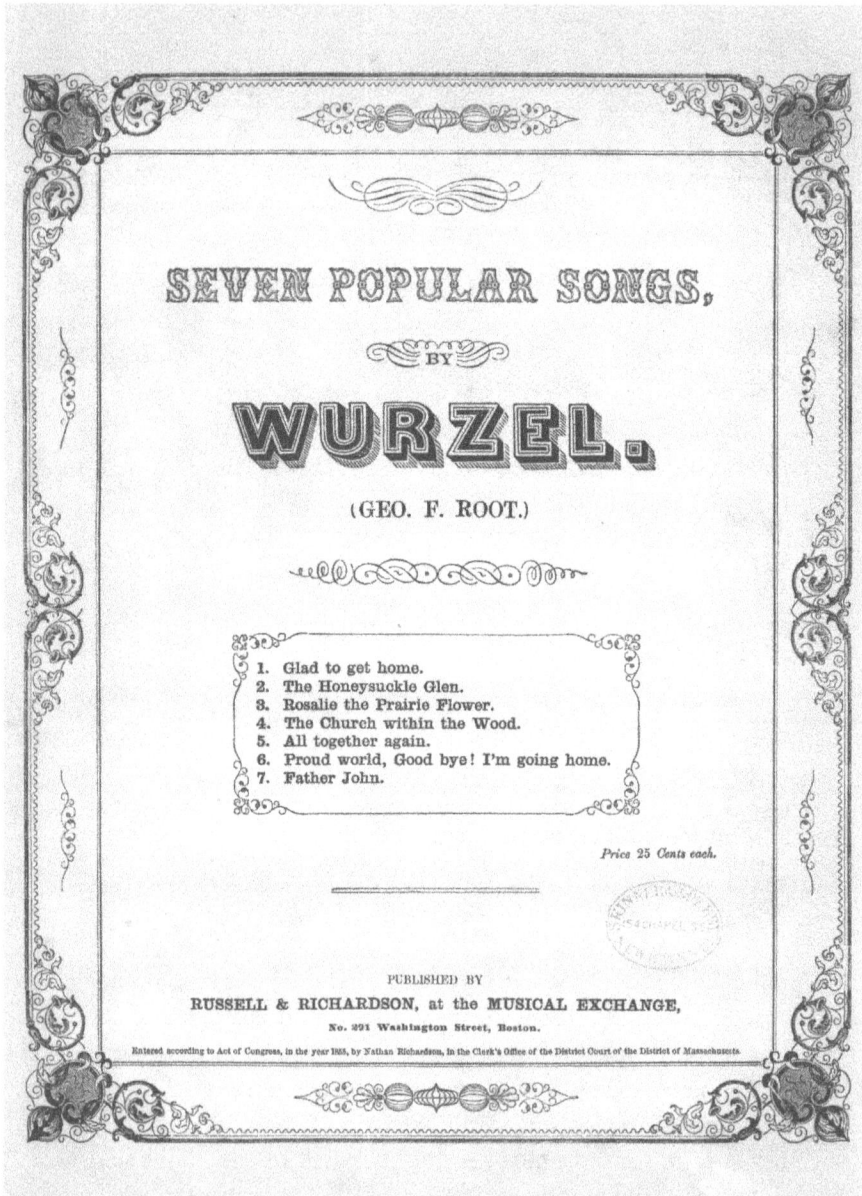

"Rosalie the Prairie Flower" reflects the musical taste of its time — a song for the popular stage and the family parlor, telling the story of a lovely child with blue eyes and flaxen hair who dies in a peaceful cottage and is remembered as the "light of that prairie home."

than a retail transaction, he could have "the lot" at the wholesale price of six hundred dollars. Richardson, unaccustomed to paying such a price, laughed at the idea. They agreed then on a royalty arrangement. In time, Richardson paid almost three thousand dollars in royalties on "Rosalie" alone.[81]

Later, thinking about the problem of "better" music, Root made what he called "a frank statement." He had "never dreamed of eminence" as a composer. Some who knew about his pseudonym, Wurzel, advised him to "aim high." Root saw so many failures among those who were aiming high that he preferred, in his words, to "shoot at something I could hit." Critics told him, "'It is nothing to write those little songs." One man in particular claimed he could write a dozen such songs in a day, so he tried it, using a pseudonym. Root observed that this man's songs. "slumbered quietly on the shelves of a credulous publisher until they went to the paper mill." Writing a simple song was easy; following the rules of music theory and composition was easy. But writing a simple, technically correct song that would "be received and live in the hearts of the people," Root found "quite another matter."[82]

Success as a songwriter did not seem to tempt Root away from teaching or from compiling textbooks. He accepted the prevailing idea that music should refine human feeling; the better and more classical the music, the greater its aesthetic, uplifting, enriching effect. This premise underlay the books he compiled for music classes, the articles he wrote for a music magazine, and his compositions. Still he was determined to write music for the popular market, since this seemed to be where his ability led.

By the 1850s Root had worked for several years with the best-known teachers in their musical conventions — updated successors to the traditional singing schools. As he remembered it, "My connection with the Teachers' Classes, and the 'Normal' recently held, and with Mr. Bradbury in *The Shawm,* had brought me more before the singers of the country."[83] He began receiving invitations to conduct musical conventions himself. This would mean taking responsibility for the entire event, working in unfamiliar places, and scheduling the conventions around his regular classes in New York. Finally he decided to try it, and his first independent class met in Sussex County, New Jersey. By the time he wrote about it the details had been lost. What he remembered was "a pleasant scene in a hilly country, with a crowd of happy people, who took kindly to my way of teaching and entertaining them."[84] His colleague William Bradbury wrote about the cost of a musical convention in 1855. Asked about "the usual expense of a conductor from New-York," Bradbury wrote, "If within two or three hundred miles of New-York City, one hundred dollars is the usual charge for four days. In places of a great distance, it is worth more."[85]

As Root remembered it, each year he became more convinced that New York was not a good place for the Normal Musical Institute. The summer heat in the city was one disadvantage; the expense was another. In 1855 he decided to leave what he called his "city work" as soon as possible and concentrate on musical conventions, the Normal Musical Institute, and writing.[86] Leaving would not be easy; the work had been pleasant and the friends, in his words, "most kind and generous." Each year the schools and institutions where he had taught had given "testimonials" of their appreciation. Members of Mercer Street Church, where he had been organist and choir director for more than ten years, presented him with a silver tea service valued at about five hundred dollars.[87]

Root's work as a teacher was both a liability and an asset in his career as a songwriter. In a sense, teaching restricted his composing. He taught the fundamentals of music theory to facilitate music reading. He was deeply interested in the learning process and in sequencing the material to be learned. He found that the more sophisticated a song was, the harder and more time-consuming it would be to learn, and that most people preferred music they could learn quickly and easily. Some of his compositions showed the effects of his having written hundreds of vocal exercises — sparse and utilitarian. Teaching was an asset in that meeting and teaching hundreds of singers in different parts of the country enabled him to accommodate the tastes and abilities of the public, to touch what he called "the hearts of the people."

4

Music for the Popular Market 1855–1861

Root believed that "emotional or aesthetic benefit by music can come to a person only through music that he likes."[1] He characterized songs the public preferred as "simple" music. These songs had a few basic chords and unadorned, easy-to-read melodies. He mentioned the songs of the Hutchinson Family (a popular singing group) and his gospel song "The Shining Shore" as examples. The value of simple music was its ability to reach all or most of the people. His sheet music titles usually reflected the current trends in popular music.[2]

In the years just before the Civil War, Root "went more among the people of the country" as he expressed it, teaching musical conventions in towns and villages where he was invited. In 1855–1861 he traveled to Maine, New York State, and New Jersey; to Washington, D.C., and Richmond, Virginia; to Mississippi River towns and the prairies of Illinois. Each year this musical convention work added to what he called his "knowledge of what the singers throughout the country needed, and could do."[3] He learned from the people he taught. In his Normal Musical Institute sessions, an "experience meeting" was designed to "get from the singers and teachers" who came from all parts of the country "some knowledge of the state of choirs, singing-schools, and music generally" in their home communities.[4]

The Normal Musical Institute was highly successful, but Root became convinced that New York City was not the best place for it, "not only on account of the heat but the expense."⁵ In 1855 he decided to move the Institute to North Reading, Massachusetts, where he had grown up. North Reading would be his headquarters, and he planned to give all his time to "conventions, Normal and authorship."⁶

He began his fall 1855 musical convention season with a return to Sussex County, New Jersey, for the first week of September. This convention culminated in concerts on Thursday and Friday evenings.⁷ A full schedule kept Root traveling and teaching in New England through September, October and November.⁸

Root had held a musical convention in Richmond, Virginia, in the spring of 1855, and the organizers had asked him to teach another one in December. The December session, called the Southern Musical Institute, met Friday, December 14, through Wednesday, December 20.⁹ The announcement promised an elaborate list of offerings, including chorus practice in the evenings.¹⁰ A fairly large audience attended Lowell Mason's lecture on "Congregational Singing" in spite of weather that was "quite unpleasant."¹¹ A newspaper reported that this convention had closed with what amounted to a music festival. The closing concert included music by Handel, Mozart, and other master composers. On two successive nights a chorus of nearly one hundred voices sang Root's *Flower Queen*.¹² The participants in this convention gave Root his first gold-headed cane. In the years that followed, he thought they would have liked to "break it over the head of the man who wrote war songs for the northern army." Writing in 1889, he believed the feeling of enmity had passed. In his words, "On both sides we did what we thought was right."¹³

Root was in Richmond on Christmas Day, 1855, when the *Enquirer* reprinted a sizzling article from the *N. Y. Evening Mirror*. "THE ABOLITION WAR BEGUN. The virgin soil of Kansas is stained with the blood of its citizens. The abolition fanatics ... have at last committed the overt act, and a civil war is begun!"¹⁴ The article continued in tones of bitter hatred.

Root's commitments took him to Southold, Long Island, in February;¹⁵ Florida (Orange County), New York,¹⁶ then Bridgeton, New Jersey, in March; and Salem, New Jersey, in April 1856.¹⁷ After the Bridgeton convention he sent the *Review* a highly complimentary report calling it "the most interesting and successful" convention thus far. The organizers had had everything — room, piano, and books — "in perfect readiness, and in good order" at the appointed time. He admitted that one purpose of this article was to encourage the same efficiency and promptness in others who were planning musical conventions of their own.[18] In May he taught in Beemersville, Sussex County, New Jersey, returning for the fifth time to the county where he had begun to teach independently.[19] From the teacher's viewpoint, the musical convention business could be contentious. In Root's words, "personal and bitter attacks upon other teachers and musicians and their systems" caused difficulty and dissatisfaction.[20]

In April 1856, Mason Brothers announced publication of "Mr. Root's New Book of Church-Music" but explained that it wasn't ready yet. Available in June or July, it would be titled *The Sabbath Bell*. This was his first book without a co-author. In words that reflected a widespread viewpoint of the time, he offered the book as "a means for improving and ennobling the heart and the affections." He was indebted to the Reverend Henry Ward Beecher for the use of many verses that had been set to music for the first time especially for this book.

Root had tried writing words for songs while he lived in New York. He cited some of the problems in using poems of other writers: a thin vowel to be sung on a high note; a wrong meter; words that failed to convey the emotional quality he had in mind; or words that had a rough, jarring quality where he wanted them to flow. After he moved to North Reading there was no one nearby to whom he could go for the kinds of words he needed. In his pleasant surroundings at Willow Farm he enjoyed "turning into rhyme" the thoughts that came to him. He attributed the success of *The Sabbath Bell* largely to these words.[21]

The Sabbath Bell contained "The Shining Shore," arguably the best-known of Root's hymns or gospel songs. It remained in a number of hymnbooks into the twentieth century. It had originated with a poem his mother chose from a religious periodical. The words began "My days are gliding swiftly by." As he read the poem "a simple melody sang itself along" in his mind. He jotted it down and went on with the work he was doing. When he returned to it, planning to add alto, tenor and bass to the melody, it seemed so simple, so commonplace, that he hesitated to add the harmony parts. Finally he decided that "someone might find it useful," and completed it. His doubts about it came back; he threw it into a wastebasket. Mary Olive rescued it and insisted that it be published. When it became widely known, used in the hymnals of several denominations and sung by Civil War soldiers on both sides, he wondered why. "It had in it that mysterious life" that made a song appeal to people. "To the musician there is

THE SHINING SHORE.

Rev. DAVID NELSON.   G. F. ROOT.

1. My days are glid-ing swift-ly by, And I, a pilgrim stranger, Would not de-tain them as they fly, Those hours of toil and danger.
2. We'll gird our loins, my brethren dear, Our heav'nly home discerning; Our ab-sent Lord has left us word, Let ev-'ry lamp be burn-ing.

CHORUS.

For oh, we stand on Jordan's strand, Our friends are passing o-ver; And just be-fore the Shining Shore We may almost discov-er.

3 Should coming days be cold and dark,
   We need not cease our singing;
   That perfect rest naught can molest,
   Where golden harps are ringing.

4 Let sorrow's rudest tempests blow,
   Each chord on earth to sever;
   Our King says, Come, and there's our home,
   Forever, oh, forever.

When Root finished writing "The Shining Shore," he was not sure it was worth keeping. He threw it into a wastebasket; his wife Mary Olive rescued it and insisted that it be published. Root believed that a composer could not know whether one of his songs had the "mysterious vitality" that would make it "live in the hearts of the people." In his own experience, he claimed, "successes are usually surprises." According to his contemporaries, "The Shining Shore" became the best known and longest lasting of his hymns. Root described the author of the words, David Nelson, as a missionary who preached against slavery.

not one reason in melody or harmony, scientifically regarded, for such a fact," he admitted.[22]

When the Normal Musical Institute opened in 1856 in North Reading, it was still what Root described as the only Normal Institute in the country specifically for teachers of music.[23] On the faculty at this session were the best-known men in their field: Mason, Webb, Bradbury, and Root. Sixty-two students from seventeen states attended.[24] Root claimed that everyone liked what he called "the picturesque old town" of North Reading. For students from what was then the west, the New England landscape was "a novelty."[25]

The Institute's day began at nine A. M. with the sound of a bell rung by one of the students. After roll call, either Mason or Root read from the Bible and the class sang a hymn. For the first hour Lowell Mason lectured on the art of teaching. Root's voice training occupied the second hour. In the third hour, Mason taught an elementary-level demonstration lesson as students took notes, knowing they would be called on to take turns teaching the same lesson in the afternoon. The class in harmony and composition followed. Here students sang chords, listened to them, analyzed them, and wrote them. One student commented that the preparation for this class kept them up until the small hours of the night. In the late afternoon the class sang glees and other short choral pieces, and three times a week they rehearsed choruses from Handel's *Messiah* in the evening.[26] On Friday afternoons about five or six o'clock, vehicles of all sorts began arriving from the neighboring towns, bringing an audience to hear the evening rehearsal or concert. In Root's opinion, Lowell Mason's chorus work on these evenings was "grand" and the glee singing under the direction of George James Webb was "exquisite."[27]

All the members of the Institute were asked to sing at the commencement of Andover Theological Seminary, about seven miles from North Reading. Their program included choruses from the *Messiah* accompanied by George James Webb at the organ. A student recalled that Root was expected to conduct; instead, he "took his place" with the basses and "sang as one of us."[28] At Willow Farm on Tuesday evening, August 19, the Root family entertained the faculty and students of the Institute. The three-months' session ended Monday, August 25. The largest hall in the Institute's building could hold only about half the people who came to hear the closing concert. One singer wrote that the "sublime strains" of a *Messiah* chorus would remain with them when they were far from the "opportunities for hearing or joining in such music."[29] The class presented Lowell Mason with a beautiful Bible and gave Root a silver baton tipped with gold.[30]

With the Normal Institute finished for the year, Root began what he called his "convention campaign" for the fall. Traveling west, he taught in Galesburg, Illinois; Indianapolis, Indiana; Jerseyville, Illinois; and Oshkosh, Wisconsin. A report from Galesburg observed that "Mr. Root is just the man for this country, and we should be glad to keep him here" primarily because of his method of vocal training.[31]

Root started 1857 with a trip on his favorite railroad, the Erie. At 7:00 A.M. Monday, January 12, he boarded a train for Hinsdale, a town in the mountains of western New York State. The weather was terrible; snow blocked the railroad and frosted the rails. His train fell behind schedule; he fell asleep and missed the place where he was to change trains. "Tumbling" off the train at the next stop, he left his hat behind. Stranded in Belvidere at 4:00 in the afternoon, he found that there would be no train to Hinsdale until 8:00 the following morning. Wrapping himself in coats and a shawl, he lay down in the depot for the night. About 11 o'clock the next morning he arrived at the depot in Hinsdale, where several people were waiting. The Hinsdale convention closed on Thursday evening; Root was expected in Cooperstown for his next convention the following Tuesday. He had planned to go there directly from Hinsdale, but when the time came he felt what he called "premonitions of coming illness." He decided to go to New York City as soon as possible. An eastbound train was due about midnight. After the closing concert he cleared up some details and rested for a short time, then went to the depot, where he waited three hours for the train. Finally the depot-master woke the young telegrapher, who after several attempts learned that the train would not arrive until morning. Root, in his words, "made the best of the softest side of the benches" and slept until the train came. He did not say what the illness was, only that his doctor in New York told him he was "not a minute too soon" in arriving. On the following Monday he was well enough to go to Cooperstown for his next musical convention, but a snowstorm blocked the railroads. Assuming that most people knew about the snowstorm, he was perplexed when he read in a Cooperstown paper that "for some reason, Mr. Root did not arrive." A teacher of musical conventions could not afford the stigma of missing scheduled classes. The *Review* published his letter of apology, and he was able to schedule a later trip to Cooperstown.

He was ill again when it was time to leave for a convention in Towanda; his doctor advised him not to go, and Root engaged George B. Loomis to take his place. Writing on February 7, 1857, Root was determined to leave for a convention in Geneva, New York, without asking his doctor.[32]

Root was in Washington, D.C., by May 4, 1857, for a highly unusual musical convention at the Smithsonian Institution. "Delegates" were invited to represent their choirs or musical associations "in the East, West, North and South," and they would all be "entertained" free of cost during their stay.[33] Sponsors chose Washington in order to attract a larger attendance than usual, and "to be near the southern states," Root remembered. He stayed longer than he had planned, joining with the Union Choir Association in a concert and a trip by boat to Mount Vernon. Cruising along the Potomac, the visiting musicians played instruments and sang. "I shall never forget that day," Root thought, nor the feelings of "awe, veneration, and gratitude" with which we gathered around the tomb of "our immortal Washington" and sang "Rest, Spirit, Rest."[34]

In 1857 the Normal Musical Institute was held in North Reading for the second year. Lowell Mason, George James Webb, and August Kreissman joined Root on the faculty.[35] In late August some 75 people were reportedly in attendance.[36] The Mason Brothers music firm promoted the Institute, believing it "destined to accomplish most important results in the musical progress of America." The company claimed to have "no pecuniary interest whatever in it."[37]

Teaching music to blind students had given Root a distinctive way of teaching harmony. He found that students could learn to identify the various chords by hearing them. He played chords on the piano; students responded by naming and describing them in the terminology of music theory, observing the traditional rules. This was a great improvement over what he called "eye" harmony. In Normal Institute classes, students brought completed harmony assignments to class and listened as the group sang the chords they had written. Root never seemed to lose his high regard for the opinions of Lowell Mason and George James Webb, and no other comments they made about his teaching gratified him as much as their approval of his method of teaching harmony.[38]

The success of his 1852 cantata *The Flower Queen* must have been gratifying as well. By 1856 *The Flower Queen* had been performed more than five hundred times. Root's associates at the *Review* editorialized about operas that were called American and that had been written in America, yet somehow failed to project the qualities expected of an American opera. From the *Review's* point of view, the widespread popularity of *The Flower Queen* held more promise of a national opera to come than "all the *Rip Van Winkles* and *Giovanni di Napolis*" that had appeared onstage thus far.[39] According to music historian Gilbert Chase, the cantata served the same purpose in America that the opera served in Europe: It was "the most popular form of extended vocal composition."[40]

Root's next cantata, *The Haymakers,* was a step in the direction of "a national opera." Subtitled an "operatic cantata," it was easy enough to learn and dramatic enough to hold the interest of singers and listeners. In his autobiography, Root gave credit to the man who had suggested that he write a secular cantata: Lowell Mason, Jr., senior partner at Mason Brothers. At the time, an interest in everyday life was one of the elements of American Romanticism.[41] According to Root, the younger Mason "took a great interest" in the work, and "to a great extent planned it," the characters and the action as well as what each piece in the cantata should be about.[42] Root began the work, sometimes writing the words first, sometimes the music, and sometimes both together.

While Root was working on *The Haymakers,* Mason Brothers published the opening chorus and a brief description of the plot.[43] Months later they advertised *The Haymakers* with more than their usual enthusiasm and promised that this new work would be available "early in the fall."[44]

Root composed most of *The Haymakers* in his new library at Willow Farm. Going to the door and looking out, he could see the fields where he had "swung the scythe and raked the hay" nearly twenty years ago. Almost every scene in the cantata had a counterpart in his farming experience. He had watched the sky anxiously and rushed to get the hay in the barn before a thunderstorm. He wrote that into the cantata. The exception was a comic character called "Snipkins" who was "purely imaginary."[45] In concert performances without costumes or scenery the part of Snipkins, the "young man from the city, unused to rural affairs" was to be omitted.

Snipkins's most dramatic moment was a "Fireman's Song." In the recitative, "Stay! Hold On!" he urged the workers to rest while he sang to them. In the song, reminiscent of the work of Henry Russell, a fireman rescued a child.

For one who grew up believing theatrical entertainments were harmful, Root got rather involved in writing "Explanations and Directions" for staging *The Haymakers*. The singers were to carry scythes, rakes or pitchforks, according to the subject of each piece, and move around the stage in the familiar motions of haymaking. For the dinner scene they were directed to pass plates and baskets around and improvise appropriate actions. The comic city-dweller Snipkins, singing, "Some folks like the country, I don't!" could be "somewhat dandified" in costume, with a monocle and gold chains. He was to improvise his reactions when, according to the plot, he ran into a wasps' nest. At one point in the score Root advised stagehands to "Commence diminishing the light about here, to represent the twilight." Before his serenade "My Katy's a Girl Beyond Compare," Snipkins was to tumble onstage "as if falling over something." The katydid was written into the song to "contradict" Snipkins's claims, beginning with "Katy never loved anybody but me." Root gave detailed directions for making the katydid sound with a device made of string, resin and a walnut shell. In a morning scene, whistles blown in glasses of water would imitate the sounds of certain birds. The "Good Morning" chorus started offstage and built as the singers came on. When William, the hired man, and Anna, the farmer's daughter, were finishing their duet, "Lo, the Clouds Are Breaking," the lights would gradually brighten to prepare for the chorus, "Rainbow! Rainbow!"

The music, as well as the words, described what was happening. As the story developed, the piano suggested sunrise, wind and rain, "the singing of the scythe through the grass," and military drums. In the thunderstorm scene the chorus swept up and down the scale suggesting the "rushing, howling wind." The trees swayed with a pattern of notes that illustrated their motions. The storm ended with a low-pitched trill in the piano accompaniment, fading away like thunder in the distance. "Crickets, katydids and other sounds of the night" enhanced the twilight scene when the chorus sang "Softly the Twilight Fades."

Like *The Flower Queen*, this cantata had a few religious moments, a musical nod to the fact that religion was a strong presence in American life. The full chorus sang "To Him Who Made Us"; a quintet sang "How Good Is He the Giver." In the final chorus, the cast sang "Thanks Be to Him Who Has Given Us the Increase."

To pre–Civil War audiences, *The Haymakers* was good entertainment. It had a love story, comic relief, a storm scene, and a heroine who sang while dreaming. One of the pieces incorporated an easily recognizable fragment of "Home, Sweet Home." A citified Snipkins who thought wasps were houseflies, and treated them accordingly, was entertaining. Root suggested that "a rustic dance" could be added to the final number "if thought best." *The Haymakers* was more dignified than a minstrel show and less demanding than an opera. Americans took it to their hearts. In the first year of its availability Root conducted it twenty times in Boston and the neighboring towns.[46]

After tea in the afternoons, students in the 1857 Normal Musical Institute at North Reading sang choruses. Ordinarily they sang pieces from *The Messiah*, but one student reported that sometimes in Lowell Mason's absence, they sang pieces from *The Haymakers* under Root's direction.[47]

The Haymakers was a people's operetta, heard in towns and cities across the country. To the composer it brought the same criticism that his successful popular songs brought. It was good, but it wasn't comparable with the works of the European master composers. *The Chicago Tribune,* however, preferred *The Haymakers* to Italian opera, which it said "walks on stilts, deals in exaggeration, and treats largely of kings, queens, dukes and nobles" while the Haymakers "is purely democratic, exalts labor, ridicules the useless city dandy, and holds up for your admiration the sturdy Farmer and his household.'"[48] The strongest criticism was written by Root's mentor and friend Lowell Mason, in a personal letter to W. W. Killip: "Which is your standard *musically*—'The Messiah' or 'The Haymakers'...? Ought we to put forth an effort to improve public taste and knowledge, or should we bring ourselves down into communion with the most coarse and vulgar?"[49] *The Haymakers* demonstrated that Root's most successful works were those based on his self-assessment that "I am simply one who ... writes music for the people."[50]

At the Normal Musical Institute in 1857, participants celebrated the Fourth of July with a picnic. Lunch was announced by the singing of a chorus, "Tis the farmer's welcome call, come to dinner!" from the forthcoming cantata, *The Haymakers*. After lunch there were "toasts, speeches, and stories." At 5:30 the whole group gathered to observe one of the widespread customs of this holiday — hearing the Declaration of Independence read.[51]

The Normal Institute at North Reading attracted crowds of visitors and a few special guests. In July 1857, *Dwight's Journal of Music,* on the classical end of the popular-classical continuum, published two articles by visitors. The unidentified writer of an article called "A Day at North-Read-

4. Music for the Popular Market 1855–1861

ing, Massachusetts" was impressed that the institute's widespread reputation had brought students from nearly every state in the union. He enjoyed the Teaching Exercise, in which a member of the class assumed the role of teacher and was subject to the criticism of the other students. He remained until darkness began to fall before starting back to Boston and, as he rode away, heard the sounds of one of Handel's choruses grow fainter. He was convinced that if the country were ever to have institutions with the high standards of a conservatory of music, such institutions must begin with gatherings like the Normal Musical Institute.[52]

On July 22 the distinguished scholar Alexander W. Thayer visited the Institute. Thayer had lived in Germany while he gathered material for his biography of Beethoven. He had close ties with Lowell Mason and was favorably disposed toward the Institute and its teachers. He described Root's method of teaching harmony in detail: How he played a succession of chords on the piano, moving on into various keys, and how the class was expected to determine, by hearing, what kinds of chords were played, whether a particular chord was inverted, which inversion was played, and so on. Thayer was generous in his praise of Root's other specialization, vocal training. "The best class teaching of vocalization I had ever seen was by Goetze, in Leipzig, and Stern, in Berlin; but in neither case did the method strike me as better than Mr. Root's," he wrote. The value of this training was evident in the evening rehearsal of choruses from the *Messiah*.[53]

On August 19, Lowell Mason's son William, an eminent pianist, came to North Reading to play for the participants. Writing to the *Review*, a student admitted that many of the Normal students had never heard "a real artist," such as Mason, at the piano. The listeners enjoyed several of Mason's own compositions, particularly "Silver Spring."[54]

Harriet Beecher Stowe, author of *Uncle Tom's Cabin*, lived at Andover, seven miles from North Reading. Her brother, the famous preacher Henry Ward Beecher, usually came to visit her in the summer. Members of the Normal Institute particularly wanted to see the Reverend Beecher, and perhaps hear him speak. Root had doubts about insisting on a visit, but a student from Geneseo, New York, W. W. Killip, went to Beecher and delivered the invitation in person. Mrs. Stowe objected; Killip urged her to come. He argued that her "Uncle Tom" was more famous than her brother Henry. According to Root's account, Beecher hesitated to come, but when Killip offered to vote for his candidate for governor, he agreed. On the appointed day the visitors came. After Lowell Mason's morning lecture, the Reverend Beecher spoke in his inimitable way for half an hour on the connections of music to the church and the home. The distinguished visitors dined at Willow Farm and attended the afternoon rehearsal of choruses and glees.[55]

Root and his wife Mary Olive, his sister Cynthia, and their brother Towner sang Mendelssohn's "Hunting Song" for the Normal Institute members. Full of enthusiasm for his friends, L. Hinsdale Sherwood called this "probably the best quartet ever heard in America"; and praised their "purity of tone, distinctness, balance of the several parts, light and shade."[56]

The customary audience for a Friday rehearsal had not been invited, but on Friday, August 21, the hall was "thronged" with listeners while members of the Institute rehearsed. Singing pieces from *The Haymakers* had become a favorite pastime during the summer; the music was as familiar as "household words," according to one report, with melodies that could "live in the heart." Wednesday, August 26, was the last day of the 1857 session. Some of the students looked at the blackboard through moist eyes as Lowell Mason wrote on it an exercise in four parts, with the words "Glory be to God on high." Everyone stood and sang this, and the Normal Musical Institute for 1857 came to an end.[57]

The Normal Musical Institute found a future in the west, as did musical conventions and the music trade. Chicago became a center for these developments. A new Normal Musical Institute, patterned on the original, began in Chicago in the summer of 1857 with C. M. Cady as director. Cady had moved to Chicago in 1856.[58] The new Institute's second term, announced for the six weeks beginning September 15, was "designed especially for the preparation of teachers of Vocal Music for the Northwest."[59]

For many of the Normal Institute students, as for George Root, teaching would lead to composing exercises and songs, perhaps hymns and anthems for their classes to sing. In a letter to the *Review* someone asked a question that, in all likelihood, many other readers had wanted to ask: How did one become a composer? There was no way to develop one's talent for composition other than hearing genuinely *good* music, the *Review* replied. "A good long residence in a European city — Berlin, Leipzig, or Paris" was recommended as the way to become thoroughly acquainted with the work of the better composers. The making of a real composer would require genius, observation and experience, and a study of the best models. Asked to recommend a book on composition, the *Review* mentioned several, but concluded, "If one is not a composer without book helps, he will never be so with them."[60]

The New England countryside was looking particularly bleak on the day Root began an article of his own for the *Review* on composing music. His mind went back to the settlers who had arrived on this day 236 years earlier and their joy in having a new home. As if by habit a four-part song came from his hand: "They came when the wintry wind rushed by, and the snow-covered pines were bending; when all was drear in earth or sky, but the sound of their praise ascending." He hadn't intended to write music when he began, but from his personal viewpoint, "any thing that excites emotion finds readiest expression in music." He went on to explain his concept of composing. Although it was commonly understood to mean creating "new rhythmic and melodic forms, and new harmonies and progressions," only a few musicians throughout history had invented harmonic and melodic forms that endured. Composers and compilers of the popular books Americans used had, through consistent practice and observation, stored in their minds what he called "the musical forms, combinations, and effects" that had impressed them as "beautiful, striking, or effective." These and the individual's originality formed a "reservoir" from which the composer drew. The writer would apply what seemed to be the appropriate musical form to the emotion or sentiment he was trying to express. The word *composing*, to Root, meant putting together. Beethoven *invented* or *originated*, but most producers of songs and other pieces of music composed.[61] Stored in Root's mental reservoir were hymns and folk songs from the colonial days; songs by Stephen Foster, Franz Schubert and Franz Abt; melodies from the works of Handel and Mendelssohn, and from the operas and minstrel shows on the New York stage. Evidently Root composed quickly and purposefully, often facing a deadline. His usual comment about his music had to do with its usefulness to the public.[62]

Root's *Festival Glee Book* was a veritable sampler of American music, 1857 style.[63] Its popular songs and current themes, such as temperance and the romance of the prairies, appealed to a broad public as well as the students for whom it was designed. It had no elementary music reading or "singing school" section and most of the songs were secular. His "operatic cantata" *The Haymakers* was printed in the back of the first edition of the book.

Root said almost nothing in his autobiography or in the articles he wrote about the foreshadowing of war between the sections of the United

States. For the *Festival Glee Book*, however, he set to music a plea for unity, "Who Would Sever Freedom's Shrine?" The author of the words was not named.

Millions of Americans felt the effects of industrialization. For the *Festival Glee Book* Root set to music a poem that spelled out the impact of steam as an energy source—"The Song of Steam."

Root included a generous selection of his popular songs in *The Festival Glee Book*. His hit songs, "Hazel Dell" and "Rosalie the Prairie Flower," were there, as were "The Old Folks Are Gone," "All Together Again," "Our Pastor," and "Mary of the Glen." A song called "Never Forget the Dear Ones" was dedicated to the Western Vermont Musical Association. "Flying Home" was subtitled "Happy News for My Mother"; "They Sleep in the Dust" honored parents. Singers using *The Festival Glee Book* could study two of the favorite pieces the Root family quartet sang: William Mason's "Slumber Sweetly, Dearest" and Mendelssohn's "Hunting Song." Root's musical setting of "The Ship of Union (Sail On, O Ship of State)" by Longfellow was written for baritone, alto, tenor and bass. A poem called "The Old Maple Tree" was set to music by George's brother E. Towner Root.

Stephen Foster's "Hard Times, Come Again No More" seemed appropriate in the last months of 1857. The financial panic of that time was called many colorful names, among them a "commercial revulsion."[64] Newspapers and other publications were full of distressing news and commentary. "The times! Hard times, is the hue and cry from all quarters of the nation," one commentator wrote. Musicians, hurt by the financial panic, showed concern for those in need. "The 'hard times' have served to develop the kindness and generosity of the musical profession to a degree which no other cause could have done" one report claimed. Many people struggled to take care of their own obligations, and yet concerts were "constantly" being given and the proceeds donated to local organizations "for the aid of the poor and suffering."[65] Banks were suspending their operation, stocks had depreciated dramatically, and the public was preoccupied with the situation. The same writer predicted that many people who had planned to study music in the coming months would "be obliged to forgo" that study and that the economic recovery would not be pleasant. The "music-dealer, the musical instrument-maker, and the music teacher, must all more or less help to bear the trials ... of so great a commercial crisis."[66] Mason Brothers publishers called the panic of 1857 a "general derangement of trade" and recommended that customers order directly from them rather than through a local music store. "We will take in payment notes of all solvent banks in the Union at par," they promised.[67]

In mid–September 1857, Root started on his fall schedule of musical conventions. He taught in three towns in New York State in a period of about three weeks. During the first half of October he taught in Ellsworth and Bangor, Maine. At Bangor approximately four hundred singers presented selections from *The Haymakers* and from Handel's *Messiah*.[68]

In the fall of 1857, Root sent a particularly informative article called "Passing Notes of Musical Travel" to the *Review*. In this article he took the readers with him from the Massachusetts hills to the Mississippi River and the prairies of Illinois. On the way to Burlington, Vermont, he and his brother Towner stopped in Andover, Massachusetts, to visit Lowell Mason. Boarding a train at Andover they chose their seats carefully, ignoring the conductor's loud announcement that there was plenty of room in the forward car, thinking the second car might be safer. They settled down with copies of the New York and Boston papers and the latest *Harper's* magazine. The train track ran along the scenic course of the Merrimac River, which powered the factories of Lowell and Lawrence, Massachusetts. Friends met them when they arrived in rain and darkness at Burlington. The next morning at the Town Hall where the convention was to take place, Root found the problem he had written about in his article on the importance of promptness. It was time to begin, the place had not been swept, there was no fire, no piano, and there were no books. One of the residents explained that people never expected to do much the first day, and that the conventions they had had in past never began on time. "We'll inaugurate a new state of things," Root told him. A few participants came in; someone brought a few of the books Root had specified from the local music store, and wearing shawls and bonnets, hats and overcoats, the few who were present began the work of the convention. During the day the room was "put in order" and the singers straggled in. With fewer than a hundred singers, Root considered this a relatively small class.

Root was scheduled to teach in Geneseo, New York, beginning on Tuesday, October 27. On the train he and his brother Towner had some of the usual problems that plagued travelers. People milled about in confusion when the conductor announced that those going to Albany, Troy and beyond must change cars. Lost umbrellas, forgotten bags, and crying children contributed to the confusion. The Roots hurried into the Albany car and settled down, only to be told that they should not have changed cars. Arriving in Troy, they found that the next leg of the journey would be by ferry, and that they *might* be in time for the train on the other side. They left the ferry to find the conductor standing beside the train, looking at his watch. They had two minutes to get their luggage from an adjacent depot and buy tickets. Root urged the conductor not to leave without them. He and Towner boarded the crowded train as it was beginning to move. At the next town many of the passengers left the train, and the Roots settled down, hoping for a quiet rest. A small boy in their car persisted in singing "Rosalie the Prairie Flower" in what Root called "the most dismal way." He consoled himself by "thinking of the next pay-day at the publishers." George and Towner Root were in Rochester, New York, on Sunday, October 25. George suggested they attend a certain church where the music was always good. Towner reminded him that he had recently told the participants in a musical convention they should not go to church "for the purpose of being musically entertained." George concluded that it was much easier "to preach than to practice." On Monday, October 26, George and Towner left Rochester. They went by train to Avon, and by stagecoach from Avon to Geneseo, New York. "The thirty miles in one hour, the twelve miles in three — but those who have rich soil must be contented with bad roads," George wrote. The miles of dragging along through deep mud led to a beautiful valley with picturesque views and well-kept farms. At Geneseo, three hundred singers were in the chorus. In spite of rainy weather, they were punctual. With very limited time together, the participants faced the problem of a closing concert. Some questioned the need for it; others thought it was an obligation to the community since students were guests in the homes of residents. Root commented that the work of the convention involved more than singing the right notes in correct rhythm; the studies must include what he called "modes of teaching" and the "true use of music in divine worship." The convention closed with a concert in a local church.[69]

On Saturday, October 31, George and Towner Root started west, stopping on the way to "take a look at Niagara," before spending the Sabbath in Detroit. On Monday, November 2, they were in Chicago. The train for Kewanee, Illinois, their destination, departed at nine in the evening. George claimed that a person could become accustomed to sleeping on a train. This time he rested comfortably for a few hours, only to be roused by such a fierce shaking that, half-awake, he thought the conductor must be pulling him out of the wreckage while asking for his ticket. There, standing over him, was William B. Bradbury. Too startled to be polite, Root asked "What are you doing here?" Bradbury explained that he was on his way to a musical convention in a town near Kewanee. For a few days they would be neighbors, Root told him. About three A.M. the train stopped for Kewanee and the two Roots stood alone on the prairie, the full moon making the boundless expanse look almost like an ocean. On Tuesday morning, November 3, the annual convention of the Central Illinois Musical Association began; it was scheduled to continue until Friday night. This meeting in Kewanee was a clear example of the way towns in the west were springing up, in contrast with the old, long-settled eastern towns Root knew. The hall where the convention met was barely large enough to hold the participants, and no building in the area was large enough for the closing concert. Two churches were under construction, so the concert was scheduled for the one that was most nearly finished. Root was startled to see that it was full of "carpenters' benches, timbers, joists, boards, shavings," and "three or four pews" half finished; this was the building in which the concert was to take place in a few hours. Residents of the town assured Root that the place would be ready in time, and it was. Neatly arranged planks served as seats; there were a few chairs, and more importantly to Root, they were all filled. He wondered at the growth of a place that, three years earlier, had one house; now it had almost two thousand residents that he called " young, enterprising, and full of vitality."[70]

At noon on Saturday, November 7, George and Towner Root arrived at Quincy, Illinois, on the Mississippi river. The water level was low; no one could tell them when they could board a boat for St. Louis. After dinner a boat was sighted, and they rushed to get on board, only to wait while great quantities of merchandise were loaded. It was almost dark when the boat left. The Roots went to their stateroom for what they hoped would be a good night's sleep. The boat's monotonous sound had lulled them to sleep when a loud scraping noise, followed by a thump and a crash, startled them awake. The captain had said this boat drew so little water she could go anywhere there was a heavy dew. In the morning the passengers discovered that the boat had run aground among the trees, one wheel was broken, and repairs would take several hours. The Roots arrived in Alton too late to go to St. Louis as planned. On Monday, November 9, they boarded an old-fashioned stagecoach that made "old-fashioned" time — twenty miles in six hours. The Jerseyville, Illinois, musical convention began on the tenth and lasted eight days. On Wednesday, November 18, George and Towner started across the prairie toward Shipman, planning to take the evening train to Chicago. They arrived in time to watch the train leave. They found a place to spend the night, but there was very little rest. George compared the prairie wind with that on the ocean. As he described it, they were rocked, not in the cradle of the deep, but in a house on the prairie. During the night they heard the crash of some unfinished buildings that were toppled by the wind. Their train the next morning ran hours behind schedule, finally arriving at Bloomington, Illinois, where they found a group of men waiting for them. These men had come to discuss music education; Root described the Normal Musical Institute and talked with them about their plans for "the Prairie State." Finally on the evening of Wednesday, November 24, George Root was at home in North Reading just in time for Thanksgiving. One more convention the following week in Morristown, New Jersey,[71] and then he could look forward to what he called "a quiet winter's work in my den." He ended this part of his travel journal with the suggestion that all musical associations make their convention plans as far in advance as possible, so that conductors could plan their travel to save time and expense.[72]

Root was scheduled to hold conventions in Connecticut, New York, and Pennsylvania in February and March 1858.[73] In Danbury, Connecticut, George, Mary Olive, and Towner Root took part in two concerts directed by one of Root's former Normal Musical Institute participants.[74] When Root arrived in Niagara Falls for a musical convention in March, he found that the singers had rehearsed his cantata *The Haymakers* throughout the past winter and were prepared to sing it in a benefit concert for the poor. The concert was judged a success and the donation for the poor was called a "handsome" one.[75]

Planners of the annual musical convention in Washington, D.C., invited Mason, Root and Bradbury to teach there in the spring of 1858. Mason had to decline due to prior engagements. The Washington singers were very disappointed. They had set their hearts on seeing the "Father of Music in America," as they called Mason, and profiting from his instruction. Musical life in Washington was not as lively as usual because, as a correspondent said, "Political subjects so engross the attention." With unprecedented generosity the managers of the convention, eager to attract a large number of attendees from the north, planned to show them the Washington sights and entertain them free of charge. "Come on, now, musical people from the North!" the letter-writer urged.[76] The convention opened April 26. A participant reported that attendance from various states was highly satisfactory and a considerable number of Washington residents were attending as well. The galleries were packed with observers. About Root and Bradbury the writer to the *Review* was careful to say "the relative merits of each are not discussed." The closing concerts received high praise.[77]

During the years of George Root's extensive travel, the Root family must have written a great many letters. One rare example is a letter to Frederick, George and Mary Olive's son. The letter includes both a message from his mother and a note from his brother Charles. "Father is at home now," Mary Olive wrote to eleven-year-old Frederick, who was probably away at school. One of a pair of horses George Root kept for his family's use had caused an accident. Now the question was whether the horse was too unreliable to keep. George and another man were testing the horse. Mary Olive described her husband as "very much tried himself." On the same sheet of stationery eight-year-old Charles wrote his own letter to his brother, telling about rabbit-hunting with Fred's dog and fishing with their uncles. Charles had begun the letter days earlier, but as his mother wrote, "his head is so full of being out doors it is very hard for him to settle down to write a sentence." He had needed three sittings to complete his very short note.[78] By this time the Roots had four children. Clara Louise would soon be four years old; Helen was two.

Meeting in North Reading again, the Normal class of 1858 was larger than any previous one and would presumably have been still larger but for the recent recession, which in some cases had resulted in public school teachers' salaries not being paid.[79] The participants analyzed the work of their classmates. Each student wrote harmony assignments that were sung and criticized by the class. In the "teaching exercise," participants took turns teaching lessons as if to a class and having their teaching analyzed by classmates as well as by Mason, Root, Webb and their assistants. In the evening chorus rehearsals, participants sang works by Handel, Haydn, Mozart, Beethoven, Rossini and other composers.[80] The gifted and well-known pianist William Mason, a son of Lowell Mason, visited the Normal class, played for them, and demonstrated the art of improvisation.[81] Ex-governor Boutwell of Massachusetts visited and lectured.[82] When news of the successful laying of the Atlantic Cable reached North Reading, it was received with a genuine nineteenth-century American response: The whole institute sang a grand "Te Deum" ("We Praise Thee, O God"), followed by the "Hallelujah Chorus."[83]

The western offshoot of the original Normal Musical Institute, called the Chicago Musical Institute, opened its 1858 session on May 17. The principal teachers were C. M. Cady and William B. Bradbury. The six-week term ended with a "Festival Week" under Bradbury's direction.[84] Preparing to close on June 25, the Chicago institute announced plans for the next term to begin May 1, 1859.[85]

Once the Normal Institute in North Reading was over, Root was an itinerant teacher again. During October he held a musical convention in Sheffield, Massachusetts, his birthplace. On his schedule were conventions in Bridgeton, New Jersey, and Fredonia, New York.[86]

A new music business called Root & Cady came into being in 1858. E. Towner Root and Chauncey M. Cady started the firm in Chicago, which in George's words was "nearly the far west in those days."[87] Chicago was a burgeoning commercial center with several music businesses and plenty of room for a new one. On December 9, 1858, the *Chicago Daily Press and Tribune* announced that Root & Cady had leased space at 95 Clark Street in the Larmon Block (the most prominent building on Court House Square), and they would furnish it as an elegant store. The paper identified George's brother, E. T. Root, as the senior member of the firm and described C. M. Cady as well-known in Chicago, with "few equals in his art." Not yet finished, the store was open on the day before Christmas and some of its departments were already selling music merchandise. On the company's sign outside, a few notes from "The Star Spangled Banner" caught the customer's eye.[88] An ad in March 1859 invited customers to visit Root & Cady for the best musical merchandise and the latest songs "at the sign of the Star Spangled Banner."[89]

Chauncey Marvin Cady had met George and Towner Root in New York. While Root taught at Union Theological Seminary, Cady was a student there.[90] The new company issued a "circular"[91] announcing that the store, located opposite the courthouse, would sell sheet music, music books, pianos and other musical instruments. The circular introduced the partners: Senior partner E. T. Root, who for the past six years had worked at William Hall & Son in New York, would be business manager. The junior partner, C. M. Cady, was a former editor of the *New York Musical Review* and of the *Chicago Musical Review* and was at this time Professor of Music at Illinois State Normal University and conductor of the Chicago Musical Union.

George Root had invested what he called a small amount of money in Root & Cady. Chicago, and the firm of Root & Cady, became for Root what he called "a new kind of business home."[92] He went on teaching and writing while he kept a hopeful eye on the new company.

While the firm of Root & Cady was getting under way, Chicago was undergoing an extraordinary process. The early buildings in the city had stood only a little higher than the water level of the lake. Drainage became a problem. Large brick and stone buildings were rising when it became apparent that the whole city, buildings and streets alike, must be raised by several feet. As George and Towner Root arrived, some buildings were at the new level and some at the old. Walking along a sidewalk, people went up and down stairs at each place where the level changed. Many streets were not yet paved. In wet weather Root saw horses and oxen wade knee-deep in mud, bringing ladies in carts which were backed up to the doors of the stores. Wood, gravel, stone, and brick were not readily available in Chicago and had to be shipped such distances that improvements were slow.[93]

Root liked the west for its freedom from the kind of social stratification New England had. He observed that social distinctions held no one back. Some of the qualities he liked in the west were exemplified in the prairie town of Kewanee, Illinois, where he held a musical convention. Eighteen months earlier there had been only a railroad shanty there. At the time of Root's convention Kewanee had fifteen hundred residents. He described them as young and energetic, "just the kind to leave the quieter East and enjoy the excitement of starting a new town." An unexpected number of these people had been members of choirs and musical societies in eastern cities; they found the idea of a musical convention in the midst of their bustling community attractive. The convention met in a hall over a large store; the closing concert took place in an unfinished church with seats improvised from whatever building materials were on the site. A few singers came in long wagons called prairie schooners. Others came by rail from places farther away. Root decided the town of Kewanee had a larger proportion of what he called "cultivated and refined singers" than he had found in country conventions in the east. He was amused by the reported rush to have houses built. One of the men in the Kewanee musical convention joked that in the early days of Chicago there had been only one carpenter. Asked when he could build a house for a new arrival, the carpenter was said to have answered, "There's Smith Monday; Jones Tuesday; Brown Wednesday; Johnson Thursday; I'll put yours up Friday."[94]

Root and the other readers of the *Review* could follow the reported performances of *The Haymakers* around the country. In the spring and summer of 1858, performances were given in Maine, Illinois, Massachusetts, New York, Connecticut, and the District of Columbia. By the end of the year, one conductor was rehearsing the cantata in Boston with Root's occasional assistance and with distinguished soloists. The *Review* said it would be performed "about the last of January" and commented, "We look for almost an operatic enthusiasm."[95]

George Root found what he called "the new and adventurous life of Chicago" so attractive that early in 1859 he rented a room in the building occupied by Root & Cady and began to use it as a library and workroom when his musical convention schedule allowed. He called his first involvement with the company "playing at business," and explained that he did none of the buying or selling.[96] Friends commented in February 1859 that the firm was "in the full tide of successful experiment."[97] An advertisement described Root & Cady as a "Wholesale & retail music depot for the north-west." They sold instruments — string instruments, from violins to bass-viols, brass instruments, and Steinway & Son pianofortes. They were wholesale agents for melodeons and for William Hall & Sons' guitars, flutes and banjos. As wholesale agents they sold all of Mason Brothers' church music books, glee books, juvenile books and other music publications, all Episcopal church music books, and all the sheet music and books published by companies that were members of the Board of Music Trade. They represented the Novello company of London, England, as wholesale agents for their oratorios, masses, and organ music.[98]

Root & Cady's advertisements in Chicago papers were more inventive and more aggressive than their competitors.' Other firms ran the same ad for months, sometimes just a modest "card." Fresh ads for Root & Cady appeared every few days. The first *Tribune* ad featured the company's trademark, the same fragment of the melody of "The Star Spangled Banner" that appeared on the sign hanging outside the store. This ad ran from January 15 to January 25, 1859. The company's ad for melodeons cautioned readers to "preserve this advertisement, for the next one will be about something else." This advice reappeared intermittently in the company's advertising for some time.[99]

Root & Cady was ready to publish sheet music, but having no presses of their own yet, they arranged with Russell & Tolman of Boston, one of

George Root's publishers, to print their first song. It was Root's arrangement of a Scottish folk song, "Oh, Are Ye Sleeping, Maggie ... as sung by J. G. Lumbard, Esq." The company's second publication[100] was a set of "Six Ballads by George Root" (with Wurzel in much smaller print below), again through Russell & Tolman. These songs had in common an impressive sheet-music cover depicting a harvest scene. The lyrics of "Only Waiting" revealed some of an elderly person's thoughts about the end of life. In the November 26, 1859, *Review*, "Softly She Faded" appeared with a note at the bottom of the page: "Published by Root & Cady, Chicago, Illinois." Root's accompaniment was designed for melodeon or organ, but for best effect he suggested that voices hum the accompaniment, "linking the tones closely together." The first verse, by an unidentified writer, ended "so 'twas she faded, as fades the twilight, So 'twas she murmured, 'Dear friends, adieu.'" Others in the set of six ballads were "My Home Is on the Prairie," "The Forest Requiem," "My Mother She Is Sleeping," and "Lilly Brook."

A set of six "Songs from Willow Farm" followed the six ballads. Their common sheet music cover pictured a tree-lined lane leading to a square, two-story house. People who had attended the Normal Musical Institute would presumably recognize this as Root's home, and readers of the *New York Musical Review and Gazette* would presumably recognize the name, Willow Farm. "Man the Ship," dedicated to C. M. Cady, celebrated the pleasures of sailing "far away from friends and home." "My Father's Bible" was a solo dedicated to George B. Loomis, one of Root's teaching associates. "On, Boys, On" was a solo for male voice with lyrics that combined two of Root's interests, boating and "the grand old prairie." "She Has Told It to the Winds" was dedicated to Adelaide Phillipps, a contralto who, after successful study and performances in Europe, came back to Boston and sang light opera. "Don't You See Me Coming" was subtitled "The Song of the Bobolink" and dedicated "To My Little 'Nell.'" Perhaps Nell was a familiar name for his daughter Helen, born in 1856.[101] The unattributed words of the song depicted a bird waiting for workmen to leave a cornfield so that he could find food there. The piano accompaniment ended with sounds imitating the chirping of a bird. "If He Can" was a solo for a female voice, its lyrics challenging a young man to ignore her.

Looking back on this period in his life, Root remembered "a constant pressure" for more music — a book, a cantata, or more songs.[102] When he was not traveling to musical conventions, writing occupied about half of his day, as it would for years to come. The *Review* announced that Root and Bradbury would share editorial supervision of the songs that appeared in its pages in 1860. Nine prominent musicians had promised to contribute songs.[103]

Root's teaching schedule for 1859 was not as full as usual. The year before, when plans for the convention season were being made, the *Review* had explained that people in many places in the west were going to be disappointed, unable to secure Root's services. There was hope, however, that this was only "a pleasure deferred," and that after a period of much-needed rest he would be once again available.[104] He traveled to Homer,[105] Cooperstown, and Afton, New York,[106] to conduct musical conventions with George B. Loomis. One participant commented that the convention in Homer was successful because there was "no fun, no foolery, no clownishness, nor comic singing." In March Root taught in Lee, Massachusetts, but he missed a scheduled three-day convention at Middletown, New York, because of illness. George B. Loomis taught in his place.

In the spring of 1859 an unsigned statement in the *Review* announced that the Normal Musical Institute at North Reading had been "suspended."[107] As early as 1857, there had been broad hints that competition among teachers was increasing. To compete with the planned 1859 Normal at North Reading, William B. Bradbury had sent an emissary to gather names on a petition for an institute in another town, with Bradbury as teacher. Signing the petition meant automatic enrollment in the proposed institute and commitment to pay the tuition. People signed the petition without realizing that the school they were supporting was in competition with Root's.[108]

Root and Bradbury had taught together a number of times, most notably in the inaugural 1853 New York Normal Musical Institute[109] and at the Smithsonian convention in 1858. Bradbury was not on the teaching staff at North Reading in 1858, but he paid "a short, pleasant visit" and "addressed the class very handsomely."[110] Geneseo, New York, was chosen as the site of Bradbury's school, scheduled to start July 6 and last for eight weeks. With the Normal Institute at North Reading suspended for this year, the *Review* was sure that many of those who had planned to be there would now go to Geneseo.[111]

On July 26, 1859, "A Happy Normal" wrote the *Review*, giving the daily schedule in a nutshell. Theodore Perkins and William B. Bradbury were the teachers. Perkins taught the men's vocal training class. Bradbury taught harmony and the "teachers' class." There was a 35-minute class in psalmody, and Perkins taught the women's voice class. A class for music reading was designed to help people read "difficult music with facility and ease." Three evening rehearsals each week focused on the works of the great masters. Carlo Bassini, a prominent voice teacher, was to give private lessons. The class numbered nearly 100 and latecomers were still arriving.

On the same page, and immediately following this report, there was an article by George Root. Writing on August 1, he explained uncharacteristically that he was enjoying a summer of quiet at Willow Farm "after eight successive summers of hard work" in the Normal Musical Institute. The rest and the change from a rigorous routine were pleasant. He had regrets which he felt were shared with a considerable number of people who had expected to spend the summer in North Reading. Applications for this summer's institute had been more numerous than ever. Serious doubts had arisen about the capacity of the village to provide hospitality for all those who would have come. He hinted at an announcement for the following year that would involve a better plan for the kind of work the Normal had done. He wrote that he was glad to see that Bradbury, together with T. E. Perkins, had begun a Normal session at Geneseo — he wished for their school "all success." Lowell Mason was at Andover, charming listeners with his lecturing on church music, Root reported.[112]

Lowell Mason, the undisputed leader in the training of teachers and church musicians (Root had called him the "master"; someone called him the "pope"), wrote privately about an "awfully dark controversy" involving Root. In a February 21, 1859, letter to W. W. Killip, a participant in the Normal Institute, Mason wrote in the space left after the letter was finished:

> Bradbury versus Root & Perkins.
> Bradbury versus Perkins & Root.
> Root versus Bradbury & Perkins
> Root versus Perkins & Bradbury
> Perkins versus Bradbury & Root
> Perkins versus Root & Bradbury.
> Every man's hand against every man.
> Every man for himself and no man for any other man.[113]

In one of his letters to Killip, Mason expressed his hatred of the "politics and chicanery" of the musical convention business. He compared teachers of musical conventions with "hungry dogs," snarling and fighting, each trying to take what one of them had. He accused the teachers of "trickery, guile, shakiness, fraud, etc." He wrote about standards for church music and for teaching. His examples of the wrong kind of music were "the little silly, unmeaning tunes that are *Bell'd* out in *Jubilee* times," evidently referring to two books — Root's *Sabbath Bell* (1856) and Bradbury's *Jubilee* (1858). Mason explained his view of "the state of things." Soon after the Normal session in 1858 Root's attitude toward Bradbury had changed completely from a feeling of bitterness to a spirit of cooperation. Mason wrote that he had been "pleading" with Root for Bradbury for a year or two. Suddenly, without apparent reason, Root had changed; the reason was "not difficult to imagine" by those who were "near the Booksellers."[114] Bradbury and Root were forming a partnership in the book business "by which they were to publish together." Mason soon entered into the partnership and the three made plans to publish several books. The first to be published under this arrangement was to be Root's. The book agreement affected the three men's plans for Normal schools; they agreed to teach two or three schools together. The first was to be at North Reading, and Mason wrote, "We all expect to go there." Two other places were being discussed — Geneseo and Chicago. Mason assured Killip that he would not teach in Geneseo. That was Killip's territory; Mason, Bradbury and Root would not encroach on it.[115]

In late summer Root sent a light-hearted letter to the *Review*. All across New England the recent financial "hard times" were passing and, judging by the information he was receiving, an unusually large number of musical conventions and festivities were planned. His present circumstances made it necessary that he go "to the west and north-west" this year, so in this letter he sent his best wishes (and enthusiastic compliments) to those who had invited him teach in their New England communities.[116] Traveling between North Reading and Chicago, Root sent a note to the *Review* from Niagara Falls, describing a theory on the "qualities of tone" and reminding the public that his mailing address would be, for the present, "Care of Root & Cady, Chicago, Ill."[117] By mid–October he was rehearsing new music with the Chicago Musical Union.[118] His musical convention in Princeton, Illinois, in November ended with a concert featuring pieces from *The Haymakers* and *The Sabbath Bell*. He sang two solos, "Rocked in the Cradle of the Deep" and "In Native Worth."[119]

All through 1859 choral groups gave their own performances of Root's cantata, *The Haymakers*. A chorus of one hundred select voices in Boston rehearsed for a performance in costume, "with scenery and action," to be given March 2 at the Tremont Temple.[120] Root surprised the cast by playing a flute part when the chorus sang "The Shepherd's Pipe." The *Review* reported that three performances had been given to crowded houses and announced a fourth performance.[121]

Root had worked hard to win the acceptance of New York critics and advocates of higher music. Now *Dwight's Journal of Music*, known for strong criticism and strict standards, called *The Haymakers* a work of "quite high pretensions," needing only orchestral accompaniment to raise it to the status of an opera.[122] Singers in Worcester, Massachusetts, were "making hay by gaslight," a correspondent wrote. On March 24 Root conducted J. R. Miller's production of *The Haymakers* there. After the performance, "The 'Haymakers'" and their guests had "an elegant supper at the Bay State House." The company returned to Boston on a special train.[123] Miller continued with performances in Fall River and Providence and with plans to take the play to Lynn and other eastern cities.[124]

It seemed an observer or a participant had only to send a few words to the *Review* and wait for the next issue to see a local production mentioned in print. Performances of *The Haymakers* in Somerville, Massachusetts, Portland, Maine, and Quincy, Illinois, received notice.[125] Lighthearted comment came from a Chicago observer: "The Musical Union are making hay on Mr. George F. Root's operetta farm, the owner acting as 'boss.'" Incidentally Root had been very busy since he arrived "in the West," with the Musical Union on Monday evenings and "dodging off to various places, holding conventions during the week."[126]

In February, 1860, Root announced plans to be in New York for two or three months, working with Mason Brothers on a new book.[127] It would be a major publication for use in churches and musical conventions. "Making music books is one of the most difficult of all departments of authorship," a Mason Brothers spokesman wrote in answer to frequent questions from would-be authors. Asked whether they published collections of church music for others beside Mason, Bradbury, and Root, the publishers claimed they would publish any good book that would prove remunerative. The company claimed that because their facilities for publishing were excellent and their experience so extensive, nearly all the music books written in the United States were submitted to them first. For a typical church and convention book the printing plates would cost from two thousand to twenty-eight hundred dollars. Manufacturing would cost from thirty to fifty cents per copy. Their closing comment may have been intended to discourage new authors: "Experience has shown that very few have the requisite taste, knowledge, experience, and ability to succeed" in authoring a book like those Mason Brothers published.[128]

The new church music collection Root had promised was titled *The Diapason*.[129] He signed the preface in June, 1860.[130] Mason Brothers published the book, claiming, "This is to be the general collection of church music for the season."[131] By December of the year in which it appeared, 32,000 copies of *The Diapason* were in print.[132] This book made its appeal to the public in a down-to-earth way through the words of exercises and songs such as "Don't Run in Debt." There was a "Song of the Smith" ("swing the bright hammer and strike the hot iron") and a round, "With practiced eye and skillful hands," about typesetting. The words of exercise 23 were timely, with references to "freedom's call" and "chains at last unbound." The words of an unattributed song called "Dame Fashion" told how men and women were bound by current styles such as thin slippers that were worn in the coldest weather.

Root's viewpoint on musical taste and its development came through in *The Diapason*. Above some of the hymns that were to be used for vocal study and practice he wrote instructions, probably the advice he would give in person. On "Menville," a Mendelssohn melody adapted by Lowell Mason, he wrote "Sing this tune until you understand and like it." Root believed that familiarity was essential in developing musical taste.

He had planned to include his new cantata, *Belshazzar's Feast*, in *The Diapason*, but instead the book and the cantata appeared separately at about the same time.[133] The cantata was subtitled "The Fall of Babylon: a Dramatic Cantata in Ten Scenes." The libretto was written "and arranged" by General B.

George F. Root in 1860. Courtesy of Lief H. Carter, his great-great-grandson.

F. Edmands, who in previous years had been associated with the Boston Academy of Music. The cantata was built around readings from the Bible or statements with scriptural references that set the scene and carried the story along. They were to be read by a clergyman, or by the conductor or a member of the choir, and they would take the place of a printed program.

"We shall now have a Normal Institute for the West and one for the East," the *Review* announced in the spring of 1860.[134] The 1860 session in Chicago would open September 12 and would welcome both teachers and non-teachers to its classes.[135] A six-week class exclusively for teachers was scheduled to begin in North Reading on Wednesday, July 11.[136]

While the Normal Musical Institute was changing and expanding, a writer to the *Review* gave a capsule account of how such schools came to be. Lowell Mason and George James Webb had called together in Boston what was believed to be the first class for music teachers ever assembled in America. In successive years the number of attendees increased until those planning to teach were gradually outnumbered by those who were not. This changed the nature of the classes to musical conventions, which by 1860 had spread to all parts of the country and were primarily occasions for enjoying music, rather than studying it. Now Root and Bradbury, and certainly Lowell Mason himself, received so many invitations to teach that they could not possibly accept all of them. Those who had "most carefully attended" classes held by Mason, Bradbury, and Root were said to be "among the most successful" teachers in the country. There followed a list of eighteen teachers who were fully qualified to teach musical conventions and apparently in fairness to Bradbury, a statement that his Normal class held the previous year in Geneseo, New York, had been highly successful.[137]

On Saturday, July 14, Root wrote to the *Review* from his home that the Normal Musical Institute in North Reading had begun. Lowell Mason was teaching; the students had looked forward to Bradbury's reappearance at this Normal and Root reported that he had fulfilled their expectations nobly.[138] Like the one at North Reading, the Chicago session was to last six weeks. There were conflicting reports on the attendance at the Chicago Normal. "This season has been one of unparalleled 'tight times,' and I have no doubt many are kept away on this account," one participant wrote on October 6.[139] The Musical Institute Bradbury had started in Geneseo, New York, the previous year went on without him in 1860.[140]

From Boston to Chicago and a fair number of places in between, Root's cantata *The Haymakers* was still performed. The Chicago Musical Union had presented *The Haymakers* near the end of 1859 with Root conducting; on November 17, 1860, they presented the cantata again. The history of the Chicago Musical Union illustrated one of Root's favorite themes — the folly of offering people music that was beyond their capacity to appreciate. He felt that most musical organizations made the same mistake. A few members would insist on performing music he described as "beyond the capacity of the chorus to perform, and of the audience to enjoy." Both chorus and audience would soon decrease in number, and the organization would suffer financially. When the Musical Union's indebtedness reached a thousand dollars, someone asked Root to conduct a production of *The Haymakers*. "Two performances cleared off the debt, and left a small balance in the treasury," Root recalled.[141] The prominent Chicago singer Jules Lumbard sang the role of the Farmer. Towner Root sang the role of Snipkins.[142]

On December 1, 1860, the second anniversary of the founding of Root & Cady, George Root joined the firm as a partner. The original partners needed more capital, and George Root's name would lend prestige to the business. The Chicago *Tribune* described him as having "a world-wide reputation" and said he planned to "devote himself" to compiling books and writing songs which could be expected to "circulate all over the Union."[143] Contrary to the *Tribune's* welcoming report, Root had no intention of giving up what he called his professional work — teaching — and no immediate plans to move to Chicago. He was pleased by the thought of being associated in business with Towner, whose work with their father in South America had been difficult and dangerous. At this point George thought his own role in Root & Cady looked like "a kind of recreation."[144]

Chicago in the summer of 1860 was working on a presidential campaign. "Wide Awake Clubs" were organized to support the candidacy of Abraham Lincoln. For the mass meetings and torchlight parades, brass bands would be essential. Root & Cady invited Wide Awakes to see "the largest and best assortment" of brass instruments, drums, cymbals and fifes west of New York.[145]

In January 1861 the country was coming apart. Congress argued compromise while opposing sides disputed possession of Fort Sumter in South Carolina. Talk of secession resounded across the south while the *Tribune* claimed that Chicago "buzzed as earnestly as if secession had never been heard of."[146] Public entertainment went on in a normal way. Playgoers could see "A Night with Dickens" at McVickers Theatre.[147] "Dixie" was called "everybody's favorite" song and was sung as part of the play *Beauty and the Beast*.[148]

Newspaper publishers did not see objectivity or impartiality as their goal. The paper was a politically oriented medium. The Chicago *Tribune* was pro-Lincoln, pro-union, and patriotic. Headlines like "Danger at Washington" alerted the public[149] while six of the southern states convened in Montgomery, Alabama.[150]

In the *Tribune,* advertisements customarily appeared on page one after the major news of the day, as well as on the inside pages. Root & Cady's ads were eye-catching. On Wednesday, April 3, the company advertised "Rock Me to Sleep, Mother, at Root & Cady's." Several other songs were advertised in separate spaces on the page with the company name added. Mixed in among the non-music ads such as one for "Gentlemen's Dress Hats" was "Kitty Ryder at Root & Cady's. A new Song by Geo. F. Root." "Kitty Ryder" was a light-hearted story about a girl kneeling at a stream for a drink of water and seeing the reflection of a young man's face. Below the title were the words "As sung by Rollin Howard Esq."[151] Howard was a popular minstrel show singer.[152]

The firm of Root & Cady found itself in the same quandary that Root faced as a songwriter: public taste determined what a composer would write and what a publisher could sell. This was a problem because Root & Cady, like George himself, believed fine music had a beneficent effect on the mind and heart. "The average taste of the West is not yet up to the standard of either Wagner or Schubert" an advertisement said when Root & Cady published a "Grand March" from Wagner's *Tannhauser* and a Schubert song, "The Secret." Friends doubted that the company would sell enough to pay the cost of publishing these pieces. But if sales were at all encouraging, Root & Cady promised, they would issue Chopin's "Funeral March" and some other "classical pieces for the pianoforte." Speaking for the public, someone wrote, "'Dixie' and 'Old Dog Tray' are the tunes for our money." Gradual, repeated exposure to the serious music Germany was producing would educate the younger generation to better music, the company's ad said, even though "hardened minds" preferred "Keemo-Kimo" and "Old Dan Tucker."[153] Root & Cady's publication of "The Secret," with English words by Geo. F. Root, was one of a series titled "Twelve Standard Songs."

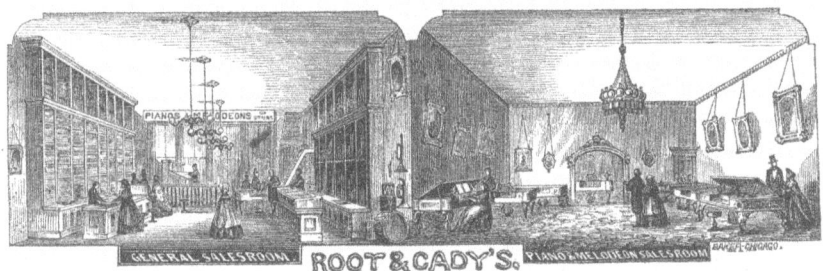

From its beginning in 1858 until Crosby's Opera House was built in 1865, Root & Cady was located in a building called the Larmon Block at 95 Clark Street. It faced courthouse square in the heart of Chicago. The trademark on a sign outside the store was recognizable as the first few notes of "The Star Spangled Banner." Images from I. D. Guyer's *History of Chicago*, 1862.

On March 14, Mrs. Cassie Mattison, a favorite Chicago contralto, gave a "Grand Entertainment of Vocal and Instrumental Music" assisted by several well-known musicians. Near the close of the program she sang the setting of "Rock Me to Sleep, Mother,"[154] that Root had composed for her.[155] His piano introduction seemed to suggest a gentle rocking motion. Mrs. Mattison had sung the role of Anna in the Chicago Musical Union's production of Root's *Haymakers* four months earlier.[156] Classical songs, even when the words were in English, usually had foreign language directions for tempo and perhaps for style: andante, allegro, presto, and the like. At the beginning of this song Root's tempo specification was "about as fast as you would read." Near the end his directive was "Earnestly and a little slower." The words, by Florence Percy, began "Backward, turn backward, O Time, in your flight; make me a child again, just for tonight."

Root & Cady expanded in March 1861 to the second floor above their store at 95 Clark Street. Pianos and melodeons were displayed in the added space. On the first floor, a counter for music and books stood on one side of the room, another for instruments and musical accessories on the other, and an office was in the back. A handsome chandelier completed the décor.[157]

On April 12, 1861, headlines from Washington warned: "Old Abe's Blood Is Up. District Militia Enrolled. Washington a Military Camp." President Lincoln had expressed little hope for peace. Pennsylvania Avenue looked like an army post. An oath of allegiance was administered to the troops in order to weed out disunionists. About one seventh of the troops refused to take the oath. All attention was turned toward Charleston harbor, where the sound of artillery was expected to be heard on the following day.[158]

The functions of music in the Civil War era are difficult to imagine today. People sang as a matter of course — in school and church and on public occasions — partly because all music was live. Listening to music meant hearing a live performance. As a favorite line tacked onto various folk songs said, "If you want any more you can sing it yourself." The grand old social tradition of the singing school was still part of community life, gradually replaced and updated by musical conventions like those Root taught. One of the social functions of music was often pictured as a young woman playing the piano, surrounded by family and friends who sang along. Diaries from the time mention music as a part of visits in people's homes. One book on housekeeping pictured the parlor piano as prominently as the kitchen stove. Another reason for the increase in music making was economic. Popular music was a growing business; sheet music sold well.

War intensified the effectiveness of music as communication, as commentary, as a means of expressing personal or public sentiment. During the war years some 10,000 new songs appeared.[159] The musicologist Charles Hamm has written that music became an actual part of events of the Civil War era and interacted with them.[160] Songs like "Take Your Gun and Go, John" encouraged recruitment. Men went to the army with rallying songs, among them "We Are Coming, Father Abraham" and "Dixie," ringing in their ears. Families mourning their losses heard their grief expressed in "Somebody's Darling" and "The Vacant Chair." Songs reinforced loyalty to a cause and warned against potential enemies living next door. Those on the "Home, Sweet Home" theme, and those whose prewar popularity evoked thoughts of home, mellowed the long evenings in camp. Comic songs, written by musicians or by the soldiers themselves, lightened stress. "Grafted Into the Army" reinforced a negative attitude about conscription. "We'll Go Down Ourselves" expressed the determination of women to support an active war. Music honored generals and commemorated battles — "The Beauregard Manassas Quickstep" did both. It was simpler to honor a hero with an instrumental piece than with a song. At least one piece written to honor a general on a triumphant occasion was re-titled when another hero eclipsed him. Through the medium of music, propaganda and political messages were spread; even controversial issues were argued. The experience of the Hutchinson Family, banned and then readmitted to a camp under General McClellan's command, showed that music could be a threat to both loyalty and morale.

George Root was arguably the leading composer of Civil War songs. All his experiences — study, teaching, traveling, writing, publishing — could be interpreted as preparation for his role as a musical spokesman for the people, particularly during the war.

5

The First Gun Is Fired
1861–1863

In April 1861, the firm of Root & Cady had begun to publish sheet music, and George Root was working on the firm's first book when, in his words, "The WAR burst upon us!" He saw the "bustling, cheery life of Chicago" become suddenly "grave and serious." People looked at each other differently. Friendly faces and light-hearted, neighborly greetings changed. Even the sunshine no longer looked the same. "The old flag had been fired upon, and that act had waked into stern determination the patriotism of every loyal heart," he wrote.[1]

Chicagoans went on a "news hunting quest" that day; the Chicago *Tribune* called it "the first Sunday of the second American Revolution." Headlines drew attention to the effect of the news on churches, in the streets, in the saloons. People crowded into hotel lobbies, hoping some newly arrived traveler would have news from the East. Fear and frustration made the news reports sound frantic, sometimes unreal. Everywhere there were questions: Had Fort Sumter surrendered? Had the fort's ammunition been destroyed? Had the military leaders of both sides met? And more realistically, how could people decide what to believe? On the same page, a special dispatch from Washington claimed that Unionists were furious when the news of Fort Sumter's surrender was announced. Clenching their fists in anger and shame, they swore vengeance. President Lincoln called for 75,000 volunteers. The East waited in fearful anxiety to find out how the Northwest would react to the war news, the *Tribune* claimed.[2]

George Root's response to the news set a pattern that he followed throughout the war. "In common with my neighbors I felt strongly the gravity of the situation, and while waiting to see what would be done, wrote the first song of the war," he recalled. The song was titled "The First Gun Is Fired, May God Protect the Right."[3] Then with each important event, and in all the circumstances brought about by the war, when Root

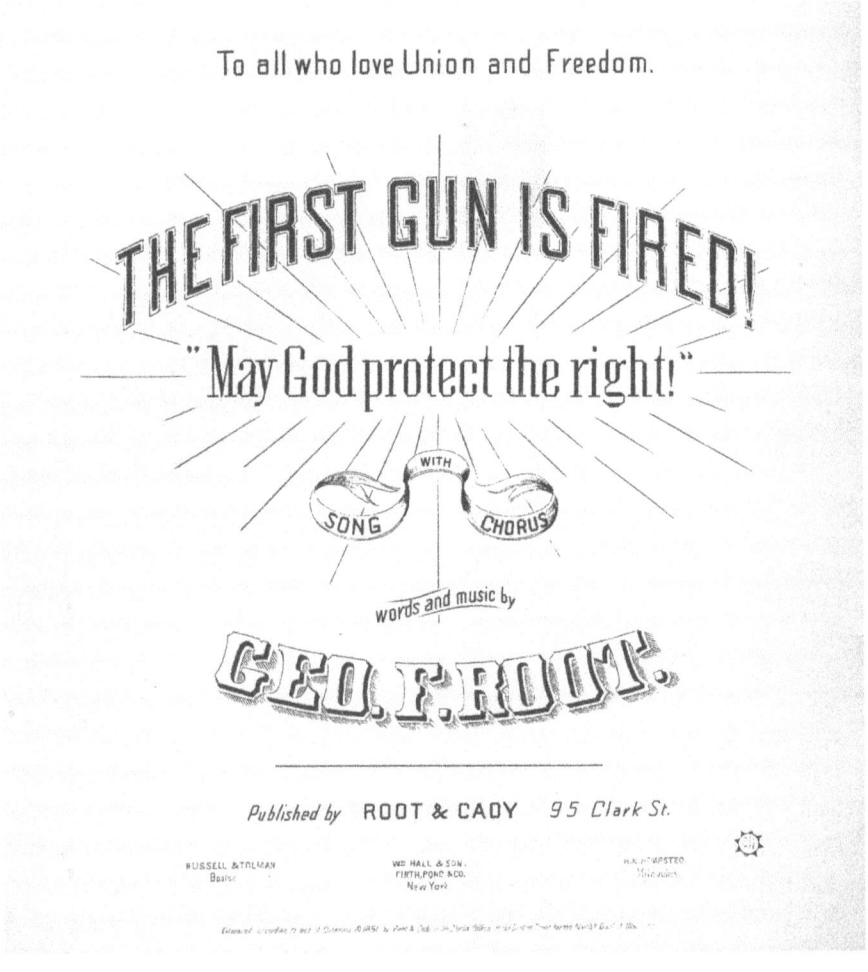

George Root described the impact of the firing on Fort Sumter as an act that "waked into stern determination the patriotism of every loyal heart." Three days after the bombardment of Fort Sumter began, "The First Gun Is Fired" was in print.

believed a song would be welcome, he wrote one. His fourteen years' experience in extemporizing melodies on the blackboard, working quickly so as to keep his class in order, gave him what he considered an advantage. He need not wait for a melody to come to him. "Such as it was it came at once, as when I stood before the blackboard in the old school days,"[4] he claimed. Three days after the bombardment of Fort Sumter began, "The First Gun Is Fired" was in print.[5] Root dedicated this song "To all who love Union and Freedom." He wrote the words, and they flowed with energy and conviction. For the chorus Root added four-part harmony to the last two lines of the verses. The song strongly resembles "The Heavens Are Telling" from Haydn's *Creation* in its melody and its harmonies. Perhaps Root was thinking of his classes who had sung "The Heavens Are Telling" and the satisfaction that had brought.

Chicago on Monday, April 15, was a colorful place, with flags floating from the hotels, the public buildings, and many of the stores. Throngs crowded the newspaper offices all day. The moment a dispatch came, a printed bulletin was issued as a means of spreading the news. Thousands read the bulletins; other thousands heard the news spread verbally. People crowded into railroad stations and swarmed the trains, looking for newspapers from distant cities. Crowds gathered in public places and listened to resolutions and pledges to sustain the government, the *Tribune* reported. In the same issue, the words of "The First Gun Is Fired" were printed, all three verses. That night the Republican party held "A Rally for the Union and Flag," in which they resolved to support the administration, "every man with his prayers, his purse and his sword." After a speech by the Republican candidate for mayor, the words of, "The First Gun Is Fired," were read aloud. The popular Lumbard brothers sang it admirably and the audience, who had been given copies, joined in the chorus."[6]

On April 18, Chicago witnessed "a night of wild enthusiasm." A huge rally raised money for the expenses of the city's volunteers. Flaming tar barrels lit the streets, which rang until midnight with martial music and the shouts of the crowds. "Choose You This Day, Which You Will Serve," the *Tribune* demanded, with drawings of two flags, "The Union Flag— The Old Stars and Stripes" and "The Secession Flag, The Rattlesnake."[7] As George Root said, war made people look at each other with different eyes. A friend, a neighbor, a family member might sympathize with the South. Loyalty could not be taken for granted.

The South expected to become a separate, independent country. The North, according to the Chicago *Tribune*, expected to reunite with the South in a single country once the war was over. While the fighting had barely begun, the question was how to reconstruct the government and the union once the fighting stopped.[8] Although death and destruction could hardly be expected to bring people back together, the idea of reconstruction appeared in the news fairly regularly.

An estimated 10,000 people took "the oath of Fealty" on Saturday night, April 20, at the Wigwam (renamed "National Hall") where Lincoln had received his party's nomination for president. The front of the gallery was still decorated with the coat of arms of each state, but on this night "the arms of seceded States were draped in mourning. The huge crowd stood, raised their hands, and solemnly repeated the words of the oath: 'I do solemnly swear, in the presence of Almighty God, that I will faithfully support the Constitution of the United States and of the State of Illinois. So help me God.'" George Root, Julius Lumbard and a group of vocalists sang "The First Gun Is Fired." The immense crowd sang the chorus enthusiastically and "with the finest effect."[9] "The First Gun Is Fired" was not the phenomenal success that some later songs would be, but for a songwriter, the sound of some 10,000 people singing a song he had written had to be inspiring. Root had given voice to people's feeling. He had come close to what Lincoln called "molding public opinion."[10] "The First Gun Is Fired" captured a historic moment and filled a need in the first days of the war.

The role of Root's music in the Civil War years illustrates a view held by the musicologist Charles Hamm: that the music of this period was so closely tied to events of the era that it became part of them.[11] As the war went on, Root's songs would become part of the war — at home, in patriotic rallies and ceremonies, in army camps, and on the field.

At the beginning of the war there was no draft and a great many men were needed. Early in May 1861, Root's second war song, "God Bless Our Brave Young Volunteers"[12] pictured men leaving "anvil, loom and plow," answering the call of duty in the tradition of their revolutionary forefathers. The words he wrote reflected the feelings of people at home and their concern for men whose duty called them to crowded army camps and bloody battlefields. The song prophesied that men would give their treasure to the home of freedom in this costly war and urged that a tribute of love and honor be offered for their bravery. The piano introduction was recognizable as the first eight measures of "The Star Spangled Banner," the last eight measures of which were used as a coda. An interlude after the second verse was recognizable as the first six measures of "America."

In a handsome ad on May 23, Root & Cady advertised Root's first two war songs and added his "Forward, Boys, Forward!" described as "A song for the volunteers themselves." Another ad on the same page offered patriotic merchandise: "Union Breast Pins," pins for scarves and coats, rings, badges, shields and cockades, as well as envelopes and letter paper, all under a memorable heading: "The Union Forever. New Styles of Union Goods Every Day."[13] The words of "Forward, Boys, Forward!" were attributed to "F. H. S." and they were stirring indeed. Among the strongest lines was "In thy strength, O God of battles, we will conquer or we'll die." The words of the chorus were strongly motivating: "Then forward, boys, forward, our cause it is just: Shall the star spangled banner be trampled in the dust?"[14]

Root & Cady, like the other publishers, issued songs the newspapers called "up to the times." Colonel Elmer Ellsworth, a popular military organizer and showman, was the first well-known officer killed. When he saw a Confederate flag flying from the top of a hotel, he raced up the stairs and snatched it down. Almost immediately he was shot dead. Chicago held an elaborate memorial service for him. The Light Guard Band played "The Ellsworth Requiem." Root & Cady announced that the requiem was on press and would be available soon.[15]

With war uppermost in their minds, George Root and his associates at Root & Cady continued to furnish songs for the popular market as well. As one advertisement claimed while promoting the Christy Minstrels' shows in Chicago, "It is better to laugh than to cry."[16] Considering his workload, Root composed a surprising number of songs for the popular market in 1861. "Jimmy's Wooing" was subtitled "A Story in Rhyme." In nine verses it outlined Jimmy's courtship and engagement to Milly, whose heart was "good as gold." Several of these 1861 songs, like "May Moore" and "Kitty Ryder," fit the pattern of the minstrel show song that was ultimately meant for the family parlor.

"O Come You from the Indies?" was subtitled "Robert's Return from the War." The unattributed words described a mother questioning a soldier about a certain regiment, asking who among its members was safe and well. As the story went on, the soldier told her they'd made a man of her son. At last she recognized him: "Robert, my own blessed boy." There were references to Lucknow, a city in northern India, and "Havelock's fights," which suggested the Sepoy Rebellion, suppressed in 1858. The melody was one that Root would reuse later, with new words and the title, "O Come You From the Battlefield?"

For Sarah Flint Root, George composed a song called "Mother, Oh Sing to Me of Heaven."[17] Root may have written the words as well as the tune; they described a "home of peace and rest" where those who had died were seen "upon the shining shore." Sarah had given her son the poem "The Shining Shore" and suggested he set it to music. By 1861 this song had reportedly been carried halfway around the world by missionaries. It was well-known in the Union army[18] and a favorite with southerners, both in the army and at home.

Sometime in 1861, Root's "Cradle Song" called "Love Thy Mother, Little One" was published. On June first of that year, a baby girl was born to George and Mary Olive Root and given her mother's name. Whether the little girl's birth inspired the song was not disclosed. The unattributed words of the "Cradle Song" sounded more like a warning than a lullaby. "Early death, led on by care" might snatch the beloved mother from her family. "Pray for her at eve and morn," the last line suggested. The melody was serene and almost sprightly.[19]

The grim words of a poem called "Have Ye Sharpened Your Swords?" brought to mind the Revolutionary War and urged men to meet a national crisis as their forefathers had. The subtitle, "A Battle Cry," may have lodged in the mental reservoir of the mind that Root had once described. The words were dark, and Root set them for men's voices in four parts.

Music, previously considered "a matter of taste and fancy," was now enlisted urgently into the army. New regiments were organizing, recruits were filling up the ranks, equipment and supplies were multiplying. By September 1861, a movement was under way to supply regiments organized in the future with complete and well-equipped bands. The western states would not be left behind. Each regimental band would ordinarily have twenty-four pieces, and players would be paid according to a strange formula seemingly unrelated to their musical assignments. The Chicago *Tribune* supported the effort to provide bands and declared, "The importance of good music in the camp and upon the field cannot be too highly estimated." There was nothing quite like it for firing enthusiasm; nothing as exhilarating; after a hard-fought battle there was nothing as

5. The First Gun Is Fired 1861–1863

soothing and refreshing as the music from home, the writer explained. "Let our regiments have music," the *Tribune* insisted, "for 'he who hath no music in his soul is fit for treason.'"[20] By February 1862, there were 17,500 musicians in the Union army, "as large a force as the whole army of the United States before the war." By the spring of 1862, 239 Union regiments had bands, the rest had fifes and drums, and the total cost was more than six million dollars a year.[21] As the war dragged on, these numbers had to be greatly reduced.

The firm of Root & Cady took part in patriotic events whenever possible. To promote public band concerts, the firm chose twenty musicians for a group called the Douglas Brigade Band. Concerts were announced for alternate evenings at two locations, Hyde Park and Michigan Avenue. The band was to play every evening for a week.[22]

In George Root's words, "The growth of our little business after the war commenced was something remarkable."[23] In late September 1861, Root & Cady was bringing in from its suppliers a thousand dollars' worth of brass and silver instruments each day for sale to bands.[24] A Chicago infantry regiment, the Nineteenth Illinois, advertised on October 3 for "A few good musicians" to complete their band. Less than three weeks later the group, with twenty-two members, received their new instruments through Root & Cady. On the evening of October 22, 1861, they were to leave Chicago on their way to join their regiment in Kentucky. The Nineteenth Illinois would make history later in the war and would be remembered in a song by George Root.

The 1861 battle of Ball's Bluff brought the war home to George Root as perhaps no other battle did; in its aftermath he composed a song called "The Vacant Chair." Men of the 15th Massachusetts Infantry all came from Worcester County, a place Root knew. For one of the young men from Worcester, Lieutenant John William Grout, Ball's Bluff was his first battle.[25] Since the previous July, Union and Confederate forces had glared at each other from opposite banks of the Potomac River in the area of Ball's Bluff, not far from Leesburg, Virginia. On Tuesday, October 22, there were "partial and disconnected reports of a fight in progress yesterday" between General Charles P. Stone's column and the enemy.[26] General McClellan had ordered Stone, with his force of 10,000 men, to keep watch on the area. What was intended to be a reconnaissance or, with discretion, a small show of force, became a military nightmare: crossing a river in the face of enemy fire.

Early reports of the battle of Ball's Bluff were optimistic. On Thurs-

Relatively early in the war, the battle of Ball's Bluff shook the confidence of the northern people. Young Lieutenant John William Grout had survived the worst of this, his first battle, and was helping the wounded across the river to safety when he was hit. Southern families mourned their own losses as well — there were at least three Confederate editions of this song.

day, October 24, a report said the results were "satisfactory to McClellan." The next day Federal losses were found to be much heavier than the early reports had indicated. President Lincoln lost a close friend, Edward D. Baker, a United States Senator from Oregon before he became a colonel in the army. Baker's regiment was virtually destroyed. Baker and Lincoln had enjoyed a visit on the White House grounds just days earlier; they had relaxed, talked about the fighting that was to come, and reminisced about their days together in Sangamon County, Illinois.[27]

On Monday the 28th, a report on Ball's Bluff from *The New York World* was picked up in Chicago. "Now comes the naked truth, in all its stunning and distressing horrors." A captain gave his eyewitness account. "We had no proper means of transit and retreat," he said. "Hundreds plunged into the rapid current, and the shrieks of the drowning added to the horror of sounds and sights. The enemy kept up their fire from the cliff above."[28] When the order to retreat came, men tried to swim back across the river to safety. Eighteen-year-old Lieutenant William Grout helped some of the wounded into boats and was trying to help others when a bullet struck him in the head.[29] He called out, "Tell Company D I could have reached the shore, but I am shot."[30] On Thursday, October 31, the *Tribune* promised, "The reckoning for the Ball's Bluff sacrifice, (for defeat it was not), will one day come." After Ball's Bluff there were changes of command in both armies. In Washington a Joint Committee on the Conduct of the War was set up, primarily to investigate the battle. Grout's body was recovered and taken home to Worcester for burial.

Henry S. Washburn[31] was a neighbor of the Grout family. When he heard about their loss he wrote a poem, "The Vacant Chair," which was published in the *Worcester Spy* in November 1861. Families were making plans to celebrate Thanksgiving; as Root explained in his autobiography, Thanksgiving was a major holiday in New England. Root set Washburn's poem to music. Later, he described this song as "mourning for the lost one."[32] "The Vacant Chair" came to symbolize many thousands of losses, in southern homes as well as northern ones. The chorus, arranged in four-part harmony, reiterated the first two lines of the first verse. The sheet music cover of a Confederate copy of "The Vacant Chair," published by Davies and Sons in Richmond, showed an armchair beside a fireplace. On a Root & Cady sheet music cover, there was a vignette showing a family seated around a dining table. One chair was vacant.

Reactions to the battle of Ball's Bluff still filled the news when friends gave a benefit concert for a favorite singer, Jules Lumbard. He had helped to introduce Root's song "The First Gun Is Fired." Root volunteered to participate in the benefit. The *Tribune* commented that the role of soloist was a new one for Root, who was better known as a teacher of vocal technique, and reported that he sang Schubert's "Wanderer" in a "most careful and easy" style.[33] Lumbard sang Root's new setting of Disraeli's poem, "My Heart Is Like a Silent Lute," with Root as accompanist.[34] The words spoke of heartbreak and dejection. The melody, in a major key, was artful and flowing.

Trying, as he expressed it, to "hit the copperhead element of the North," Root composed a song called "Stand Up for Uncle Sam, Boys."[35] Copperheads were among the members of the Peace Democrat party, northerners who believed the war should be fought to restore the Union, not to destroy the South or to bring about emancipation. Some of them wore an image of the Goddess of Liberty taken from the copper penny. Root & Cady advertised this as "A spirited and capital song for the times."[36]

"The blight of war has not reached us," the Chicago *Tribune* declared on Thanksgiving Day in 1861. Financial chaos had threatened its businesses, but as 1861 went on, trade had flourished and money had grown more plentiful. Confidence was restored. Problems that had plagued businesses elsewhere had only made Chicago's trade stronger, bringing new sources of wealth and signs of future prosperity. Now Chicago and the *Tribune* could boast about palatial residences, new business firms, and new streets that had been laid out while old ones were being improved..[37] The war situation was as frustrating as the commercial scene was encouraging. After eight months of war the North was still on the threshold of a concerted war effort. The *Tribune* predicted that the battle to decide the outcome of the war would be fought within hearing of the Capital. On the last day of 1861 the North looked back on unprecedented events. More than half a million men were in winter camps. Six hundred thousand were stretched from Kansas to the Chesapeake Bay, waiting to engage the rebel forces. There was a trace of desperation in the *Tribune's* suggestion that the government start the New Year with definitive plans for action.[38]

Through the years Root traveled by train, by coach, and by wagon through good weather and bad, teaching in dozens of places. The cold of late December and early January usually accompanied him from one musical convention to another. Near the end of December 1861, he taught conventions in Le Raysville, Pennsylvania, and Attica, New York.[39] On January 15, 1862, he began a musical convention in Morristown, New Jersey, about 30 miles west of New York City. A "Circular" invited all singers and music lovers to attend and become members of the Morristown convention. The circular stressed the importance of being present the first day and on time. Those attending were asked to "provide themselves" with Root's book, *The Diapason*. Root promised to furnish them with *The Glee Book*—presumably his *Festival Glee Book*. There was an unusual request in the circular: Soloists and those experienced in quartet singing were asked to come prepared with pieces they could sing in a concert.[40] In February Root's teaching schedule took him to the town of Bryan, Ohio,[41] then to St. Joseph, Michigan, where the singers had never experienced a musical convention. They expected to see a show like those given by traveling musicians.[42]

Storms, cold temperatures, and snowdrifts accompanied Root's musical convention in Beloit, Wisconsin, in March 1862. In McGregor, Iowa, he taught another "first ever" convention.[43] During the first week of April, he taught a three-day class in Wooster, Ohio.[44]

While Root was traveling and teaching, the war was constantly on the minds of people at home in Chicago. On January 6 the *Tribune* trumpeted its opinion on the war in an article called "The Shorter Catechism." The central question was about the purpose of the war. The *Tribune* answered boldly: "To save the country, and let slavery take care of itself," while putting down everything that stood in the way of Union. A week later the paper urged an "active" war and described the generals as reluctant to move against the South because "They have friends there."[45]

The Hutchinson Family were well-known singers, focusing now on abolition. Later in the war the Hutchinsons would be instrumental in the spread of George Root's most influential song. In January they created a series of incidents that illustrated the power of a song. They started on a planned series of concerts in army camps on January 24, 1862, with the "commendation" of Secretary of War Simon Cameron and a permit from General George McClellan. Their most noteworthy song was "We Wait Beneath the Furnace Blast," in which the words of a poem by John Greenleaf Whittier were sung to the tune of the venerable Lutheran hymn, "A Mighty Fortress Is Our God."[46] The *Tribune* called the song "too hot for the pro-slavery commanders." General William B. Franklin called the song "incendiary" and said it "deserved to be suppressed." McClellan agreed with Franklin and ordered the generals of his various divisions not to allow the Hutchinsons to sing for the soldiers in their commands.[47]

At this early point slavery was one thread in the tangle of wartime problems. Thousands of northern men had volunteered to fight for their country, but in many cases the abolition of slavery had not been the major cause of their volunteering. Military and government policymakers would have preferred to fight for union or reunification. A *Tribune* editorial observed, "For nine months the war has been managed on the policy of putting down the rebellion mildly, and saving slavery." The goal had been to conduct the war in such a way that, "whether the rebellion succeeded or failed, the condition of no human being should [be] changed." Twenty thousand lives had been sacrificed; debts of four hundred million dollars had been incurred. Appalled by the cost of war in lives and resources, and perhaps by failures on the battlefield, people called for "active war."[48]

News that the Hutchinsons had been refused admittance to the camps of McClellan's command created a stir in Colonel Farnsworth's regiment, camped at Alexandria. Farnsworth and his officers immediately issued an invitation to the Hutchinsons, who gave a concert in a Methodist church there. The church was packed; the concert closed with the "John Brown Song," the soldiers joining heartily in the chorus: "Glory, glory hallelujah, his soul is marching on." Secessionists in the community claimed the church, which belonged to the southern branch of Methodism, had been desecrated by the singing of "Free Soil" songs. Violence was threatened by both sides. Some of Farnsworth's soldiers immediately hung posters announcing another concert for that evening. During the evening concert a minister preached an anti-slavery sermon.[49] According to a persistent popular account, President Lincoln told his cabinet the Hutchinsons' songs were among the kinds he wanted the troops to hear.[50] Thereafter, the Hutchinsons were welcome to sing wherever they wished.

Chicago prided itself on its appreciation for fine music. At the same time, new songs in the popular style appeared in a steady flow and the city attracted well-known performers. In March Root & Cady brought out a new song, "Our Captain's Last Words," by an obscure composer, Henry Clay Work.[51] He was a gifted songwriter; his melodies were irresistible. His words were poetic and at the same time natural. In less than a month two presses were printing "Our Captain's Last Words," and Root & Cady was trying hard to keep up with the demand.[52] L. M. Gottschalk announced a concert in Chicago for April 15; Christy's Minstrels advertised "New acts, new features, new faces," one of whom was "D. Giovanni." McVicker's Theater announced the last night of "Shakespeare's Roman Tragedy, Julius Caesar."[53] Advertised in the same newspaper column, and illustrating the democratization of musical taste, there was another ad for Christy's minstrels, as well as an ad for a Philharmonic Society concert offering Beethoven's *Symphony No. 6* (Pastoral) together with music by Verdi, Mendelssohn, Weber, and Meyerbeer.[54]

In May 1862, Root & Cady, thriving on the business generated by war, expanded its facilities, particularly for publishing sheet music. Also in May, Isaac D. Guyer published his *History of Chicago*. It appeared to be a genteel form of paid advertising with descriptions of the city's "commercial and manufacturing interests" and articles about the men who had played significant roles in business and industry. Among the eighty-eight entries were descriptions of three music businesses. Guyer called Root & Cady the "originators of music publishing in the West, and the *only* house having their facilities." The firm had recently extended its facilities by adding a music composition house where they could "prepare their own illuminated title pages and sheet music" for printing. Their elegant store on the first and second floors at 95 Clark Street was described as a gathering place for "sociable, musical, loving spirits."[55]

War disrupted the regular sessions of Root's Normal Musical Institute. The 1862 Normal in Wooster, Ohio, lasted six weeks. Attendance was good, but excitement about the war was distracting. Recruiting officers and an occasional war meeting made it difficult for teachers as well as students to give all their attention to their classes. Root and his associates were always ready to participate in the war meetings. He recalled that the new war songs, sung by a fine chorus made up of Normal students, helped recruiting and roused the enthusiasm of the public. When the war began, Root, like most people, thought it might last as long as a year. Now, as he said, "the magnitude of the undertaking began to appear." So many men were going to the army that he decided to suspend the Normal until the war ended.[56]

C. M. Cady, one of the founders of the company, was in charge of advertising, and Root & Cady's ads were as innovative as any the Chicago *Tribune* published. On April 12, 1862, a mysterious announcement appeared under the heading "New Advertisements" on page one of the *Tribune:* "KINGDOM COMING." For the next week the cryptic words "Kingdom Coming" appeared without explanation in the paper's pages. Apparently the ad was effective in arousing the public's curiosity. On Saturday, April 19, the *Tribune* explained that Root & Cady had just published a serio-comic song by Henry C. Work, titled "Kingdom Coming." In it, a slave "advertised" his runaway master.[57] Three days later a notice promised the public a performance of the song at the opening of Christy's Burlesque Opera House in Kingsbury Hall.[58]

In a roundup of musical news in Chicago on May 2, 1862, the *Tribune* noted that George Root was in Boston, working on a book of Sabbath School music, and added that Work's "Kingdom Coming" was sure to become as well-known as "Dixie" and to "take its place in the North." A musician was arranging "Kingdom Coming" as a quickstep for the Light

Guard Band. Minstrel show singers, theater orchestras, and rural concert performers were singing and playing it in all parts of the country.[59]

In retrospect Root described his first impressions of Henry Clay Work and his gift for composition. Unexpectedly one day early in the war, a young man was sent up to Root's workroom from the store below, bringing a song for Root to examine. The song was "Kingdom Coming." The young man was serious and quiet and poorly dressed. Root looked at the song, then at the young man, in astonishment. The manuscript was elegant; the melody was captivating; the situations it described were comical. Root concluded that it was "exactly suited to the times." He was pleased to see that the words and the melody fit together in a way that brought Gilbert and Sullivan to mind. Had Work really written this, the words as well as the music? He had, was the modest answer. Root asked what his occupation was. The young man was a printer. "Would you rather write music than set type?" Root asked. He would. If this was a sample of the work he could do, he could give up the printing business, Root told him.[60] As the person in charge of publications, Root needed songwriters and Henry Clay Work was an inimitable one. Like the young Root arriving in Boston, he had found the right place at the right time.

Henry's father, Alanson Work, was called "a fearless anti-slavery advocate."[61] Alanson spent his days in welfare work for the slaves and actively helped the Underground Railroad. At one point he was imprisoned for it. Henry's lyrics showed the single-minded conviction of one who grew up in the center of this.

The next ad for "Kingdom Coming" showed a drawing of a man running. A few words from the song accompanied the drawing. "He seen a smoke way up de ribber, whar' de Linkum gum-boats lay. He took his hat, an' lef' berry sudden, an' I spec he's run away."[62] Root & Cady could hardly keep up with the orders for "Kingdom Coming." "It is whistled, sung, hummed and instrumentalized everywhere, in fact it is one of the institutions of the day," the publisher claimed.[63]

On Wednesday, April 16, 1862, President Lincoln signed a bill designed to end slavery in the District of Columbia. On the same day, Root & Cady advertised Henry Clay Work's new song, "Uncle Joe's Hail Columbia." Printed with the first eight measures of the song was the gist of the new law: "'An Act for the release of certain persons held to service or labor in the District of Columbia' has this day been approved and signed. Abraham Lincoln, Washington, April 16th, 1862."[64] The familiar song title "Hail Columbia" now had new meaning. Work's lyrics began "Uncle Joe comes home a singing, Hail, Columby!" Work had reached back into history for the basis of this song. Chicagoans had heard the traditional "Hail Columbia, happy land" on virtually every public occasion. It was not the national anthem, but when there was a need for a musical expression of patriotism, this Revolutionary relic came to mind. Joseph Hopkinson, son of a signer of the Declaration of Independence, had written the words of this 1798 song and they included the phrase "Rallying round our liberty."

By 1862 the public needed a great rallying song. "Why has the war produced no national Anthem worthy of the name, and no eloquence fit to rank with the world's masterpieces?" the Chicago *Tribune* wailed. The public needed a "Marseillaise," or a hymn with the grandeur of Luther's, or something with the power and magnetism of Patrick Henry. The present war was a revolution, an event as historic as those that had gone before, the paper declared.[65] Day after day newspapers described war rallies and patriotic meetings. Those reports still evoke torchlit streets, recruiting posters and bands playing "Yankee Doodle," "Hail Columbia," and "The Star Spangled Banner." The pages for 1862 illustrate the need for something new to sing and play, something that would capture the moment and become part of it. In the summer of that year Chicagoans read chilling reports about McClellan's army in the vicinity of Richmond. By the Fourth of July, terrible fighting had gone on for six days with Federal losses of 12,000 to 15,000 men. "For the first time since secession showed its head, the Republic is in real *danger*," Chicagoans were warned. People swung like a pendulum, the paper said, between elation when there was a report of success and despair when a defeat was announced. Governors of some states were petitioning Lincoln to call for more troops.[66]

Root composed his most significant song in response to Lincoln's call. Newspaper reports on "The New Call for Troops" and "How the People are Responding" came from across the Union states. Boston reported, "The war spirit is up in Massachusetts." Detroit reported that a great meeting of citizens was held at City Hall to respond to the president's call for troops. Indianapolis and Buffalo sent reports of rallies. Closer to home, Freeport, Illinois, recruited another company and sent it to Camp Douglas near Chicago. Not all war rallies were peaceful. At a second rally in Detroit, "Patriotic resolutions were passed, amid much disturbance, and the meeting came to a premature adjournment."[67]

On Saturday, July 19, the Chicago Tribune urged, "TO ARMS! TO ARMS! MEETING OF LOYAL CITIZENS OF CHICAGO.... Let the people rally to-night." The paper called this the "Second Call" for troops. Men were urgently needed. "Skeleton" regiments in the field must be filled.[68] This one rally became three. Bryan Hall was jammed and overflowing; Metropolitan Hall was full; five thousand people gathered in the Court House Square. At Bryan Hall, J. G. Lumbard sang "The Marsaillaise." A poem, "Three Hundred Thousand More," was sung to the tune of "The First Gun Is Fired." At Courthouse Square, Frank Lumbard with two others sang "The Red, White and Blue," the entire audience joining enthusiastically in the chorus.[69]

Root's account of writing "The Battle Cry of Freedom" captures the spirit of the moment — urgency, patriotism, a need to act. "I heard of President Lincoln's second call for troops one afternoon ... immediately a song started in my mind, words and music together: 'Yes, we'll rally round the flag, boys, we'll rally once again, shouting the battle-cry of freedom!'" He "thought it out" that afternoon, and wrote it the next morning in his workroom at Root & Cady. As he remembered it, the ink was hardly dry when the Lumbard brothers, Chicago's outstanding singers of the war, came to the store asking for something to sing at a war meeting that was about to begin in the courthouse square. They sang through the song once, then rushed to the steps of the court-house, followed by a crowd that had gathered to listen while they practiced. Jules Lumbard sang the verses; his brother Frank's "trumpet tones" led the refrain: "The Union forever, hurrah, boys, hurrah." By the time they reached the fourth verse a thousand voices were joining in the chorus.[70]

The *Tribune* published a rousing description of this "GREAT WAR MEETING" held Saturday, July 26, in the courthouse square. A crowd of 20,000 took part in "the second uprising of our patriotic people since the new call for volunteers." The paper quoted the lengthy speeches verbatim, and added that after a speech by a Mr. Arnold, a new war song by George F. Root was sung by a well-trained chorus of voices, with J. G. Lumbard singing the solo and the Light Guard Band accompanying the singing. The words of "The Battle Cry of Freedom" were printed in the article. This issue of the paper also carried the first advertisement for "The Battle Cry of Freedom." In the ad, four measures of the song were printed in musical score, the words under the notes.[71]

Dena Epstein, in her definitive history of the Root & Cady firm,

"The Battle Cry of Freedom" exemplifies musicologist Charles Hamm's saying that music interacted so closely with the events and circumstances of the war that it became a part of them. A vibrant artifact of the war, this song is heard in films and documentaries and on numerous individual recordings.

questioned the date of the first performance of the song. According to the *Chicago Tribune*, the courthouse square meeting Root described as the occasion of the first performance took place Saturday, July 26, 1862. According to Epstein, the first performance took place two days earlier, on Thursday, July 24, at a Board of Trade war meeting and was reported in the *Tribune's* July 25 issue. The Light Guard Band played while the

Board of Trade, where the price of grain and "the traffic of tradesmen" occupied each normal day, became a recruiting office. A reporter saw young men, the employees of commission houses, "stepping up and enrolling themselves"; merchants "contributing lavishly towards their support" while the walls were "reverberating patriotic strains." After a speech by the Honorable Isaac N. Arnold, the audience heard "The Battle Cry of Freedom, words and music composed by George F. Root."[72]

The "Battle Cry of Freedom" became a part of the Civil War and of American history. It reverberated through the spring election campaign of 1863; rolled across battlefields such as Murfreesboro, the Wilderness, and Vicksburg; heralded the raising of the flag at Fort Sumter when war ended. Root explained his theory about songs that endure. He believed some music has a "mysterious quality which makes it live, while all the rest fades away and is forgotten." It was not a matter of aesthetic quality. The music might be of the highest type or the lowest. He thought back to the time when he was an unsophisticated listener. Every tune that produced what he called "the thrill of that mysterious life" then was "still alive" in "the hearts of the people," he wrote.[73]

When the "The Battle Cry of Freedom" came out, Root sent the first copy, as he usually did, to Mary Olive, who was still at their home in North Reading, Massachusetts. James R. Murray, a friend and former student of Root's, had volunteered and was in camp in the nearby town of Lynnfield. When Mary Olive heard this, she and Root's father went to visit Murray and wish him well before he went to the front. They gave him the new song.[74]

Less than two months after "The Battle Cry of Freedom" was published, Root added a second set of words.[75] The original had been a recruiting song, a patriotic response to Lincoln's call for public support. Root called the original a "Rallying Song" and the new version a "Battle Song." As the "seventh thousand" copies of the original version came off the press with a colored title page, the words of the "Battle Song" faced the first page of the music.

"We will rally round this glorious old flag of ours until the Union is restored," Illinois Governor Yates told a crowd of ten thousand in Chicago on August 1, 1862. Then the Lumbard brothers and a "powerful" chorus sang "The Battle Cry of Freedom" "capitally."[76]

While the war years dragged on, Root's "The Battle Cry of Freedom," often called "Rally Round the Flag," was heard in all sorts of circumstances. Clara Barton, the pioneering war nurse, reportedly sang it while tending the wounded at Fredericksburg in early December 1862.[77] Men of the Fifty-fifth Illinois regiment sang it at the battle of Chickasaw Bayou in the Vicksburg campaign later that December.[78] Chicago's Lumbard brothers were sent to Vicksburg to sing in hospitals and entertain the troops with free concerts; one of their songs was "The Battle Cry of Freedom."[79] Schoolchildren in Maryland sang it while "cheering Federal troops marching north to Gettysburg" in June 1863.[80] Captives in a Confederate prison at Danville, Virginia, sang it in the late days of the war.[81]

Sometimes a song was the last thing one would expect to hear. A brigade of the Union Ninth Army Corp, attacked from their flank, was driven back with heavy losses on May 6, 1864, in the battle of the Wilderness. They re-formed their line and turned to face the enemy. At that crucial moment a voice from the Forty-fifth Pennsylvania Infantry began: "'We'll rally round the flag, boys, rally once again, shouting the battle cry of freedom.'" Other voices joined the song. It spread to the next line of soldiers. Gradually the singing blended with the sounds of burning brush, crying wounded, blazing muskets and shouted commands.[82] Such instances illustrate the peculiar role of music in nineteenth-century American life, as well as the romanticizing of war experiences in retrospect.

One evening George P. Upton, a correspondent for the Chicago *Tribune,* sat on the deck of a gunboat wondering what an enemy force close by would do the next day. From a troop transport ship in the convoy he heard a clear tenor voice singing "The Battle Cry of Freedom." An answer came from the enemy's position, a similar voice singing "Dixie." The first singer responded with a song about hanging Jeff Davis from a sour apple tree. Then there was silence. "There was no song of the war time that equaled 'The Battle Cry' in popularity and patriotic inspiration," Upton wrote.[83]

Root & Cady issued several variants on George Root's great war song. The most impressive was "Battle Cry of Freedom, Grand Caprice de Concert" by Louis Moreau Gottschalk. Audiences had heard Gottschalk play his transcription and had responded "with the greatest enthusiasm." Root & Cady paid him five hundred dollars; pessimists said they would never recoup their investment, but almost three hundred orders for the piece came in before the publication date.[84] Gottschalk's piece was published in Europe as "Le Cri de Delivrance, Caprice Heroique," Opus 55, by B. Schott's Sons and dedicated, as the Root & Cady publication was, "To my friend, George F. Root." In 1864 Gottschalk wrote in his diary that he believed "The Battle Cry of Freedom" should be the national anthem.[85]

Root described his reaction to the success of his "Battle Cry of Freedom." "The testimony in regard to its use in the camp and on the march, and even on the field of battle, from soldiers and officers, up to generals, and even to the good President himself, made me thankful that if I could not shoulder a musket in defense of my country I could serve her in this way."[86] He heard a number of reports about its use. The story that moved him most was told by an officer who had been at Vicksburg. An Iowa regiment sent eight hundred men into battle and "came out with a terrible loss of more than half their number; but the brave fellows who remained were waving their torn and powder-stained banner, and singing "Yes, we'll rally round the flag, boys." Years later, in the closing concert of a musical convention in Anamosa, Iowa, Root received a note asking him to sing his "Battle Cry of Freedom." He read the note to the audience and told them the story of the Iowa regiment at Vicksburg. "Here is a soldier who lost his arm in that battle," a voice called out. Root asked the veteran to come forward and stand with him while he sang. "It was hard work," Root remembered, "and there was hardly a dry eye in the house." Another of Root's favorite stories about the song was published in *The Century* magazine. This story illustrated how, in Root's words, time had "changed the terrible realism of the march and the battle-field into tender and hallowed memories."[87]

Just days after General Lee surrendered in April 1865, Union and paroled Confederate officers were staying in neighboring houses. The former Confederates heard the Union men singing. "I shall never forget the first time I heard 'Rally Round the Flag,' one of the Confederates was quoted as saying. He was on picket duty, he recalled, on a rainy night during the Seven Days battles. Just before the bugle was to play "Taps," a soldier on the other side began to sing; others joined, and finally it seemed the whole Union army was singing. One of the Confederates expressed the amazement of many: Having beaten the Federals back for six consecutive days, they could hear them now singing "Rally Round the Flag."[88]

"Munitions of war" were advertised repeatedly in the pages of the Chicago *Tribune*. This was a familiar term, originally referring to the prodigious effort of the arms industry to supply the troops with weapons. The Colt factory had fifteen hundred men producing weapons; the Sharp's Rifle Company worked around the clock. Another manufacturer was to deliver a thousand mortar shells, weighing two hundred pounds each, in twenty days. Other products, from tin cups to engines, were essential to the army. Root & Cady headed one of their advertisements "MUNITIONS OF WAR" to make the point that music was a vital part of army life. The ad listed band instruments, fifes and drums, and "a book for the times," the "Army Regulations for Drum, Fife and Bugle." Some of the firm's songs were mentioned in the ad: Henry C. Work's "Take Your Gun and Go, John" and "Uncle Joe's Hail Columbia"; "Wrap the Flag Around Me" by Taylor, Root's "Battle Cry of Freedom" and "De Day ob Liberty's Comin.'"[89]

"De Day Ob Liberty's Comin" was subtitled "Wurzel's Liberty Song." By this time it was no secret that Wurzel (the German word for Root) was the pseudonym of George F. Root. His words for this song expressed the belief that bondage would end in the foreseeable future and pictured Lincoln as advocating payment to former owners for freed slaves. In the third verse the slave was pictured as offering military service in exchange for emancipation.[90]

Like Root's "Battle Cry of Freedom," a poem called "We Are Coming, Father Abraham" was a response to Lincoln's call for more troops. Early musical settings of the poem answered on behalf of "three hundred thousand more." Several composers, including Stephen Foster, set the poem by James Sloan Gibbons to music.[91] When the quota was raised to six hundred thousand men, Root & Cady published "Father Abraham's Reply to the 600,000!" The music was "adapted and partly composed" by George Root. There was no further explanation of the origin of the tune. The words, in four verses, acknowledged state after state, including what were then the western ones, for sending more men.

The Chicago *Tribune's* tone betrayed doubt, frustration and even fear in an article called "The Present Aspect" on September 5, 1862. Until now, the people of the North had always believed that the power and resources of their government could ultimately crush any force the enemy could bring against them. This belief had sustained the public after the disaster of Bull Run; it had held off despair through the inactivity and endless entrenching on the banks of the Potomac. There had been more than enough time to enlist, drill and arm a force such as the world had never seen. And yet, the enemy seemed more powerful than ever: Re-conquering positions he had lost, marching into places once thought to be safe, and threatening Washington with an army that, in the face of the best Federal troops, steadily approached the capital.

The public could not know that President Lincoln had already decided to emancipate the slaves.[92] Feelings were strong on both sides of this, the most divisive issue of the time. Some thought of emancipation as a first step toward enlisting former slaves in the Union army. While many loyal supporters of the Union, in Illinois as elsewhere, were still strongly opposed to emancipation by proclamation, the names of Chauncey M. Cady and George F. Root were among those listed on an appeal to the president, calling for a decree of emancipation as "a sign of national repentance as well as a military necessity."[93] Lincoln had told his cabinet on July 22 that he planned to make such a proclamation. With opinions at home and in the army so strongly divided, he waited for a favorable moment to announce it. The battle of Antietam on September 17, and McClellan's wire announcing that it was a Union victory, set the stage. The *Tribune* called it "the grandest proclamation ever issued by man" and rejoiced that all slaves in the Confederacy would be free.[94]

Responding to the Emancipation Proclamation, Chicago musicians volunteered to sing at the inevitable mass meeting, where the public would "endorse" the Proclamation. A "full chorus" was ready to sing "The Battle Cry of Freedom," "Fill Up the Ranks," "Father Abraham's Reply," "Kingdom Coming," "Our Country Is in Danger," and "Abe's Gone and Did It," among other songs. The music firms H. M. Higgins and Root & Cady would provide soloists (including the Lumbards) and several musical societies would join in the choruses. Three bands, the Light Guard, the Great Western, and Vass & Dean's were scheduled to play.[95] On Saturday night, September 27, 1862, an estimated 10,000 people "ratified" Lincoln's proclamation in "Union Mass Meetings" at Bryan Hall and Court House Square.[96] On the following Monday, Chicagoans read the various speeches verbatim in a report that called the Bryan Hall rally a "magnificent demonstration."[97]

The war made itself felt in two books Root published in 1862, *The Silver Chime* for Sunday Schools and *The Silver Lute* for "Schools and Academies." By now, families were familiar with Root's "Vacant Chair" and the painful circumstances it described. In *The Silver Chime*, "One Place is Vacant" described a similar situation, but from the children's point of view. Just days after publication was announced, *The Silver Chime* was selling more than a thousand copies a day in the eastern states.[98]

The Silver Lute "for schools and teachers" was a historic publication, "the first music book ever prepared, stereotyped and printed in Chicago."[99] It opened with the basics of note reading and followed with "song-lessons," arranged step by step in order of difficulty, which prepared the student for its large assortment of songs. With some of the songs there were suggestions for physical exercises to be done while singing. An entire section of the book was titled "Songs of Union, Songs of Freedom, and of Our Beloved Fatherland." In the preface, Root encouraged children, while their fathers and brothers were on the battle-fields, to sing songs that promoted courage, heroism, and support of "the government and free institutions" of their country.

In this book an unattributed song called "After the Battle" pictured a grim scene where "sheaves of the dead" lay on the ground. Children also found Root's "Battle Cry of Freedom" and "Vacant Chair" here. "Make Your Mark" and "Be Careful of Your Money" reinforced familiar advice. There were songs on current themes: "I'm Glad I Am a Farmer," "O'er Prairie," "I Have No Mother Now," "Never Forget the Dear Ones," and a "Temperance Rallying Song." A month after publication, almost all the first edition of 10,000 copies of *The Silver Lute* had been sold, the publishers noted. In its first year, sales exceeded 1,000 copies a day.[100]

The Chicago Board of Education held an "Interesting Discussion on Musical Text Books" early in November 1862. After a quarrelsome session focused more on personalities than textbooks, the Board adopted Root's *Silver Lute* as the music textbook for Chicago schools. One board member said he "did not know much of the book named, but thought if the compiler had selected more and written less, it would have been an improvement."[101] In the last three months of 1862, Root & Cady printed more than 31,000 copies of *The Silver Lute* and explained "the binders cannot keep up with the demand."[102]

On Christmas Day, 1862, the Chicago *Tribune* wished "to all men everywhere, except traitors," a very merry Christmas. This morning, as children found stockings full of gifts "from the wrinkled old man whose steeds were reindeer," people were urged to remember those sad households where a son or brother was missing. Many of the absent ones lay beneath southern soil or suffered in hospitals; many homes were bleak from the "cold embers of poverty." While they enjoyed the holiday, people were urged to remember the soldiers and the poor.[103]

On this Christmas Day Root & Cady announced publication of two "stirring war songs from the pen of Geo. F. Root." R. Tompkins wrote the words of both songs. "Oh, Haste on the Battle" listed generals who had tried with varying success to lead Union forces.[104]

As 1862 came to an end, the Emancipation Proclamation would soon go into effect. Some people in the North felt it shifted the purpose of the war from saving the Union to freeing the slaves. Abolitionism was an explosive ideology and a matter of degree. At one extreme, the Hutchinson Family singers had been prohibited temporarily from singing their abolitionist songs. At the other extreme were people who tried to ignore the subject. "Call 'Em Names, Jeff"[105] described a scene in which southern leaders decided to call all Union soldiers "Abolitionists" in order to create dissent among them. The words cast this most serious subject matter in a comical light. Root & Cady boasted that "Call 'Em Names, Jeff" would "not be likely to please your Secession neighbors, if you are so unfortunate as to have any," and suggested that sarcasm was often more effective than argument. The company advertised this song as "a genuine and earnest gush of patriotic feeling."[106]

On the night of January 12, 1863, crowds in Chicago celebrated the issuing of the Emancipation Proclamation with a "popular uprising." "The great public heart was stirred to its very depths," the *Tribune* said. Political leaders and government officials made speeches. Early in the evening Bryan Hall was filled to capacity and a reported 10,000 people stood in the street along the side of Court House Square. Someone said the First Baptist Church was available; it promptly filled to capacity as well. Still thousands were outdoors, trying to get within hearing distance of the men who were speaking. At Bryan Hall "Messrs. Root, Cady and Tillinghast" sang "Call 'Em Names, Jeff."[107] Whether this was George, Towner, or their brother William Root was not explained.

From the time the Nineteenth Illinois Infantry was formed in the Chicago area, people there followed the regiment, mostly through newspaper reports. In the battle of Murfreesboro (Stone's River) at the end of December 1862, the men distinguished themselves in the kind of incident that made legends. The *Tribune*'s reporter told how long lines of Confederates emerged from the woods with a demoniac yell, charging "almost to the very muzzle of the cannon." The Union forces fired a veritable sheet of flame; the earth shook; rebels in the front line were "literally swept from the field"; smoke obscured everything. Ten minutes later hundreds of dead, dying and disabled men lay on the ground; "their blood soaked and reddened" the earth.[108] On January 10, the same reporter went out looking for Chicago men, asking about their experiences. One awful scene stayed with the men who had been there. During a fierce rebel assault, Union General Negley saw that his left flank was about to crumble. He rode to the front, looking for troops to strengthen that part of the line. "Who'll save the left?" he shouted. Colonel Scott answered immediately, "The Nineteenth, Sir." Scott, a Chicago native, led a charge against the Confederate force and was wounded.[109] When Chicagoans saw the words "Who'll Save the Left?" as a song title a few months later, many of them remembered the story. The cover of the sheet music explained that the song was intended "To perpetuate the glory of the brave men of the Nineteenth Illinois and their companions in arms who fell at Murfreesboro." Tompkins's words described the Nineteenth Illinois attacking across fields littered, as eyewitness accounts said, with the bodies of the dead and the disabled. By sunset the men realized that "the charge was triumphant, the great battle won."[110]

Some six months after the battle Colonel Scott died of the wounds he received in the historic charge at Stone's River. Chicagoans found the order of his funeral procession printed in their newspapers. Bands played and the "Citizens' Corps" marched. In the next day's *Tribune* all the verses of "Who'll Save the Left?" were printed with a description of the funeral.

In mid-January 1863, George Root sang in a benefit concert for the Sanitary Commission, a civilian organization working to help sick and wounded soldiers and their families. He sang "The Passing Bell" and Henry Russell's "Ivy Green." "Our Chicago concert goers should know Mr. Root better," a reviewer suggested. The concert closed with "Rally Round the Flag" sung by one of the Lumbard brothers, with the entire company joining in the chorus. Root and Miss Tillinghast played the accompaniment. The concert was repeated on Monday, January 26. This time the Chicago Musical Union sang Root's "Oh, Haste On the Battle" with the audience joining in the chorus.[111]

In 1863 the firm began to publish a periodical called *The Song Messenger of the Northwest*.[112] Root & Cady announced its debut with a striking advertisement on page one of the Chicago *Tribune* that displayed the magazine's masthead with an image George Root had chosen — a dove carrying a banner with the words "Song Messenger of the Northwest." The ad promised eight pages of new vocal music and eight pages of reading matter in each issue.[113]

In a statement of its purpose, the publishers explained that *The Song Messenger of the Northwest* was intended for both ends of the cultural spectrum. "Our Aim is simply this: While making a musical paper especially for 'the people,' to furnish one which shall be of interest and value to the most highly cultivated artist." Henry Clay Work, the composer of "Kingdom Coming," was the first editor. The first issue featured "John Prosy's Talks by the Fireside," "Frank Whiteside's Introduction to Society" [by the editor], and an article on "Modern Improvements," signed "Phax and Phiggers." An article called "What We Saw at the Concert" complained that a woman's hat obstructed the view.

For the first issue of the *Song Messenger,* George Root had written a personal message "To Friends and Acquaintances." It was casual, friendly, down-to-earth. He had come to a decision. "It seems best that I should have a home in Chicago, and by the first of May I hope that will be a fact accomplished. "Willow Farm remains the same," he wrote, evidently assuming that readers knew that was his family home in Massachusetts.[114] He introduced members of the Root & Cady firm to readers. His brother E. Towner Root with C. M. Cady had "started in business here in '58." He had visited them as often as his convention tours took him westward. He had grown to like not only "the pleasant business" they were building, but the city and its "genial inhabitants." "Almost before I knew it," he wrote, "I became full half a Chicagoan, and one of the firm of Root & Cady." E. Towner Root "attended to the business detail in all departments." Chauncey M. Cady was in charge of finances and general management and George himself managed the publications. His brother William was a member of the office staff.[115]

By the time the third issue of the magazine came out Root had been to Massachusetts and brought his wife and three daughters to their new home in Chicago.[116] In this issue[117] his letter had a casual tone, somewhat like the popular humorists of the time. He described the journey by train as lasting through two nights and parts of two days without stopping. During this time he was "in charge of a party of little folks and ladies." At the time of his writing, the family was "nearly settled in a very pleasant home." He advised readers that "we shall be happy to see you when you come this way. I do not say with old Mr. Crusty, 'If you ever come within twenty miles, *stop*'; but will gladly welcome you *here*."

In the first *Song Messenger* issue, dated April 1863, songs captured moments when a societal evil was about to end and families were sending their men to the army. "Clear the Way" was marked with the monogram GFR. Neither slavery nor abolition was mentioned specifically in the words of the song. The words promised that "a brazen wrong" was about to be conquered and urged "men of thought and men of action" to "clear the way"[118] for this to happen. "Gone to the War" was a quartet marked with

5. The First Gun Is Fired 1861–1863

"Gone to the War" was published in the first edition of Root & Cady's magazine, *The Song Messenger of the Northwest*, in April 1863. The words were unattributed. The melody, marked "Air," is on the third staff line.

Root's monogram. Evidently never published in sheet music form, this was arguably one of Root's finest songs. The unattributed words conveyed strength and conviction as well as resignation. "Lulu Wilde, or the Song of the Octoroon" described a slave's thoughts on a future in which "the cruel days of bondage" had ended.

The Copperhead threat was strong enough in the spring of 1863 to cause a controversy in Chicago. When the mayor vetoed a proposed patriotic rally, his political critics accused him of giving in to Copperhead pressure. The *Tribune* urged "Loyal Men of Chicago, to the Rescue! RALLY TO BRYAN HALL" and promised a glorious gathering of loyal Union men. About eight o'clock on the evening of April 9, a splendid rendition of Root's "Battle Cry of Freedom" by Vaas and Dean's Light Guard Band "fired the audience with enthusiasm." The hall was jammed with people, listening to speech after speech. Frank Lumbard closed the rally by singing "The Red, White and Blue." The audience joined in the chorus. The *Tribune* called this the largest and most enthusiastic gathering of loyal Chicagoans since the rebellion began.[119]

"Rally round the ballot box," the *Tribune* urged on April 21, during the election campaign for Chicago's local offices. Slogans, this time sounding more patriotic than political, were interspersed with the news. One slogan proclaimed "The Battle Cry of Freedom at the ballot box today."[120]

On April 20, 1863, a rally described as the largest ever held in New York City met at Madison Square in response to a call by the Loyal League. The crowd was estimated at 50,000. Speakers stood on platforms in four locations. Red, white and blue hung from flagstaffs, from lines stretched across streets, and from the sides of the speakers' stands. At stand number one, Dodworth's band played patriotic songs. After a particularly long speech on the duties of patriots in wartime, the Hutchinson Family sang Root's "Battle Cry of Freedom" and "Glory Hallelujah" ("The John Brown Song"). General Winfield Scott, aged veteran of America's wars since 1812, spoke from the balcony of the Fifth Avenue Hotel. Later, sitting on the balcony in the late afternoon chill, he asked for a shawl. None was available, so someone brought a heavy American Flag and wrapped the old general in it. The admiring crowd applauded.[121]

6

Rally Once Again 1863–1865

In the spring of 1863 Chicagoans knew there were people in their midst who sympathized with the South, enough people to create a threat in their communities. All across the North there were reports of peace movements. To calm the people's fears, Union Leagues organized in support of Lincoln and his party. Music would help to carry the message the leagues wanted to convey. George Root put together *The Bugle Call,* a sixty-page paperback collection of songs "for Union Leagues in the North, our Army in the South, and Loyal people everywhere."[1] He intended *The Bugle Call* to inspire "a greater love for the Union, and a sterner determination to protect it to the last." The first song in the book was titled "The Bugle Call" and was signed with his monogram, the letters GFR one on top of the other in the space of a single letter. The words warned that "Traitors lurk on every hand" and urged people to "Help the brave men in the field" to fight for truth and justice. This song was followed and reinforced by Root's 1861 anti–Copperhead song, "Stand Up For Uncle Sam, My Boys."

Root had invited submissions from the public for this collection. When the book was finished his worktable was still stacked with what he called "more than enough capital pieces" to fill another volume. These pieces had been left out for lack of space and for the sake of variety, he explained. He saw in these submissions the outpourings of people's hearts. These were songs that "*would be written*, impelled perhaps by the loss of a brother," or other loved one, or by love of home or country "or a hate of traitors, open and secret," and he commented: "That which comes from the heart goes to the heart."[2]

A poem called "The Skedaddle Rangers" from the *Steuben Republican* was set to music, though the book didn't say by whom. The words addressed "fair weather patriots" who shook in their shoes, sneaking away "with the cowardly throng." The chorus featured the words "Skedaddle I-O."

"Stand by the President," an unattributed song in *The Bugle Call* urged. Its message was reassuring: "Though traitors breathe their discontent, and southern hosts rebel; stand firmly by the President, and all will yet be well." Both versions of "The Battle Cry of Freedom" were in the book, one with the original words ("Rallying Song") and the other with the words of the "Battle Song."

Henry Clay Work's songs in *The Bugle Call* voiced contrasting opinions about army life. "Brave Boys Are They" faced the grief of war frankly and openly.[3] His "Grafted into the Army" expressed a negative opinion of the draft.[4]

Root & Cady needed more songwriters, and in 1863, as George Root remembered it, Philip P. Bliss sent him a song manuscript and a letter asking for a flute in exchange for the song. Root published the song with a few corrections and sent the flute. Some time later Bliss wrote again, suggesting that he would like to relocate to Chicago if he could find suitable work. Root & Cady engaged him as their representative to the towns around Chicago, where he held musical conventions or gave concerts or in some other way drew attention to the company as a source of musical merchandise. He continued with Root & Cady and the firm published his music until the dissolution caused by the Chicago Fire. Eventually he joined the evangelist Dwight L. Moody as a solo singer. Bliss wrote many of the best-known gospel songs of the time.[5]

George Root and *Song Messenger* editor Henry Clay Work fell into an unfortunate disagreement in the summer of 1863. Work had assumed editorship of the *Song Messenger* on the condition that he would be "independent and untrammeled in the expression of his views on all subjects." He was responsible for the editorial department of the paper, so "the conduct of the paper should also rest with him." Senior partner George Root admitted "We rarely see what the editor writes until it is in print," and this was the case with an article titled "The Old Tunes" published in the June 1863 issue. Compilers of church music books were changing the tunes their great-grandfathers had loved. Work said this violated the sacred associations a tune carried with it, associations with church and school and fireside. He said when these old tunes were sung, "Even the sensations and emotions, so long forgotten, again take possession of us."

Work followed his June article with a stronger one in July. He had found the hymn tune "Bartimeus" in "a modern music book, "hardly recognizable, mutilated, with the liquid melody, so to speak, streaming from every vein." He printed the original melody of "Bartimeus" with its "dear peculiarities" followed by the altered version. Each of the rugged, primitive, untaught qualities had been changed. He urged compilers, composers, and publishers of church music books to preserve the traditional songs. "We beg of you — don't presume to remodel them according to *your* ideas of propriety, or the lyric fashions of the day," he wrote. He could "never let the matter rest," he threatened, "until we see a reform."

In the August issue of the paper Work tried to be fair. "We will admit at least as many articles in favor of the plan of altering old tunes as we do against it." George Root felt he had to write a reply in order to "relieve the publishers from a false position." He felt Work was attacking Lowell Mason, whom Root regarded as the most important living figure in American church music. Root shared Work's respect for the old tunes; he recalled his grandmother's singing them in the parlor at Willow Farm. His years of teaching the basics of music theory and harmony determined his response. He concluded that "Every compiler of church music has to ask himself this question — shall I reprint the old tunes with faults or untasteful places in them?" Also in the August issue of the *Song Messenger* Work apologized, but the damage was done. He had "arranged with the publishers" to place the editorship of the paper "in other hands." He would still write articles occasionally, he promised. More importantly, Root & Cady would still publish his songs.

The first issue of Root & Cady's *Song Messenger* had announced that the Normal Musical Institute was scheduled to meet in Chicago throughout the month of June. George Root was fully involved with this session[6] when the news brought "Startling Intelligence" from the army. There was "A Heavy Rebel Force in Pennsylvania." Confederate troops were moving toward Harrisburg; a bridge over the Susquehanna River was in flames.[7] It was an anxious time for the people at home in Chicago. The Copperhead view was that Washington and Baltimore could be taken, and that a revolution could occur in the north resulting in disunion and peace. The *Tribune's* writer argued that instead of peace, this could mean continuous war with "new and more fearful outpourings of blood, — war in every neighborhood and school district in the land." As always, the *Tribune* urged support for Lincoln and his government.[8]

People who had never heard of Gettysburg, Pennsylvania, would soon find it in their vocabularies. A Special Dispatch to the *Chicago Tribune* described a hotly contested fight there on July 2. Late in the day Union troops were "forced to retire ... in some disorder."[9] The three-day engagement ended July 4. It was a decisive victory for the Union army, which one observer said "has worked hard, suffered much, has been abused, has been thought to be of no account," but which had in fact "written a page of history" that would "be forever honorable in the book of time."[10]

After the Battle of Gettysburg, the Reverend T. Newton Jones of North Reading, Massachusetts, wrote a poem titled "Within the Sound of the Enemy's Guns." It described a moment of victory, of silencing enemy guns and capturing them. Root set the poem to music. The dedication read "In Remembrance of Gettysburg."[11]

Not long after the battle of Gettysburg, there was rioting in New York City and in some other places. A national conscription act had required all able-bodied men in the North, ages twenty to forty-five, to make themselves available for service. The act spelled out exemptions from the draft and permitted substitutes. The draft brought contradictory reactions—from fevered patriotism to actual violence. A Chicago paper called the three-day riot in New York City "The Ripened Fruit of Copperhead Teachings."[12] The paper described people wondering whether Victor Hugo, author of the currently popular novel *Les Miserables,* could have written a scene more awful than the riots in New York. Among the actual scenes had been horrors that would "make a novelist blush"; mob scenes "reeking in murder, revelling in atrocities...."[13] Some of the responses to the draft were sarcastic. Under the pseudonym Artemus Ward, Charles F. Browne wrote "The only sons of a poor widow, whose husband is in California, are not exempt, but a man who owns stock in the Vermont Central Railroad is."[14]

"Exempts" were men who found legitimate ways to avoid being drafted into the army. The Reverend T. Newton Jones contributed a poem called "Exempts" to the *Song Messenger.*[15] It appeared in the August 1863 issue. In eight verses the Reverend Jones blasted the men who tried to find an exemption to keep them out of the army. While the wealthy could hire a substitute or pay a fee rather than enlist, a man who was not wealthy became an involuntary soldier.

Henry Clay Work's "Kingdom Coming" was "the most successful patriotic song published in the West," Root & Cady said, and it had been the most successful "for nearly a year and a half." Now they announced a sequel called "Babylon Is Fallen." The "massa," who "went and run away" in "Kingdom Coming" had become an officer in the rebel army. A policy of enlisting blacks in the Union army was adopted, and in the sequel "By a curious coincidence, [his own slaves] took him prisoner one day." The story seemed to have nothing to do with ancient Babylon but Work, the son of a minister, "borrowed from holy writ, the great idea of the day — the downfall of despotism." In Revelation 14:8 were the words "Fallen, fallen is Babylon the great," the August issue of the *Song Messenger* explained.

"The first concert of freed men has been held," a Dr. Eddy of the *North Western Christian Advocate* wrote, and the first song was "Kingdom Coming." As the escaped slaves sang "The whip is lost, the handcuff broken," Dr. Eddy wished Henry Clay Work could be there to hear them.[16] Sixty to eighty contrabands "sang several plantation songs and then gave their own rendition of '"The Battle Cry of Freedom,'" Eddy wrote.[17]

James R. Murray, one of Root's "Normal" students, wished both Work and Root could have heard their songs, "Kingdom Coming" and "The Battle Cry of Freedom," as he had heard them sung by the troops in camp. "They are great favorites with us," Murray wrote. He was in the 14th Massachusetts Heavy Artillery at Fort Ward, Virginia, "on the outer line of the defenses of Washington." Fort Ward could not be taken, he wrote, "nor can they surround and starve us out, as they did at Harper's Ferry."[18]

"The Battle Cry of Freedom" came back to Chicago in story after story. In September 1863 the New York *Musical Review and Musical World* reported that "In either Grant's or Rosecrans' army it only needs to be started to be caught up from camp to camp, till it spreads for miles over the whole army." The general commanding a division of the Army of the Cumberland reportedly ordered the colonel of each regiment to "start the 'Battle Cry' whenever the army goes into action."[19]

On the Fourth of July, 1863, Root's "Battle Cry of Freedom" rang out from the cupola of the Court House in Vicksburg, Mississippi, according to a report in the *Cincinnati Gazette*. Two men from the Fourth Ohio Independent cavalry climbed into the cupola and hung their flag there. When the crowd of officers, soldiers and civilians below saw this, someone began to sing, "Rally round the flag, boys." "'The words 'Down with the traitor! up with the star!'" floated over the conquered city, laden with a meaning they never had before," one observer wrote.[20]

In the fall of 1863 Union troops in General Blair's brigade made repeated assaults on Vicksburg, each time losing "a ghastly proportion" of their men. Finally ordered to stop, they "came out of the smoke of that terrible carnage" singing "Yes, we'll rally round the flag, boys."[21] After the fall of Vicksburg, a band greeted Mrs. Ulysses S. Grant with an impromptu serenade that included the "Battle Cry" while she was in St. Louis on her way to join her husband.[22]

Private Robert Knox Sneden was imprisoned in Richmond quite near Libby prison. On the night of December 1, 1863, he heard men in Libby prison singing. He wrote that the loudest song he heard was "Rally Round the Flag."[23] Someone brought a rebel newspaper into the prison where Sneden was being held. News of Confederate defeats at Lookout Mountain and Missionary Ridge lifted the spirits of the prisoners, who sang from the time darkness fell until approximately midnight. Sneden mentioned "Rally Round the Flag" and "The Star Spangled Banner" in particular. A guard's warning to stop the "infernal howling" had the opposite effect— according to Sneden the prisoners sang louder.[24]

"On the Field of Battle, Mother" was "certainly remarkable, even for the author of the 'Battle Cry' and 'Vacant Chair,'" Root & Cady's *Song Messenger* said. The words were "written by a wounded soldier and found in his testament after his death" by a woman who was caring for the men in a military hospital. The poem evoked a heartrending image, one that would appear with increasing frequency in accounts from the battlefield. After a battle the forces often found it necessary to stay in their positions and to leave their wounded on the field through the night. The soldier who had written the words did not survive his wounds.[25] In September Root & Cady advertised "Just Before the Battle, Mother"[26] with their "Latest Sheet Music." The words were not those of the soldier's poem, "On the Field of Battle, Mother." Root & Cady explained that a mistake was made "in regard to these words." It was the same song, the company claimed, but with new words. Whatever the reason was for changing the words, the effect was to change the song from a description of lonely death on the field to one, in Root's words, "picturing the condition and thoughts of the soldier on the eve of an engagement." "Just Before the Battle, Mother" spread across the southern states as well as the north, appeared in Confederate songsters and, looking as though it had been notated from memory, in sheet music issued by J. W. Davies and Sons of Richmond.

Songs like Root's "Battle Cry of Freedom" and Work's "Kingdom Coming" were already "part and parcel of the history of the Rebellion," a

In 1865 someone "forgave" Root, evidently in a letter, for composing "Just Before the Battle, Mother," and accused him of lowering the standards of music by writing "degrading" songs that would sell. A Root & Cady spokesman replied that Root's music held "healthful and ennobling sentiments."

Tribune ad said. With "the whole horizon ... illumined with the lightning of war" loyalty to a cause was more needed, and less taken for granted, than ever.[27] On the strength of its war songs, Root & Cady was thriving. The Chicago *Tribune* was "gratified to note the almost unparalleled success of this music publishing house." Every day large orders were received from music dealers in the east. *The Silver Lute* was selling more than a thousand copies a day and copies could not be printed and bound fast enough to keep up with the orders. Ten thousand copies of a new edition of *The Bugle Call* had just been issued. This would enable the company to fill orders that were two weeks behind. There was "apparently no limit" to the demand for sheet music from every quarter, the *Tribune* observed.[28]

Root & Cady gave what a *Tribune* writer called "a munificent present" to the ladies who organized a Sanitary Fair in Chicago. The present was a seven-octave piano valued at $500. The organizers realized the full value of the piano by means of a raffle.[29] The company also placed a bid of $2,100 for the original manuscript of Lincoln's Emancipation Proclamation, planning to issue facsimiles to be sold for the benefit of the Sanitary Commission. The manuscript was to be presented to the Chicago Historical Society after the company received "a percentage of profit on the cost of manufacture."[30] Their bid was unsuccessful.

An unseemly dispute between Root & Cady and Steinway, the eminent piano makers, came to light in the fall of 1863. Root & Cady had advertised Steinway pianos vigorously, although they sold those made by several companies, and had printed endorsements of Steinway by eminent musicians.[31] One Root & Cady ad for the rival Worcester pianos the year before said "Steinway had better look to their laurels." This was "rather more than we could comfortably digest," Steinway and Sons wrote. The two companies exchanged insulting letters. Finally a letter to a Root & Cady client fell into Steinway's hands. In it Root & Cady advised a client to buy a Worcester piano and claimed they "could scarcely recommend" the Steinway instrument. Root & Cady claimed that until recently Steinway's dealings with the company were fair and "gentlemanly" and all the pianos they sent were "magnificent." In the last year Steinway had "often failed to send" the instruments they promised. When pianos were defective, Root & Cady claimed that Steinway "found it easier to call in question the evidence of our senses, than to share our losses." Steinway appointed another firm, Smith and Nixon, as their agents in place of Root & Cady. This would seem to have ended the controversy, but it did not.

Both firms published long quotes from the correspondence between them in a variety of journals.[32] Root & Cady accused Steinway of "blackguardism." Steinway accused Root & Cady of "bringing a lady's name before the public," an uncouth deed in 1863, by writing about Mrs. Hovey's piano that had a cracked sound board.[33] Whether George Root was the spokesman for Root & Cady in the quarrel with Steinway is not stated. Letters between the companies were signed with the company names.

Near the end of 1863 Chicago's music businesses were succeeding beyond their expectations while "The War in Virginia" was at a standstill again, according to the Chicago *Tribune*. A council of war was held, but the circumstances were found to be discouraging. In the December cold it would be impossible to care for the wounded. Rations and forage had nearly run out and the roads were bad.[34] The Chicago *Tribune* blasted General Meade and his associates for what it called "The Great Fizzle." A report from Meade's headquarters said the army had crossed the Rapidan River and "the falling back to our present position was accomplished without loss of men or property." This, in the editor's opinion, was "How Not To Do It."[35]

"Musical Matters in Chicago" were "in a flourishing condition" in December 1863, according to Root & Cady's *Song Messenger*. "Noisy brass bands" played on the balconies of the minstrel show halls, inviting the public to hear the latest popular songs. At the same time the city's musical societies were doing their best to "furnish musical food for the cultivated taste," performing the works of "the masters." Root & Cady advertised George Root's new song "Will You Come to Meet Me, Darling?"[36] in extravagant terms. It was rather in advance of the musical education of the masses, the paper explained somewhat apologetically. "And yet, like the beautiful productions of Schubert, of which it reminds us, it possesses a popular vein, and will win its way to the popular heart."[37] The song had only a few chromatic tones and a few departures from the most common chords. The question "Will You Come to Meet Me, Darling?" was directed to a loved one who was already in heaven. The verses were to be sung as solos. After the last verse the quartet refrain, which ended "Darling, I am here to guide you home," was to be sung as softly as possible.

In a Grand Concert at Bryan Hall in Chicago, George Root sang his tribute to the Nineteenth Illinois Infantry Regiment on Saturday evening, December 5. Later in the program he sang "Pieta Signore" by Stradella. J. G. Lumbard closed the program with William Vincent Wallace's song,

"Flag of Our Union."[38] Yet another "Mass War Meeting" designed to stir "The War Spirit in Chicago" was held in Bryan Hall on Thursday evening, December 16. Men made long, ardent speeches. The crowd saw Frank Lumbard on the platform and "unanimously called" for him to sing. "He complied, giving the 'Battle Cry of Freedom' in splendid style, the audience and band joining in the chorus."[39]

Root held a strong opinion on presenting the music of the masters to the public. He explained this in answer to letters from people who wanted to perform choral music that was more difficult than his cantatas. These singers were looking for music to "interest and improve us, and, at the same time *take* with the public." He advised the letter-writers to sing music that was "above the popular taste," a standard oratorio or mass, or Schiller's *Song of the Bell*. But he warned, "There is no way to make it *take* at the concert but by making the audience learn to like it, as you learn to sing it; and this can only be done by giving them an opportunity to become familiar with it." If an audience could hear a musical society's rehearsals of Mendelssohn's *Elijah*, for example, then at the concert they would "have some idea of its wondrous beauty." As it was, Root said, "No audience in this country has yet liked this or any other similar work, as simpler things are liked."[40] Root's constituents knew what they liked; unfamiliarity was the first and strongest barrier to cultivating musical taste.

The death of Stephen Foster in January 1864 made Root think again about what made a melody find its way into people's hearts. "There is something — vitality, inspiration, call it what you please, a mysterious power that seems to live in certain melodies." That something causes songs "to spread like wild-fire among the people, awaking delight and exciting emotion in all but those who are enveloped in prejudice and self-conceit." No one had written as many songs with this vitality as had Stephen Foster. Root said he had modeled his own "first attempts" at songwriting on Foster's songs. Though Foster's songs were technically correct, Root explained, "people *feel* his music, they don't *think* it." A composer did not recognize the "mysterious life" in his own songs. He believed it would come where the composer least expected it.[41]

A song called "Weeping, Sad and Lonely" or "When This Cruel War Is Over" certainly had the quality Root called "mysterious life." With words by Charles Carroll Sawyer and music by Henry Tucker, the song had been published in 1863 by Sawyer and Thompson of Brooklyn. "We hear it sung everywhere, at all times, and by all classes," *The Song Messenger* said. No one knew how to "insure a successful appeal to the popular heart." Simplicity seemed to be essential, but thousands of songs "published but unsold" showed that simplicity alone was not the answer. To become popular, a song must have "a prominent or favorite idea with the people for its subject"; but how to configure the rhythm and the melody, and when to present the song, "every writer must decide for himself."[42]

Root & Cady received letters and an occasional song manuscript from James R. Murray, a former student of George Root's. Some of his letters came from Harper's Ferry and from the outer defenses of Washington. A Freedman's Village was built on the grounds of Arlington House, the former home of Confederate General Robert E. Lee. Murray, now in the First Massachusetts Heavy Artillery, reported that the former slaves had "nice little cottages," a large school, a chapel, and workshops where trades were taught. Murray was asked to teach one of the classes in the very large Sunday School. For him the experience of being in the chapel and watching as the former slaves came in was unforgettable.[43]

"Look here for another new song to-morrow," Root & Cady's *Tribune* ad teased again and again. Root composed steadily, helping to feed the company's insatiable presses. His "Brother, Tell Me of the Battle" spoke for families who yearned to know what was happening to their loved ones. "Comrades Hasten to the Battle" looked at war through the eyes of a mortally wounded soldier who urged his comrades to "Leave me here alone to die." "Oh, Will My Mother Never Come?" spoke for a stricken soldier, yearning to see his mother a final time, realizing that it was not possible. The song ended "Farewell, my gallant comrades, I'm on my journey home."[44] The Chicago *Tribune* called Root "the most popular song writer in America" in the spring of 1864. Four of his war songs were selling "by the thousand."[45] By mid–April, "Just Before the Battle, Mother" was reportedly selling at the rate of a thousand copies per month."[46] That spring Root composed a sequel, "Just After the Battle."[47] The unattributed words described a battlefield scene that had occurred far too many times. Lying among his fallen comrades, the injured man knew he must wait until dawn for help.

Like the Union, the Confederacy needed songs to urge men to action. A Confederate edition of "The Battle Cry of Freedom" was published in 1864 by Johann Schreiner, who had founded a music publishing house in Macon, Georgia, and branch stores in Savannah and Augusta. When the war made metal scarce and cut off the supply of printing materials,

Schreiner's son Hermann put a pistol in his pocket and went to Cincinnati to buy music type[48] so that the firm could continue publishing. The Schreiner edition of "The Battle Cry of Freedom" credited Hermann as composer and William H. Barnes as the writer of the words. Barnes's words pictured a Confederacy attacked, invaded, subjected to aggression.

In 1864 George L. Bidgood of Richmond published a Confederate "Army Songster" dedicated to the Army of Northern Virginia. In it a southern version of "The Battle Cry of Freedom" was titled "Rally Round the Flag, Boys!" and subtitled "A Battle Song." The words of the chorus began "Our rights for ever, hurrah! boys, hurrah! Down with the tyrants, raise the Southern Cross." Root's original words were used in the rest of the chorus.[49]

In mid–November 1864, Major James A. Connolly was with Sherman's forces when they burned Atlanta. His diary described soldiers, many of them drunk, racing on foot or horseback in streets that were lined with walls of fire. The night was as bright as midday. Crowds gathered around some of the finest buildings and sang "Rally Round the Flag" while the buildings burned, then sang and danced again when pillars and roofs fell to the ground. No description or picture had presented nearly as clear an image of hell as this, Connolly wrote.[50]

Neither the north nor the south was unanimous in support of its government. Soldiers returning to Illinois were shocked to find Copperheads "persecuting" Unionists, as the *Tribune* expressed it. Confederate sympathizers were burning Unionists' barns and their hay and grain stacks, destroying their fruit trees and poisoning their cattle. Knights of the Golden Circle, "cheering for Jeff Davis and the Southern Confederacy, and damning Lincoln and the 'Abolition war'" met once a week for military drill.[51]

Music continued to be a means of showing patriotism and supporting the war. "Go and hear the best War Songs and Patriotic Ballads, so many of which have originated in Chicago," the *Tribune* urged. George Root and some eight or ten other musicians gave a Patriotic Concert at the Hyde Park House. The Illinois Central Railroad announced that it would take passengers to the Hyde Park section of the city at half fare for this occasion.[52] On Washington's Birthday, Arlington's Minstrels climaxed their show with "The Battle Cry of Freedom." As they sang it, a picture of George Washington "rose as if by magic and was suspended in mid air." The scene "electrified" the audience. The curtain fell in "a perfect storm of applause" (as newspapers often expressed it), and the applause continued until the scene was repeated. The hall was "filled to suffocation" for this performance, a reporter wrote.[53]

In popular entertainment the effects of war mingled with the usual themes. In one instance a minstrel show in Chicago featured Duprez & Green's New Orleans Minstrels and Brass Band, "Consisting of twenty-four great Ethiopian Stars." Part One of the program offered an "Operatic chorus" from *Ernani*, a "comic song" called "Martha Jane," an overture called "The Downfall of Fort Sumter," a song called "Good Old Friends," and a presentation called "Grand Excursion to Niagara Falls." Part Two included the "Mocking Bird Song," "The Returned Contrabands," a comic song called "Fight for Uncle Abe," "The Wall Street Brokers," "Oh, Mother I've Come Home to Die," a "Stump Speech on the Present Times," and a "comic banjo song entitled 'Go Ahead Grant.'"[54]

At Root & Cady, success bred confidence in their advertising. "Preserve this advertisement, and look here to-morrow," their ads said on several occasions. Their gifted songwriter Henry Clay Work had written a song the *Tribune* said would make it possible to "perform the difficult feat of laughing and crying" at the same time. "Corporal Schnapps" detailed the "mishaps and adventures of a patriotic soldier of Teutonic origin."[55]

In the spring of 1864 Root & Cady published Henry Clay Work's temperance song, "Come Home, Father." A statement printed above the first line of the sheet music set the scene: "'Tis the Song of Little Mary, standing at the bar-room door while the shameful midnight revel rages wildly as before." The words of the whole song appeared in the June issue of *The Song Messenger* with the promise that the company would send a free copy of the sheet music to anyone who could read the words without weeping. The next issue of the magazine said free copies had been sent to ten people and interpreted this to mean that, given their readership, this meant one in a thousand had been able to get through it with dry eyes.[56]

Root's song called "I'se On De Way" looked at the war through the eyes of a former slave who was now a soldier in the Union army. President Lincoln, under increasing pressure from politicians, military officers, and black spokesmen, had encouraged the enlistment of black men.[57] By the beginning of 1864 they were enlisting in increasing numbers and preparing to fight for the Union. Lieutenant Oliver W. Norton of "Company K," U.S. Colored Troops, wrote his sister that the soldiers in his camp were singing "Rally Round the Flag, Boys." "They sing with the heart," Norton wrote. Hundreds of former slaves were waiting for recruiting officers to enlist them.[58]

In the face of considerable opposition, Col. John A. Bross, brother of *Tribune* editor William Bross, formed a regiment of black soldiers in the Chicago area. "Come forward and prove yourselves MEN," Bross urged the recruits, "and when the Union is saved you will be endowed by a grateful people with the rights pertaining to free men."[59] By March 20, 1864 Bross's 29th U.S. Colored Volunteers numbered 600 men. Two days later they were ordered to join General Burnside's 9th Army Corps.[60] George Root, using his pseudonym Wurzel, "arranged and composed" a "Freedman's Song" for this regiment. The song appeared in April, while the regiment was drilling and training. The first verse began with words that seemed to recall Bross's advice to the recruits: "Oh now we'se men...." Ole Ben" in verse three presumably meant General Benjamin F. Butler, who was the first to call blacks "contrabands." A piano interlude was printed at the end. It was bouncy and spirited, like an accompaniment for dance steps.

On June 2 Bross's regiment reached Alexandria, Virginia, on their way "to join Grant's army in the siege of Richmond."[61] They had reached the Richmond-Petersburg area when Pennsylvania troops, many of them coal miners, dug a tunnel under the 400 feet of earth between Union and Confederate positions at Petersburg and placed explosives at the far end. A long fuse was lit in the early hours of July 30. The fuse malfunctioned; men risked their lives to repair it. The earth shook, then erupted. Men, animals, equipment and earth were blown high into the air. A huge crater opened and men struggled to fight their way across it. Louis T. Wood, a colored private in Bross's regiment, saw five men die one after the other, carrying the regimental colors. Finally Lieutenant F. W. Chapman saw the colors pass into the hands of Colonel Bross, who rushed ahead shouting, "Men, follow me!"[62] Another observer reported that Bross "rushed upon the top of the fort, drew his sword, took his hat in his hand and cried, 'Rally, my brave boys, rally!'" The men rallied just as Bross fell.[63]

A story was told of black soldiers singing at the time of the battle of the Crater, not the song Root dedicated to them, but a chant that seemed to grow out of a kind of group meditation. It seemed to follow a custom among black troops, a way of creating the group's own spontaneous song. Men sat on the ground, each group in a circle of its own. For a long time there was silence. Finally one voice and then another chanted a few words, almost as though offering an idea. One man sang "We looks like men a-marchin' on, we looks like men of war." He sang this over and over, with slight changes, until other singers began to join in. The song spread from group to group, some people adding harmony, until several hundred men were singing.[64] Perhaps Bross's men remembered what he had said to them months before: "Come forward and prove yourselves men." Bross's speech may have echoed in the first verse of the Wurzel song: "Oh now we'se men, for de Pres'dent's pen done made us free."

On the day Colonel Bross died at the Crater, the Chicago *Tribune* announced the death of another Chicago officer, Colonel James A. Mulligan. Both men died saving their regimental flags. George Root remembered: "When our brave Colonel Mulligan fell, his last words were 'Lay me down and save the flag.' The day after the news of that event reached us, the song bearing that title was issued."[65]

A few days after the war began Mulligan, a young lawyer and former clerk in the Office of the Interior in Washington, called for the formation of an Irish unit to serve in the army. This became the Twenty-third Illinois Infantry Regiment, called by Chicagoans the "Irish Brigade." Other Irish communities formed their own units, and Chicago's Irish Brigade has been overshadowed in history by a more famous one.[66] On June 14, 1862, Colonel Mulligan and his men left Chicago for Annapolis. Accompanied by two bands and the applause of the spectators lining their route, they marched to a railroad depot. Three trainloads of soldiers moved out of the depot while the Light Guard Band played "The Girl I Left Behind Me."[67] On July 24, 1864, Mulligan was wounded in a battle at Kernstown, near Winchester, in the Shenandoah Valley of Virginia. A squad of his men saw him fall. They were trying to carry him off the field when Confederates charged and were about to capture the brigade's colors. Mulligan saw this and shouted an order: "Lay me down and save the flag." The men hesitated, reluctant to leave him, and he repeated the order until they obeyed. The Rebels captured him where he lay before his men could get back to him. Mulligan died in enemy hands.[68] Root set to music one of several poems based on Mulligan's last order.

Perhaps Mulligan's order was made more urgent by the memory of an incident the *Tribune* had called "Our Latest Disaster and Disgrace"[69] three years earlier. Assigned to hold the town of Lexington, Missouri, the regiment faced a much larger force commanded by General Sterling Price.

They guarded nearly a million dollars taken from the local bank and buried under Mulligan's tent. On September 13, 1861, they were driven into their fortifications and besieged. For the next five days the two commanders waited, Price for his ammunition train and Mulligan for reinforcements. During this time Confederate volunteers gathered from all across Missouri. On September 18 they surrounded the garrison and took control of its only source of water. Mulligan's regiment, badly outnumbered, fought a desperate artillery duel with Price's men, who were reinforced by Missouri volunteers shielding themselves with bales of hemp. After a few hours Mulligan's subordinate officers began to surrender independently. General Price sent a message to Mulligan suggesting a truce. Mulligan refused and the firing began again. Finally Mulligan met with his officers; they voted to surrender and Mulligan did. To keep their Irish Brigade flag from capture, the men of the regiment tore it in pieces and distributed the pieces among themselves. Mulligan was captured on September 20 and exchanged on November 25, 1861. Its officers having been captured, the brigade was mustered out of the army by General Fremont on October 8, 1861. Reactions to these events were mixed. There was a sense that the regiment had been disgraced, and yet when Mulligan returned to Chicago he was received as a hero. While in Washington on a lecture tour of the eastern states he asked President Lincoln to restore the regiment to service. It was restored on December 10, 1861, and served at Harper's Ferry, in the defenses of the upper Potomac and in the Department of West Virginia before the battle at Kernstown.[70]

The death of Colonel Mulligan was deeply felt in Chicago. A band and a guard of honor met his remains when they arrived in the city. The *Tribune* published the order of the funeral procession, including organized groups such as the Fenian Brotherhood. On August 3 the *Tribune* described his funeral in detail; in the same issue the paper reported that the song "Lay Me Down and Save the Flag" was "taking like wildfire" and that clerks at Root & Cady did "little else than deal it out." For the past two days the publisher had had two presses working exclusively on it.[71]

Root & Cady's music was "up with the times," the Chicago *Tribune* said.[72] Their sheet music advertising included "Home Songs of the War" such as "From the Red Battle-Field," "Emancipation," "Softly Now, Tenderly, Lift Him with Care," "The Drummer Boy's March," and "Mother, When the War Is Over."[73] *The Song Messenger* presented a new song called "On the Red Field of Blood" (music by George F. Root) in its May issue, followed in June by the anonymous "In Again, Boys" and Root's "Comrade, I Will Guard Thy Mother." In the spring of 1864 Root, the senior partner in Root & Cady, had charge of "publishing operations" which, added to his labors as composer and compiler, kept him "fully occupied," *The Song Messenger* reported.

Two more of Root's songs published as sheet music in 1864 took the viewpoint of the soldier. "Kiss Me Mother, Kiss Your Darling" spoke for a mortally wounded soldier.[74] "Can the Soldier Forget" gave assurance to a soldier's "beloved ones at home" that he remembered his departing promises.[75]

On May 9, 1864, a map, spread across the tops of three columns on the *Tribune's* front page, showed "The Present Situation in Virginia." The Confederates had been "Forced to Retire With Heavy Loss" and General Grant was "Left in Possession of the Field." That night Frank Lumbard brought a huge crowd to its feet to join him in singing "The Battle Cry of Freedom" at a war meeting in Bryan Hall. The building was filled from top to bottom, "as it is only filled when the heart of the people is thoroughly aroused," a reporter said, and the crowd "made the very walls shake" with their enthusiasm. The Light Guard Band played; several generals and distinguished gentlemen made speeches. Under Grant the army was "making her first real movement," one of the speakers said. The meeting adjourned with "three cheers for General Grant and all the other Generals in the field."[76]

At home and in the field, Root's "Battle Cry of Freedom" was one of the recurring musical themes. Two companies of the Chicago Light Artillery came home from war on Monday, July 25, and the city's "loyal citizens turned out *en masse* to receive them." The Light Guard Band welcomed the veterans with martial music, a parade to Bryan Hall, and as a finale, the "Battle Cry of Freedom," "the chorus being enthusiastically given by the audience."[77]

"WE'LL RALLY ROUND THE FLAG, BOYS," the New York *Tribune* headed its account of a moment in the battle of the Wilderness. The Chicago *Tribune* picked up the New York reporter's eyewitness account. He described a night when troops were lying behind temporary fortifications of earth, logs and rails and were kept down by sharpshooters' rifle fire. A solitary voice began to sing "Rally round the flag, boys." Untold numbers of men, tired of the tension and the darkness and the sporadic gunfire, joined in the song. "Thousands" of voices shouted the chorus:

"The Union forever, hurrah, boys, hurrah!" It was a strange scene "amid all the sickening horrors of war"; so many had been killed, so many horribly wounded. "But not one is forgotten by THE PEOPLE," the reporter said.[78] Other horrifying reports from the Wilderness described sparks flying and setting the underbrush on fire. Some of the wounded soldiers "perished in the burning woods."[79]

Again and again the people in Washington were alarmed as Confederate forces threatened to attack the city. On July 10, 1864, the threat was serious enough to send President Lincoln and his family home to the White House from their suburban summer residence.[80] This time General Jubal Early's men occupied the town of Frederick, Maryland, not far from Washington. "Thanks to Gen. Wallace and the Railroad Company," a reporter wrote, "the 3d Maryland regiment of veterans from Monocacy arrived just in time and promptly marched to the front, singing 'Rally round the Flag, Boys.'" The *Tribune* said the success of "the Maryland raid" was enough to "humiliate the Northern people."[81]

Union troops were camped in the Shenandoah Valley on a fine autumn evening, evidently around the time of the battle of Cedar Creek, which took place October 19, 1864. The sound of a solo voice came from the spot where a bonfire blazed on a hillside. A listener reported that the song was "reinforced" by the leading singers in each neighboring regiment. The melody spread "like a contagion," gaining strength as it went. To one listener it seemed the whole corps was "drawn into the chorus: "Yes, we'll rally round the flag, boys, rally once again, shouting the battle-cry of freedom!'"[82]

When Lincoln was nominated to run for re-election, Chicago held a "Grand Ratification Meeting." A soloist, W. M. Smith, sang the "Battle Cry of Freedom," substituting the words "We'll hurl the *Copperheads* from the land we love the best" for the original *rebel crew*. The audience approved the change enthusiastically.[83]

On July 12 the Union Club held a Republican campaign meeting at Metropolitan Hall. "The first gun of the campaign was fired most effectively," the *Tribune* said. Speech after speech praised Lincoln; "the audience was large and enthusiastic." Several songs were presented, at least one with "original verses" about current candidates. A quartet sang Root's "Just Before the Battle, Mother," and as the meeting ended, "the vast audience simultaneously rose and joined with the Lumbard brothers in the glorious strains of the 'Battle Cry of Freedom.'"[84]

Campaign songs could be created quickly and easily by fitting new words to familiar tunes. They could be disseminated readily in pocket-size paperback booklets like the "Lincoln Campaign Songster" and "The Republican Campaign Songster." The melody of Root's spirited "Battle Cry of Freedom" carried at least two rousing parodies that were sung by Lincoln supporters. The words of "Rally for Old Abe" began "Let's rally for 'Old Abe,' boys, let's rally once again, fighting for our homes and our Union." The chorus proclaimed "It's "'Old Abe'" forever, hurrah, boys, hurrah! We are no traitors — all for the war."[85]

"Rally Round the Flag," Chicagoans read among the headlines on September 1, 1864. The presidential election campaign was "fairly open." On that day a "Grand Union Rally" filled Metropolitan Hall, "notwithstanding the dampening effect of the great peace convention," which had just closed. The peace party had nominated General George B. McClellan for president. Lincoln supporters claimed "the fires of liberty have been once more kindled in Chicago" with their rally, which opened with "that glorious old tune, "'The Battle Cry of Freedom'" played by the Light Guard Band."[86]

During the political campaign season someone wrote another parody using the tune of Root's "Battle Cry of Freedom." This one called the war a "holy cause." The chorus began "For Lincoln and Johnson, Huzza, boys, huzza! Down with rebellion and on with the war." The last of the four verses urged, "Then rally, Wide Awakes, we will try it once again, singing the holy cause of freemen." [87]

Root & Cady entered the political campaign, advertising that "a gentleman of this city will pay a premium of ten dollars each for five Union Campaign Songs, to be sung to each of the following tunes: 'Old Shady,' 'Uncle Ned,' 'Out of the Wilderness'...." The words should be "cheery," humorous, full of "thrusts and sharp hits" at McClellan, Davis, traitors, and "peace sneaks." The award would be based on "the telling effects the songs will have upon the people" rather than "literary merits." Manuscripts were to be sent to George F. Root at Root & Cady. He and H. M. Smith would be the judges. The winning songs would appear in the *Tribune;* Root & Cady would pay the winners as soon as the award was made. Two weeks later the *Tribune* advertised "Six Campaign Songs" rather than five, "Adapted to Familiar Tunes" and "Issued on a single sheet." The songs were "suitable for use at Union Meetings, Barbecues, &c." and were available "from the *Tribune* Company."[88]

The chorus of "The Battle Cry of Freedom" served as a masthead for the *Tribune*'s November 4, 1864, issue announcing Lincoln's reelection.[89] Chicago celebrated the re-election with a parody on Root's "Just Before the Battle, Mother."[90]

Half a continent away "the Pacific states," California, Oregon and Nevada, had all voted for Lincoln, an ecstatic correspondent wrote. Cheering crowds filled the streets of San Francisco when the election results were announced. Each time a band in the street began to play, the crowd called for "Rally Round the Flag, Boys." Each time the band complied, the crowd drowned the sound of the instruments with "the thunder of their voices." Men formed an impromptu parade following the band with a flag waving and the crowd singing. Ladies waved handkerchiefs from the windows. Finally the correspondent went home "at a late hour in the morning." The excitement went on unabated. Usually at this hour the correspondent heard the sound of the sea. This morning he heard crowds singing, "The Union forever, hurrah boys, hurrah!"[91]

Root & Cady's business prospered in the final months of 1864. They had printed more than 250,000 copies of sheet music in 1863[92] and they were using an average of one ton of paper per week. Now they invested in two new steam presses, one for sheet music and the other, like the one *Harper's* magazine used, to print books and *The Song Messenger*.[93]

By the time the new presses arrived, Root had completed a book that would be printed on one of them. He described *The Musical Curriculum*[94] as "a course of study" designed to teach piano, voice culture, and harmony. Related skills such as music reading, performance, accompanying, transposition, modulation, and thorough bass would be introduced. As always, "the cultivation of musical taste" was its larger purpose. He had started this book about ten years earlier and had soon realized that it was an enormous project. While he continued his regular work—compiling books and composing songs and cantatas—he thought often about this project and looked forward to the time when he could go on with it. When the time finally came, "no epicure ever sat down to a table laden with dainties with a greater relish" than he to this "long anticipated work," he wrote. He thought his training as a teacher and his experience as a writer would enable him to do this work quickly and with confidence but he had not, in his words, "spoiled more than twenty sheets of good music paper" when he "came across an element or an idea" that should have been placed earlier in the sequence of lessons and exercises. With "a long breath which some folks might call a sigh" he began again. Time after time he or one of his musician friends found some lapse in the order and "progressiveness" of what he had written. He was working on what he called "new ground"; there was "no model for this book."[95] In a detailed introductory section called "A Method of Teaching," Root explained that there were two ways of teaching, a shorter and a longer. "The shorter is to tell all things to the pupil, the longer is to have him find out all he can himself." The teacher should not do for the pupil what he could do for himself. Root explained how he would teach each section of the book. In a paragraph on "Metronome Marks" he gave directions for devising a homemade metronome. Tempo markings were to be placed at measured points on a length of tape with a bullet or lead weight at one end. Holding the tape at the point where the appropriate tempo was marked and allowing the weighted end to swing would approximate the desired tempo.

A song called "The Dying Soldier" appeared in *The Musical Curriculum* with no attribution of the melody or the words. The words described a bloody battlefield where a mortally wounded man faced a lonely death. With no hope of help, he bid his loved ones "a long farewell." The song ended with an expression of calm assurance.

By the latter part of the war "Tramp, Tramp, Tramp" was an inevitable song. For many months Chicagoans had seen photographs and read news reports of starving prisoners of war. On Friday evening, September 23, a public meeting was held in Bryan Hall "in honor of our recent victories." Both the Light Guard and the Great Western bands played. A former prisoner of war at Andersonville, Georgia, told about the sufferings of prisoners there. Predictably, the meeting closed with the "Battle Cry of Freedom," the "audience joining in the chorus."[96]

On New Year's Day, 1864, Robert Knox Sneden was imprisoned again near the infamous Libby prison. He wrote in his diary that he had heard the Libby prisoners singing on New Year's Eve. In the building where Sneden was, some three hundred men sat on the floor in the moonlight, singing "Rally Round the Flag" with particular emphasis on the line "Down with the traitor, up with the Stars" directed toward their guard. On the following morning the guard warned that more such "howling" would result in their being sent to Belle Isle prison. The men disrupted roll call by jeering and moving around in line, so that the guard had to call the roll four times in order to confirm that no one had escaped.[97]

On July 4, 1864, Sneden was in Andersonville. A few prisoners made

LIBBY PRISON, Richmond Va.

TRAMP! TRAMP! TRAMP!
THE
PRISONER'S HOPE.

The music of this song can be obtained at the well known **Music-Store** of Frederick Blume, 208 Bowery, New York.

In the prison-cell I sit,
 Thinking, Mother dear, of you,
And our bright and happy home, so far away!
 And the tears they fill my eyes,
 Spite of all that I can do,
Tho' I try to cheer my comrades, and be gay.
 Tramp, tramp, tramp! the boys are marching;
  Cheer up! comrades, they will come,
 And, beneath the Starry Flag,
 We shall breathe the air, again,
  Of the Free-land, in our own beloved home.
   CHORUS: Tramp, tramp, &c.

In the battle-front we stood,
 When their fiercest charge they made,
And they swept us off, a hundred men or more;
 But, before we reach'd their lines,
 They were beaten back dismayed,
And we heard the cry of Vict'ry, o'er and o'er.
  Tramp, tramp, tramp! &c.

So, within the prison-cell,
 We are waiting for the day
That shall come to open wide the iron door
 And the hollow eye grows bright,
 And the poor heart almost gay,
As we think of seeing home and friends, once more.
  Tramp, tramp, tramp! &c.

Ten illustrated Songs on Notepaper, mailed to any Address on receipt of 50 cts. Published by Chas. Magnus, 12 Frankfort St. N. Y.

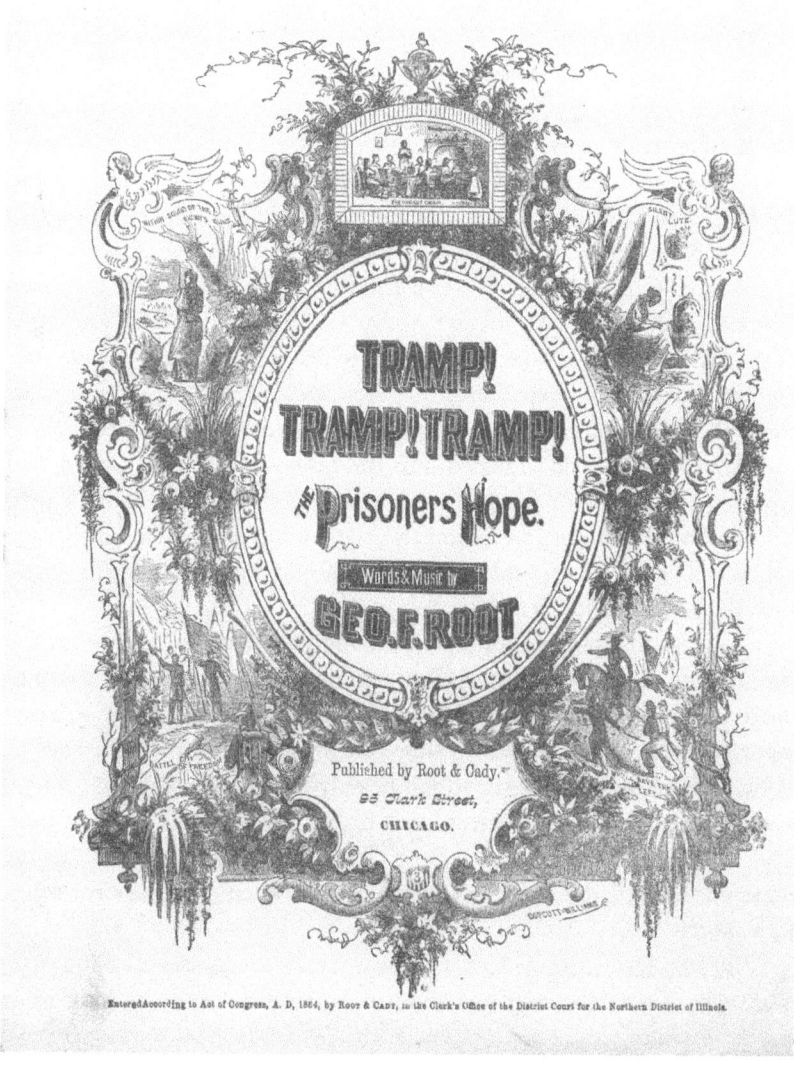

Root & Cady devised an elaborate collective cover for several of Root's songs. At the top a vignette showed a family gathered at their Thanksgiving table; the title of "The Vacant Chair" appeared under the scene. "Tramp! Tramp! Tramp!" sold almost 100,000 copies in its first six months.

Opposite: By the end of 1864, reports of the treatment of men in prison camps had grown uglier and more shocking. In his words for "Tramp! Tramp! Tramp!" Root took the prisoner's point of view and subtitled the song "The Prisoner's Hope." This broadside shows Libby Prison in Richmond, Virginia, where prisoners reportedly sang Root's "Battle Cry of Freedom" occasionally. Broadsides were half-sheets of paper with the words of a popular song printed on one side. They were cheaper and easier to distribute than sheet music.

patriotic speeches; others discussed their "desperate condition." There was no chance of being exchanged and little hope of seeing their homes again unless Sherman's army could reach them. Two hundred prisoners gave three cheers for "The Old Flag"; hundreds of others sang "Rally Round the Flag" and "The Star Spangled Banner," Sneden wrote.[98]

As 1864 drew to a close, reports about prison camps grew uglier. On Thanksgiving the story of Private J. L. Elder came to light. He had been captured and sent to six different prisons, one after the other. He spoke of the lack of meat and the men who were driven insane by their imprisonment.[99] Prisoners knew that if they stepped across the "dead line" they could expect to be shot. Thoughts of cruelty and deprivation at Belle Isle[100] and Andersonville had crowded into the public mind. Newspapers had reported the arrival of the steamer *Constitution* at Annapolis with men who had been prisoners in Savannah. Five hundred fifty had left Savannah and now a surgeon said not more than two hundred of them would survive. Some of these had lost their sanity.[101]

Against the background of dismaying prison camp descriptions, a regiment of new volunteers marched through the streets on their way to board steamboats that would take them to the war front. One observer reported that the men began to sing "We'll rally round the flag, boys"[102] as they marched. Rain began to fall heavily as they went "*tramp, tramp, tramping*" through muddy streets with drums beating and banners flying. The reporter's "tramp, tramp, tramp" may have lodged in what George Root once called the "reservoir of the mind" where materials for songs were stored.

In late December, 1864, the New Year's Extra issue of the *Song Messenger of the Northwest* was about to go to press and the song Root was expected to write for it was not ready. "We must have that song or we can not get the paper into the hands of the people by New Year's Day," George's brother Towner urged. "Go write it now while it is on your mind."

Root titled the song "Tramp, Tramp, Tramp, or The Prisoner's Hope." His words voiced confidence that imprisonment would end with the arrival of Union forces. Two hours after beginning he handed the finished song to his brother. Together they "tried it over." Towner's comment stung a little: "'I must confess I don't think much of it, but it may do." George was "inclined to agree with him about the music" but disappointed, too. He had "grown quite warm and interested in writing the words." He would remember this song as "a further confirmation ... that in my case successes were usually surprises."[103]

John M. Hubbard, a Chicago singer and songwriter, claimed he was the first to sing "Tramp, Tramp, Tramp" in public; he said the first performance was at a skating rink. Skating was popular then. The management of one rink decided to give a percentage of a Saturday evening's receipts to the Sanitary Commission. On Saturday afternoon Hubbard, Captain A. R. Sabin, Will Root,[104] and Martel Clark went to Root & Cady on Clark Street to rehearse. George Root was in his study in the rear of the store. He gave the men the manuscript and they rehearsed it. That evening they sang the song repeatedly for the crowd at the skating rink. By the time they went home everyone knew at least the chorus, if not some of the verses.[105]

Early in 1865 Root's "Tramp, Tramp, Tramp" kept the clerks and the shipping department of Root & Cady busy. Almost every evening the song was heard at the Academy of Music and other theaters. A group called Kelly and Leon's Minstrels, visiting Chicago, sang it regularly.[106] As Root remembered it, "Tramp, Tramp, Tramp" had "a short life — less than a year, but in that time our profit on it was ten thousand dollars."[107]

While Root's "Tramp, Tramp, Tramp" was spreading across the country, Root & Cady announced Henry Clay Work's newest song, "Marching Through Georgia." [108] Written from the soldier's viewpoint, this new song was addressed to the people at home who followed General Sherman's distant progress through whatever news they could get. A musical reflection on Sherman's march, it had the exultant spirit of Work's earlier song, "Kingdom Coming."[109]

When the people in Chicago learned that Charleston, South Carolina, had been evacuated, Henry Clay Work set the news to music. His new song "Ring the Bell, Watchman" was "just the thing to celebrate the fall of rebel cities which are just now, like ripe apples, dropping in General Sherman's basket" the *Tribune* claimed, and added, "When loyal people want such songs, they are always sure to get them from the teeming press of Root & Cady."[110]

The firm had thrived on the sale of war songs, music books and all kinds of instruments. Now, sharing in the confidence and optimism of northern businesses, Root & Cady planned to open a branch store at 109 Third Street[111] in St. Paul, Minnesota, early in 1865. They appointed M. L. Temple as manager. His family was ready to move and he was traveling to meet them when he drowned in the Mississippi River. William A.

Root, George's youngest brother, and D. H. Elliott were appointed managers in his place.[112] Except for a listing in a St. Paul city directory, the branch store disappeared.[113]

Late in March, 1865, the end of the war was in sight. Sherman and Grant were closing on the Confederacy like the jaws of "a terrible vise." The *Tribune* hoped Root & Cady were "not *too fast*" in "bidding 'Jeff. Good-Bye.'"[114] The company had just published a song called "Goodbye Jeff!" by Philip Paul Bliss.[115]

About ten o'clock on the morning of April 3, news of the fall of Richmond came to Chicago, and in the words of one observer, "exultation ruled the day." The Court House bell rang and bulletins appeared in various parts of the city. Business was suspended. An eager crowd surrounded the *Tribune* office, scanning the news and shouting themselves hoarse. The number of flags "found at an hour's notice" was "astonishing." Then came the processions, too many to count. A reporter saw a merchants' procession headed by Bowen Brothers' wagon bearing the inscriptions 'Sheridan & Co.,' 'Richmond,' 'Abe Lincoln,' 'Spottswood,' &c., and a band playing "The Battle Cry of Freedom." "Draymen and express wagons" paraded and "a large number of men with arms locked in 'union' followed, keeping steady step to the music." and "shouting for joy." Many other processions followed this one. When the people were tired of marching, the city's bands stood and played while "the air rang with shouts." Chicagoans were so accustomed to War Meetings with speeches and music, they gathered almost automatically in Court House Square and in Bryan Hall, where Mr. J. Rickey sang "The Battle Cry of Freedom" in "splendid style, the whole audience joining in the chorus."[116]

An exultant *Tribune* called the rebellion a thing of the past on April 4. Headlines announced "The rebel citadel has fallen. Richmond is ours!" and "The Old Flag Floats Over the Rebel Capitol." Both Richmond and Petersburg were evacuated; Richmond was in flames. Lee was retreating and Grant was "in Close Pursuit." In the same issue of the *Tribune* Root & Cady's ad offered "Ring the Bell, Watchman," "All Hail to Ulysses," and "Good-bye, Jeff." The ad was headed "SING! SING! SING!"

According to one report, black soldiers who had been assigned to help "hold the entrenchments" six or eight miles from Richmond marched into the city "with banners flying, drums beating, shouting the 'Battle Cry of Freedom' and chanting 'John Brown's Soul is Marching On.'" After a few hours in the city they moved out in pursuit of the retreating Confederates.[117]

6. Rally Once Again 1863–1865

On Sunday, April 9, General Lee surrendered to General Grant at Appomattox Court House, Virginia. The news reached Chicago a little after nine o'clock that night. The *Tribune* immediately "placarded" the dispatch in the windows of its building and sent the news to the Chief Engineer of the Fire Department. The Court House bell began to ring and crowds gathered immediately at both the *Tribune* office and the Tremont House hotel, filling the night with cheers and shouts of joy. They sang the "John Brown" song, "The Battle Cry of Freedom" and "Praise God From Whom All Blessings Flow" with what a *Tribune* reporter called "great fervor and great effect."[118] Bonfires were lighted "in all the principal streets." At 1 A. M. a reporter wrote his eyewitness account: a band was "promenading the streets playing national music." Cannon were "roaring" and rockets "blazing."[119]

"No American jubilee is considered complete unless a procession forms part of the programme," Chicagoans agreed, and the next day "a few prominent individuals" announced that a parade would take place in the afternoon. "Everybody became possessed to join a procession, and in numerous instances, two or three, and sometimes only one, formed into line on their own account, and marched through the streets, to the tune of 'Tramp, tramp, tramp,' or some other soul inspiring air." Washington too was "intoxicated with joy." On Monday, April 10, businesses and government offices were closed. Crowds gravitated to the grounds of the Executive Mansion one after another, making "popular demonstrations." At 12 o'clock President Lincoln appeared. People waved their hats or swung their umbrellas; ladies waved their handkerchiefs. When quiet was finally restored, Lincoln told the crowd he knew he would have to make a speech that evening or the next, so he would wait until then to speak. He saw that there was a band with the crowd. He had always liked "Dixie." He "insisted" that his armies had "fairly captured it." He had consulted the Attorney General, who said the song was "ours." He asked the band to play it; he stood listening at the window. When the music ended he called for three cheers for General Grant and "all under his command." The band played "Hail Columbia" while the crowd moved away "to call on other officers of the Government." [120]

On April 14 Root's "Battle Cry of Freedom" celebrated the raising of the Stars and Stripes at Fort Sumter. The flag was the same one that had hung over the fort when the war began. A crowd estimated at three thousand traveled to the fort. The Reverend Henry Ward Beecher delivered a two-part speech with a rest period in the middle, during which a band played. Beecher predicted that a day would come when the country would feel no regional separateness, "no North, no West, no South, but one United States of America."[121] A later account said it was Lincoln who determined that the flag-raising ceremony would be held on the anniversary of the fall of the fort. According to this account William B. Bradbury led the crowd in singing his song, "Victory at Last," followed by Root's "Rally Round the Flag."[122]

Fanny Seward, daughter of Lincoln's secretary of state, described the horrendous events of April 1865 in her diary. She was helping to care for her father, who had been seriously injured in a carriage accident. On Sunday, April 9, President Lincoln visited Seward, lay down beside him on his bed and described his visit to Richmond and to a hospital where he shook hands with thousands of soldiers. That evening news of Lee's surrender came to the Sewards. On the evening of Good Friday, April 14, Fanny and her sister-in-law watched from their window as a torchlight procession passed on its way to the White House, the band playing "Rally Round the Flag." Late in the evening Fanny sat with her father in his darkened room. Her brother came to the door. Lewis Payne, one of John Wilkes Booth's co-conspirators, forced his way into the room and attempted to kill Seward. Later Fanny Seward watched as Major General Henry Halleck, Chief of Staff of the Army, Secretary of the Navy Gideon Welles and Secretary of War Stanton came into the room and stood around Seward's bed. Fanny heard one of these men say President Lincoln had been shot.[123]

The "TERRIBLE NEWS" came to Chicago in a Special Dispatch written April 14, 1865. The President and Mrs. Lincoln were attending a performance of *Our American Cousin* at Ford's Theater when someone came into their box and shot Mr. Lincoln in the head. The assassin jumped from the box and ran across the stage flourishing a dagger in his hand. The actress Laura Keene and the leader of the orchestra recognized the man as "J. Wilkes Booth," the actor who was "a rabid secessionist." [124]

On Wednesday, April 19, a funeral for President Lincoln was held in Washington. Chicago closed its businesses and opened many of its churches for special services. The New Jerusalem Church (Swedenborgian) announced a service to be held in the Temple on Adams Street at noon.[125] George Root, his wife, and several members of their family were members of this church.

Chicagoans followed the journey of Lincoln's funeral train as it was

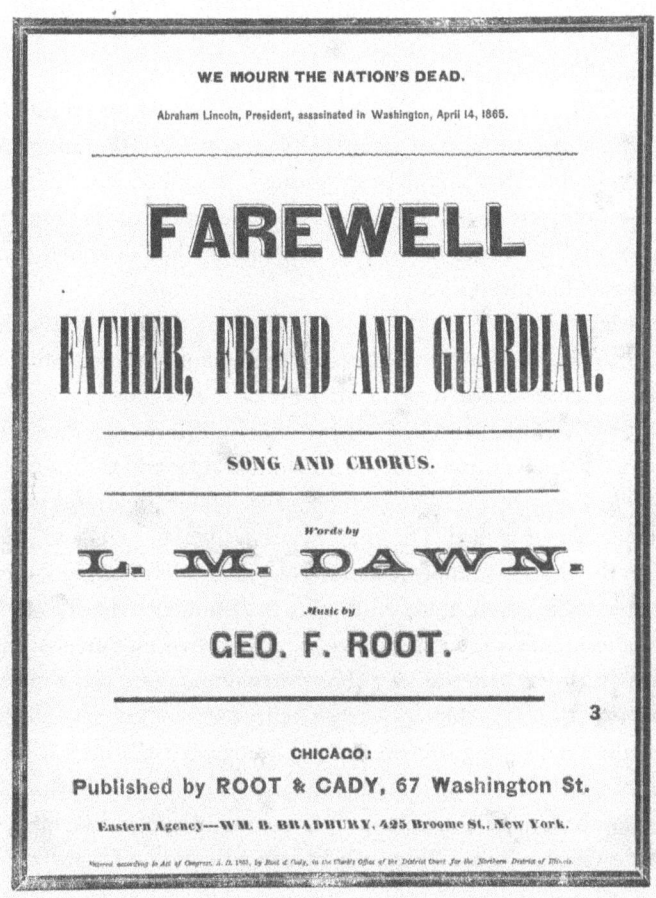

Lincoln was buried in Springfield, Illinois, May 4, 1865. George Root's "Farewell Father, Friend and Guardian" was one of six pieces sung in the funeral service. Also on that day, this song was sung at a huge gathering in Chicago following the reading of Lincoln's last inaugural address.

reported in their newspapers. Springfield, Illinois, was busy preparing for the burial. "The Capitol will be appropriately fitted up; two hundred of the best singers in the State will constitute the choir, and the best bands of Illinois and Missouri furnish the instrumental music,"[126] one report promised.

Root set to music what he called "the grief of the nation"[127] in a song called "Farewell, Father, Friend and Guardian." The words by L. M. Dawn described the people's grief, mingling with their sorrow for their own loved ones who had fallen. The song appeared in the May issue of *The Song Messenger of the Northwest* and in sheet music.

During this period of widespread public mourning for President Lincoln, there was private grief in countless places for the lost soldiers. A song called "Comrade, All Around Is Brightness" described a soldier's dying moments on the battlefield. The words were meant for those thousands at home who might never know where their soldiers had died or what their final moments had been like.[128]

On May 1, Chicago held its own funeral for the dead president. An estimated 36,000 people marched in the procession with his coffin. Some five thousand school children marched, many carrying miniature flags fringed in black. Two hundred boys in Reform School uniforms marched. Men of the Ellsworth Zouaves, the Nineteenth Illinois Infantry, and the Chicago Light Artillery marched. Lodge members and laborers marched with their groups. Politicians marched. The Great Western Light Guard Band played.[129]

From the time the funeral train arrived until it left Chicago, the city's singers gave their services. At midnight on Monday, May 1, and again when the President's body left the city, three hundred members of the various German choral societies sang. For thirty hours there was almost continuous music — solos, duets, quartets, choruses — sixty-seven different pieces in all. The leading soloists, Mrs. Thomas, Mrs. Miller, Mrs. Matteson, and Miss Main contributed; organists played, and choruses under the direction of Hans Balatka sang.[130] Someone, during those long, bleak hours, sang George Root's "Farewell Father, Friend and Guardian."[131]

At Joliet, Illinois, some twelve thousand people gathered, a brass band played funeral music, a choir sang, bells tolled and minute guns fired. Many of the towns built huge bonfires while people waited through the night for the train. It came to Wilmington, Illinois, at 3:00 A.M. Lexington at 4 a.m, Towanda at 4:30, Bloomington at 5 A.M., and Funk's Grove (probably its last stop before Springfield) at 5:30.[132]

Lincoln was buried in Springfield, Illinois, on May 4. On the same day Chicagoans gathered in Bryan Hall to "listen to an oration upon the life, character, and services of our late lamented martyr President." On the stage a life-size bust of Lincoln stood on a flag-draped pedestal. A choir sat on one side of the stage, the "City Clergy and invited guests" on the other. Six pieces of music were sung in the funeral service.[133] The reading of Lincoln's last inaugural address was followed by Root's "Farewell

Father, Friend and Guardian." The final speech of the day was printed in its lengthy entirety in the *Tribune* on May 5.

In May, 1865, Root & Cady moved to their new store in the Crosby's Opera House building. One exuberant writer said the store was "fitted up" in "the highest style of art, and with every convenience."[134] Crosby's Opera House was designed to hold 2,400 people. Masks of comedy and tragedy ornamented the arch at the entrance to the main concert room. Cherubs blowing trumpets decorated the corners of the room. A system of steam heat was installed; "the water works" were "so arranged that casualty by fire will be rendered impossible." Four stores occupied the ground floor, two of them "already secured by music dealers," a third to be a "ladies' restaurant."[135] The *Tribune* printed the opinion that Chicago was becoming a sophisticated city.

As Root remembered it, Root & Cady moved into Crosby's Opera House after buying several smaller music businesses. Eventually the company occupied a building across the alley behind the store. Their printing office and steam presses were in this rear building. Pianos and organs were displayed on the main floor. On the second floor there were rooms for band and orchestra instruments and smaller merchandise. Root's workroom was also on the second floor. In it he generated books and songs and "looked after the publishing interests of the house."[136]

June 1, 1865, was designated a "National Fast Day." In Chicago a Citizens' Committee of One Hundred planned "eulogistic services" in memory of President Lincoln to be held in Crosby's Opera House. The Reverend O. H. Tiffany was scheduled to speak on the "Life, Character and Public Acts" of President Lincoln. George F. Root was scheduled to conduct the singing of the hymns.[137]

The war's end brought a period when Root's songs looked back on the conditions of the war and dealt with the transition to peacetime. "On both sides we did what we thought was right,"[138] he claimed.

Former prisoners of war made their way home as best they could, north or south. On May 22 Chicagoans learned of a list of "Illinois Soldiers Starved at Andersonville." A soldier had copied from the hospital register a "shocking catalogue" of names that would fill "nearly three columns" of newspaper space. In the same issue of the *Tribune* "Starved in Prison" was partly editorial comment and partly an unabashed promotion for George Root's new song with that title. "Strong emotion, guided by true thought moves the world for good. We therefore welcome the aid

In May 1865, the firm of Root & Cady moved into the elegant new Crosby's Opera House and published this piano piece by George Root's son Frederick to commemorate the occasion.

of this song, coming as it does from one who has so many times during the war given the means for the expression of the emotions of the loyal people." The paper called the melody "very plaintive and affecting." Years later Root commented that he "voiced the feeling of the people in regard to the treatment of prisoners" in this song.[139] As he had done with "Battle Cry of Freedom" and "Tramp, Tramp, Tramp," he wrote both the words and the music of "Starved in Prison."

Returning soldiers were passing through Chicago in great numbers when Root set to music a poem called "They Have Broken Up Their Camps."[140] The words described soldiers, many of them wounded or scarred, "bringing back the dear old flag in glory." A song called "Good Bye Old Glory"[141] summarized the war experience and rejoiced that it had ended. After "Four weary years of toil and blood" there would be no more bugle calls and no more fighting. In the chorus, men bid hardtack "a fond adieu." The problem of reconciliation had been a public concern for some time before the war ended and now it came to the forefront. Root set to music a long, tedious poem called "North and South." He arranged it as a duet and marked the voice parts "North" and "South." Verse 1 was labeled "1861" and verse 5, "1865." The finale assumed a reconciliation "in one great Union sweetly blest."[142] "My Beau That Went to Canada"[143] told the story of a young man who had left the country to avoid military service. His fiance suggested that he need not return, now that the war was over.[144]

The popularity of "Tramp, Tramp, Tramp" was "entirely unprecedented," the *Tribune* said on June 29, 1865. One music house in Boston had ordered five thousand copies, "undoubtedly the largest single order ever given for one song in the United States." The Board of Music Trade, meeting in Niagara Falls, sent back an enthusiastic report to Chicago stating that 100,000 copies of Root's "Tramp, Tramp, Tramp" had been issued in about seven months.[145]

Root offered a "Sequel to 'Tramp, Tramp Tramp'" called "On, On, On, the Boys Came Marching! or the Prisoner Free."[146] Again he wrote both words and music. His words pictured fifty thousand men marching "like a grand majestic sea," rejoicing that "the cause we starved and suffered for" was won.

George Root's name was a household word, friends at the *Tribune* said in a burst of hometown pride. Chicago was taking its place among cultural centers; Root & Cady was "known through the length and breadth of the land as the publishers of songs that have gone into every household." Furthermore, "A song bearing their imprimatur needs no other guaranty to secure an immense demand" from the major music houses of New York and New England, the paper boasted. Their music nourished "home sentiment, morality, religion and temperance."[147]

In the fall of 1865 Root & Cady published George Root's new "Singing Book" titled *The Coronet*. In it were several war songs, but the distinguishing feature of the book was its break with the tradition of previous books designed for singing schools and musical conventions. Root and his contemporaries had used hymns, anthems and other church music as instructional material for years. *The Coronet* was based on the assumption that teachers felt "serious objections to the use of church music for mere musical cultivation, as well as for musical entertainment." This new approach offered "cheerful, (often lively)" music for classes. One topic that the *Coronet* had in common with earlier instructional collections was a section on "Qualities of Tone." Singers learned to use their voices to convey the feelings expressed in a song — joy, sorrow, fear, reverence, and so on. Root advised against keeping the same quality of vocal tone without regard for the meaning of the words.

Wartime themes mixed with more ordinary ones in the arts and entertainment. Late in 1865 an art gallery opened in Crosby's Opera House, where Root & Cady's fine music store was. The works by American artists were a revealing sample of what people saw during those years. George Inness's "Coming Storm" and "The Wreck" were shown; Gifford's "Moonlight on the Hudson" was there. G. P. A. Healy exhibited his "War" and "Peace." "General Sherman is the 'War,' and Peace is a benign-looking, portly Bishop, with whose countenance we are not familiar," a commentator said. "John Brown's Grave" by Richards was called "a lovely little piece of desolation." Chromo lithographs of Church's "Icebergs" and his "Heart of the Andes" were not well received.[148]

Root's persistence in writing "the people's" music had resulted in criticism before and in 1865 it happened again. An unidentified critic charged Root with lowering the standards of music by writing songs that would sell. Songs like "Just Before the Battle, Mother" were "degrading" and "undignified," he said. "Mr. Root is Forgiven," a Root & Cady associate using the pseudonym "Village Blacksmith" replied. "Just Before the Battle, Mother" was "intended for the simple tastes of the great mass of the people, not for the musically sophisticated." If the song had been written "in a higher style," people would not have understood it or used it. A songwriter had to choose between writing in the popular style or *"not writing for the people at all."* Friends at Root & Cady remembered that "a greater man" than Root once said "Let me write the songs of a country, and I care not who has the making of her laws."[149] Two months later the firm defended Root and "Just Before the Battle, Mother" more strongly in the *Song Messenger*. Their spokesman accused the critic of underestimating the people — those who farmed the land, explored the seas, engaged in trades and manufacturing, built railroads and produced newspapers. The public dealt with "the practical interests of society" and was "the only competent judge" of art and artists.[150]

Daily papers carried both news items and advertisements for shows, concerts and new books. In December 1865, Chicago offered Dickens's novels in bookstores, *Uncle Tom's Cabin* on stage with a new finale called "the Triumph of Freedom," and Kelly and Leon's Minstrels with a new program that included "The Colored Troops of 1864" and "Poor Old Jeff." Before the year ended *The Barber of Seville* played at Crosby's Opera House, *Beauty and the Beast* held the stage of Colonel Wood's Museum, and *Rob Roy; or Old Lang Syne* played at McVicker's Theater. Popular art, literature and music turned with the eyes of the public toward the west once more. Root's new song "Away on the Prairie Alone"[151] described a girl, a marriage proposal, and two young men, one very prosperous and the other dear to her heart.

Root's teaching had been interrupted by the war. In the closing days of 1865 the Illinois State Teachers' Association held a three-day convention in Joliet. Root led the singing at the opening session, taught an afternoon class, and led a two-hour evening session of "musical exercises."[152] To introduce Root & Cady's new "Juvenile Musical Quarterly" called *Our Song Birds* to the participants, he distributed copies of the first issue. The co-editor of *Our Song Birds* was Benjamin Russell Hanby, son of the Reverend William Hanby, a founder of Otterbein College and a station-master on the Underground Railroad. B. R. Hanby had worked as a minister until conservative parishioners objected to his use of musical instruments in the church. He decided to resign rather than participate in the division of a congregation. When he came to Root & Cady he had already written "Darling Nelly Gray" which in 1856 was one of the most popular songs in the country.[153] His "Ole Shady; the Song of the Contraband" was a hit song in 1861.[154] In the October 1866 issue of *Our Song Birds* Hanby's "Up On the Housetop" was published under the title "Santa Claus." While he was with Root & Cady, Hanby wrote Sunday-school songs, a number of which remained in use for some years. [155]

Our Song Birds was designed for Sunday School and the "Social Circle." In the first issue, called "The Snow Bird," were "The Freedman's Appeal." asking for understanding in the aftermath of slavery; "How It Marches, the Flag of Our Union"; and "The Soldier's Motherless Daughter" (words by Paulina, music by B. R. Hanby), Three Temperance songs warned against the effects of alcoholic beverages. "Have You Sold Your Matches, Tom?" pictured children in poverty and their attempt to earn what they could as street vendors. For this song Root set to music the words of James R. Murray, one of his younger associates at Root & Cady.

Looking back on his work from "The First Gun Is Fired" to "Good Bye Old Glory," Root described it in these words: "When anything happened that could be voiced in a song, or when the heart of the Nation was moved by particular circumstances or conditions caused by the war, I wrote what I thought would then express the emotions of the soldiers or the people."[156] In the years to come his music would continue to reflect what was on the people's minds.

7

A Future Full of Promise 1865—1871

As 1865 was coming to an end the Chicago *Tribune* printed a "Prospectus for 1866" describing the future as "full of the promise of greatness" and declaring that the nation was "being born again."[1] Northerners, energized by victory, were ready to take on such varied problems as railroad monopolies, poverty, and voting restrictions. A major issue in the reformers' minds was the intemperate use of alcoholic beverages. Root & Cady, attributing its success to providing for the "tastes of the great musical majority,"[2] published George Root's new collection of temperance songs and explained the need for it. "President Johnson informs us that slavery is dead and the rebellion is crushed. We believe that the moral force of music should be directed against the next greatest evil that threatens our land, viz., Intemperance. Hence, *The Musical Fountain*."[3] In June of the following year Root & Cady issued a second edition of the book with twice as many pages.

In the preface to the new edition Root suggested that the reform advocated in *The Musical Fountain* was beginning to influence Congress to support a "cold water platform"; he announced that some temperance organizations in the east had ordered a thousand copies each. He believed the first edition had "helped to swell that great tidal wave which has just reached Congress and floated off Senators upon a cold water platform." Congressional Temperance Societies were being organized. Inevitably "The Battle Cry of Freedom" had a new set of words on the theme "Shouting the battle-cry of Temperance" and a chorus that began "Cold water forever, hurrah, then, hurrah!" Henry Clay Work's "Kingdom Coming" became "The Temperance Sheep." "Tramp, Tramp, Tramp," with new words by M. B. C. Slade, became "Rise, oh, Rise to nobler manhood! Dash the tempting cup away!"

Root gave "Come Home, Father" by Henry Clay Work a prominent place in this book. In the preface he called Work "the pioneer of the grand temperance awakening" that took place at the close of the war. Root & Cady had already published Work's "Come Home, Father" in sheet music form. The song was a tremendous hit.

What most people called "taking the pledge" was a significant first step for those who supported the temperance movement. Thousands promised they would not drink alcohol. "Promise Me,"[4] to the tune of Root's "Just Before the Battle, Mother," told a compelling story from the mother's point of view. She had lost one son at Lookout Mountain; another had starved in Belle Isle prison. The song ended with a feeling of desperation: "Oh! 'twere worse than both the others, if my boy should go astray!" The answer followed in "I Promise," with words by M. B. C. Slade set to the tune of Root's "Just After the Battle."

Also in *The Musical Fountain,* "The Prodigal Son" recalled a familiar Bible story and used the music of Root's "Glory! Glory! or the Little Octoroon" which had appeared the previous month in a *Song Messenger Extra*. New words by W. O. Cushing began, "Ring the bells of heaven, there is joy today, for a soul returning from the wild." The chorus, originally "Glory! Glory! How the freedmen sang!" became "Glory! Glory! How the angels sang." One hundred forty years later, "Ring the Bells of Heaven" still appeared in a few hymnals.

Root's temperance song "Mabel,"[5] a story in three verses, was published as sheet music in 1866, the same year as *The Musical Fountain.* "Mabel" brought the death of a young woman, as found in "Hazel Dell" and "Rosalie the Prairie Flower," to the temperance cause. The writer of the words was not identified.

Reconciliation between North and South was on Root's mind. A song called "Foes and Friends"[6] described the last moments of two soldiers, former enemies, fallen on the bloodstained earth. "Lying, dying, side by side, a softened feeling rose" as they realized it was "fate" that "made them foes." The song ended sadly: Two young daughters "on Hampshire's hills, and Georgia's plain, were fatherless that night." The words of Root's "Glory!

Glory! or the Little Octoroon,"[7] published this time as sheet music, told the story of Little Rosa finding her way like thousands of former slaves to a Union encampment, following the army and looking for a new life. In 1866 the word *octoroon* was in common use; an octoroon was a person with one-eighth African-American ancestry. A play by Dion Boucicault titled *The Octoroon* drew crowds to McVicker's Theater in Chicago. The words of "Columbia's Call"[8] urged the country toward the kind of reconciliation that would "make her people one again." The memory of battle was still fresh in these lyrics, but "Now that the minute guns are cold" people must "Be friends and brothers, as of old." A song called "For All and Forever, the Flag of the Free"[9] used imagery to recall the sacrifices people had made.

Writing what Root called "people's" music meant writing about current events as well as social concerns. General Philip Sheridan, much admired for his victories in the Civil War, was military governor of Louisiana when a riot erupted. President Johnson relieved him of duty, but the northern public was strongly supportive of Sheridan. By mid–March 1867, Sheridan was on duty again as military governor of Louisiana and Texas. Public loyalty to him may have inspired the poem "Honor to Sheridan," which included the line "As we dwell with pride on his battle ride, let us speak of his civic glory."[10]

In Root's *Forest Choir,* "a collection of vocal music for young people" in "Day Schools,"[11] a vocal exercise reminded children that men in their families or in their neighborhoods had fought in the recent war. The words began "Three cheers for our heroes, not those who wear stars," but for the "rough, wrinkled and brown" common soldiers. Another exercise in *The Forest Choir* described a rural fireside and the delight of a mother and three children at the unannounced arrival of their returning soldier. "Fourth of July" by George Root had four verses, one of which honored "those who at Vicksburg kept Fourth of July." Another song in *The Forest Choir* advocated freedom for "all our country" where life would go on "Without a lash, without a chain."

Root included Benjamin F. Hanby's Christmas song, "Up On the Housetop" (titled "Santa Claus"), in *The Forest Choir*. Well into the twentieth century, "Up On the Housetop" was widely known as a children's song. Root & Cady's music periodical for children, *Our Song Birds,* had been Hanby's idea.

Moral values were very much a part of the public school curriculum. *The Forest Choir* offered temperance songs such as "Take the Pledge" and

"The Young Temperance Volunteer" and songs such as "Study Hard" to remind students what was expected of them. With *The Forest Choir* as their textbook, children sang about what they were studying. A multiplication song, a geography song, and a "Grammar Lesson" reinforced nonmusical concepts. The "Grammar Lesson" illustrated parts of speech: "How things are done, the adverbs tell, as *slowly, quickly, ill,* or *well.*" To be proficient singers, students needed to learn the Italian names for scale tones. Each line of an exercise called "Strange Stairways" was sung on the scale tone its English homophone suggested. It began: "The first step of the stairway was made of unbak'd bread, *do*. The second was a sunbeam that shone from overhead, *re.*"

Root & Cady had been growing and prospering in the years since the Civil War. In 1866 the *Chicago Tribune* had printed a long article about the company, using their success in the music business as an example of Chicago's becoming a sophisticated city. Root & Cady built "an archway beneath the alley" to connect the basement with pressrooms on Randolph Street. The front sales room was serene, while at the back of the building pianos swung on a crane and in the basement packages were made up and shipped. On an average day the company prepared and shipped packages "for nearly every Northern State, for the Provinces, for the Pacific coast and for Europe." The *Tribune* writer added that later generations would realize the songs Root & Cady had published were part of the country's Civil War–era history.[12] As 1867 was coming to an end, the firm presented what their *Song Messenger* called a unique "Musical History of the Late War" to the Historical Society of Chicago. This was a bound volume of the Civil War songs they had published.[13]

George Root used the *Song Messenger* as a link with people—students and former students, associates and customers. In an article called "Repairing Damages," he explained that he was recovering from a serious illness and trying to return to work. God permitted suffering, he wrote, but the suffering was as great a proof of his love as "the reward that follows obedience."[14] Long periods of hard work were said to be the cause of this illness. For quite some time Root and those who were close to him had feared that he might never again be strong enough for the kind of work he had done. In his autobiography he gave no precise date, although he mentioned that the problem arose when his convention work was at its height and he was about thirty-eight years old (August 1858). In his words, "I used to have occasionally a nervous reaction at the close of my four days' work that affected my head unpleasantly." As the growing business confined him more and "some large obligations" made him "anxious," the symptoms occurred more often and lasted longer. Finally, in Root's words, his illness "came to stay." Among the business obligations Root mentioned could have been the acquisition by Root & Cady of the sheet music plates belonging to other publishers: Ziegfeld, Gerard and Company; Mason & Hamlin of Boston; H. T. Merrill & Company; and Henry Tolman. The Tolman purchase consisted primarily of "standard works" and by itself totaled about thirty thousand printing plates.[15] During 1867 and 1868 Root & Cady increased its sheet music publications to almost seven times their original number.[16]

Doctors called Root's illness a condition of the brain and recommended that he stop working and go on a long voyage, perhaps to Europe. A seasoned traveler, he did not have the courage to face a sea voyage at this time, even though the head of the Curwen family of music teachers and publishers invited him to London to hear a chorus of several thousand voices sing his music. Someone Root called "a medical friend" in the Boston area recommended Butler's method of weight lifting and Root decided to try it. After three months he purchased a set of Butler's weight lifting equipment and had it sent to his Chicago residence. After six months he "began to work a little." Root credited Butler's method of weight lifting with his full recovery from the illness. He and his business partners "furnished the capital" for a place where the system could be offered to the public and appointed Dr. Frank Reilly manager. Reilly called the establishment the "Health Lift." It remained in business until the Chicago fire of 1871.[17]

The *Song Messenger* routinely announced the classes George Root taught and often followed up with reports on them. For the month of August 1868, Root left James R. Murray in charge of his department at Root & Cady while he taught in a Normal Musical Institute in Winona, Illinois. As Root recalled it, this was his first Normal Musical Institute since the war. He was principal of this session,[18] but, as he said, "the younger men were now coming to the front." One of the younger men was his son Frederick, who had taught in the Winona institute the previous year with O. D. Adams as principal.[19] Preparing for what the *Song Messenger* called "an extended Convention tour," Root and his son were scheduled to teach in Vermont, Massachusetts, New York, Pennsylvania, Iowa, and Illinois between mid–October and mid–December 1868.[20]

In June 1868 Root published a major book of church music titled *The Triumph*. He restated the prevalent belief that singing was supposed to "exercise and strengthen the good affections" or emotions. He explained that "singing is not only an expression, but an exercise of our emotional nature" and summarized: "If we do a right action, the first effect is upon ourselves." For the study of music theory the book provided elementary, intermediate, and advanced instruction. In the preface Root acknowledged "contributors and special friends" whom he called "prominent musical men in different parts of the country." Through some new technology the autographs of I. B. Woodbury, Lowell Mason, Thomas Hastings, and William B. Bradbury were reproduced, each one appearing with a hymn by that composer. Root's signature, ornate and scrupulously neat, was reproduced at the end of the preface. He acknowledged the valued contributions of associates within the firm of Root & Cady: P. P. Bliss, James R. Murray, and his son Frederick W. Root.[21]

As Root remembered it, while the Republican Convention of 1868 was going on his mind was elsewhere. But when he heard about the enthusiasm for Ulysses S. Grant, he "stopped to write a song." John Hogarth Lozier, once chaplain of the 37th Indiana Infantry, had already written a poem to commemorate a message Grant sent from the battlefield at Spotsylvania, Virginia, after days of brutal fighting, telling General Halleck that he proposed "to fight it out on this line if it takes all summer." Root set

This photograph of George Root is attributed to John Carbutt and dated 1868. Purchased from Hanzel Galleries, Chicago.

Lozier's poem to music and when Grant's nomination was announced, the new song was sung.[22]

Root & Cady took part in the political campaign of 1868 by publishing a collection of campaign songs titled "The Grant Songster." The company's logo on the cover was a lyre in a circle with R&C entwined. Newspapers, magazines, broadsides, and public speeches were the media of the time; political campaigns needed music. The most efficient way to create a campaign song was to write new words for a well-known tune. In "The Grant Songster" Root's "Battle Cry of Freedom" became "The Ballot Box of Freedom." New words to the tune of "Just Before the Battle, Mother" began "Just Before Election, Andy" and continued "we are thinking most of you while we get our ballots ready — but be sure they're not for you."

Other topics of popular interest suggested the material for songs. The country had watched from a distance while the first transcontinental railroad was being built. When it was completed Root recognized the occasion with a song called "The Pacific Rail Road."[23] The date of the ceremonial driving of the golden spike, May 10, 1869, appeared below the song title. In the same year *Gates Ajar* was a widely read inspirational book designed to bring comfort to those who had lost loved ones in the Civil War. Root dedicated a new song called "Somewhere" to "the Readers of *Gates Ajar*." The poignant words suggested that for each person there was someone with whom to share a life.[24]

Americans loved stories that vindicated the humble or the downtrodden or the disrespected. In the winter of 1870 an actor named George Holland died in New York City. Only a few people recognized his name, but his funeral made news in papers across the country and gave George Root the nucleus of a song. On the cover of the sheet music Root outlined Holland's story: "His friend, Joseph Jefferson, called upon a clergyman of one of the Episcopal churches" and asked him to hold the funeral in his church. The answer was "No," but there was a "little church around the corner" that might agree to conduct the service. Jefferson reportedly said "God bless the little church around the corner!"[25] Root was credited with both the words and the music of this song. The refrain ended "All honor give, while good deeds live, to that little church around the corner." *The Song Messenger* commented that since the war, Root had written only a few songs, and then only "when subjects of importance present themselves." The incident described in this song was "one of them."[26]

Many Americans were looking westward, drawn by opportunity and adventure. In 1870 Bret Harte was famous internationally as the author of *The Luck of Roaring Camp and Other Sketches*. Like Root, Harte was an eastern man who liked and admired the west. His travels and experiences there enabled his writings to bring a lively image of the west to the rest of the country. Harte's poem, "Poverty Flat, or Her Letter," pictured a newly wealthy heiress taking a moment during a festive ball to write to a young man with whom she had fallen in love before her father struck "pay gravel." Root's setting of the poem[27] had a music-hall quality and traces of his minstrel show songs of the 1850s. It showed his aptitude for the theatrical. A four-measure piano interlude reflected the references to dancing in the first and second verses. Root specified that these four measures be played slowly and softly after the last verse.

News of war between France and Prussia roused sympathy in Chicago, where there were numerous immigrants and visiting musicians of both nationalities. Root dedicated a new song "To the Friends of Prussia," titled it "Banner of the Fatherland,"[28] and signed it with his pseudonym Wurzel, the German word for root. The following year he composed a song for "the Producers' French Aid Organization, Chicago" and titled it "Hear the Cry that Comes Across the Sea."[29] As he had done in the song about Prussia, he wrote both words and music of this one and gave it the subtitle "Rallying Song and Chorus." Verse and chorus both began with three martial tones like those that characterized the chorus of "Tramp, Tramp, Tramp."

Dwight L. Moody, the famous evangelist, suggested that Root & Cady publish a book based on the topics specified in the "National Sunday School List." The list, used by several of the large Protestant denominations, gave a topic for each Sunday School lesson throughout the year. George Root replied that this suggestion would be carried out "as far as possible" in his forthcoming book, *The Prize for Our Sunday School*. [1870]. The gospel song was becoming a forceful presence in church music; Root's "Jewels," which he included in *The Prize*, illustrated the trend. This song appeared in a number of church music books well into the twentieth century. It was short, easy to learn, and rhythmically strong. It had a primitive quality, somewhat like the early shape-note hymns. The words by the Reverend William O. Cushing were based on a line from scripture and suggested that children were God's jewels.

George Root considered the 1870 Normal Musical Institute, held in

South Bend, Indiana, "the banner normal thus far." Six vocal training classes met simultaneously each day; each class was designed for a specific voice category. Since its inception in New York City in 1853 the Institute had met in Massachusetts, Ohio, Illinois, Minnesota, and Wisconsin. Of the original four principal teachers, only Root was still active. Several times during this session Schuyler Colfax, then vice president of the United States and a resident of South Bend, visited the Institute. Since participants had come from seventeen states and Canada, Colfax suggested that this be re-named "The National Musical Institute."[30]

Root's son Frederick had come home from Europe to teach in the 1870 Institute. For some months Frederick and his brother Charles had traveled in Europe, hearing fine music and looking for "gems of foreign music" to add to Root & Cady's stock. William Lewis, a violinist who worked for Root & Cady, was in Europe at the same time buying musical instruments for the company to resell.[31]

According to Lydia Avery Coonley, this photograph shows George F. Root about 1870. Mrs. Coonley was a member of Root's extended family. Her son, John Stuart Coonley, married Root's granddaughter Louise. *New England Magazine,* January 1896.

Root & Cady had intended, when the company was founded in 1858, to emphasize classical music at least as much as popular songs. By 1866 the company was addressing itself to the "musical masses of America," claiming their war songs had "hit the popular heart."[32] In 1871 their *Song Messenger* advised teachers, composers, and publishers to "Study the People" and to be constantly aware of their tastes, abilities and "wants." This was an "essential requisite" for success. In the opinion of the *Song Messenger's* writer, teachers as well as publishers were "tradesmen with wares to sell." Consequently, "if they do not keep the kind of wares that people want, they must expect to go into bankruptcy and shut up shop." Among the teachers, composers and publishers who owed their success to a "sympathetic study" of the people and their music, the writer named Thomas Hastings, Lowell Mason, I. B. Woodbury and George F. Root. He also warned against trying to sell the music of Mendelssohn to people who preferred "Shoo Fly."[33]

Root's protégé James R. Murray explained "Simple Music" by comparing it with the novels of Charles Dickens. Before Dickens, novelists wrote mostly about the upper class, Murray observed. If a person from the lower classes was featured in a story, it was invariably discovered at the last moment that the hero or heroine was actually "of noble birth" and had been "stolen from the cradle by gypsies." [34] "We appreciate wit, humor, intellectuality, patriotism and historical romance, but that which takes hold of us most" in the arts "is a truthful portrayal of home scenes and home affections" with "a healthy moral sentiment," Murray wrote. As examples he cited Louisa Alcott's *Little Women* among novels, *Rip Van Winkle* and *Chimney Corner* among plays, and Root's *Haymakers* in music.[35]

In the years prior to the Chicago fire, Root & Cady's magazine, *The Song Messenger*, provided rare word pictures of their elegant store and their publishing operation. One of these was a virtual tour of the premises as a they appeared in August 1868. Visitors coming into the store would see floors and furnishings of oak and black walnut, "oiled and polished." Shelves on the left held sheet music — thirty thousand titles in brown paper folios. On the right were imported goods, violins and strings. Farther along there were enclosed desks for the cashier and for the *Song Messenger*. In the center of the room were private offices and the mail order department. The second half of the space was filled with pianos, organs, and smaller musical instruments; "hundreds," Root & Cady claimed, "in all conceivable styles of case and finish." The basement was as crowded and noisy as the main floor was serene. Huge stacks of books stood ready to sell. Approximately two thousand copies of Root's *Musical Curriculum* stood in a stack six feet square and seven feet high. Farther back the shipping department packed "two to three wagon loads" of music and books each workday. Across an alley the visitor found Root & Cady's printing office. Four steam presses and seven plate presses ran while "an army" of compositors set the type for music books and the *Song Messenger*. On the day of this virtual visit two music books were being printed. Finally, the visitor was invited to go "around to No. 79 Dearborn street." Upstairs, Room

4 was George Root's workroom with his library and piano. Here he had written *The Musical Curriculum, The Triumph,* "Tramp, Tramp, Tramp," and "a host of other songs that now are as familiar as 'household words,'"[36] the *Song Messenger* said. In this, "Geo. F. Root's sanctum," a timid beginning songwriter would be greeted warmly. If his song were accepted for publication, it would be produced on Root & Cady's premises.

Mail was delivered to the store four times a day, typically 100 to 125 letters in each delivery. Employees opened them, took out any money, and entered the orders in a ledger. Each order went to the head of a department: pianos, string instruments, tuning, and so on. William A Root, George's brother, handled orders "from the Eastern houses" for books or music. The staff must finish the orders before the next mail came. Root & Cady had "One cardinal principle: that "every order must be filled and sent off the same day that it is received."[37]

In January 1871, Root & Cady's spokesman reported on the company's successes: "1858–1871, what an eventful epoch!" When the company was formed, "Chicago was in the Far west" and everyone looked to the Atlantic seaboard for their sheet music and music books. Now it seemed "a good thing published in Chicago" had the same chance of success "as if it bore the imprint of Boston or New York." The company claimed its Civil War songs proved this, and now Root's book, *The Triumph,* had, for its time in print, "the largest sale ever reached by any book of church music published in America." His Sunday School book, *The Prize,* had sold 75,000 copies.[38] Both Chicago and the firm of Root & Cady had enjoyed a period of burgeoning prosperity.

The *Song Messenger* reprinted an article from the Congregationalist paper, *The Advance,* estimating that Root & Cady's sales were about $400,000 a year and that sales in the first half of 1871 were almost $100,000 more than in the same period of any previous year. William S. B. Mathews, a friend and associate, wrote that Root & Cady manufactured and sold more sheet music and more music books that any of the New York publishers.[39]

Thinking back on what he called "the memorable autumn of 1871," Root listed the books Root & Cady had published in recent years and gave some of the statistics on their sales and profits. He mentioned the company's publications by various authors such as H. R. Palmer and P. P. Bliss. "In pianos, organs, band instruments and general musical merchandise we had a large trade and carried a heavy stock," he wrote. The company's spaces on two floors of the opera house and another space of the same size in the building behind it "were filled to overflowing." For example, 90,000 copies of *The Triumph* stood stacked and ready. Because the books intended for fall classes were expected to be sold "in a few weeks," they were not insured.[40]

The summer had been dry; in the past year Chicago had had 600 fires.[41] Root lived in Groveland Park, about four miles from Root & Cady.[42] Between three and four o'clock on the morning of October 9 someone woke Root to tell him that his neighbor Jerome Beardslee was waiting outside to see him. Root tried to light the gas but there was none. He dressed quickly and hurried downstairs. Beardslee told him that a great fire was burning downtown. Beardslee's store was gone but he had gotten his books

Root & Cady's music store in Crosby's Opera House burned in the Chicago Fire of 1871. Root described the experience of seeing "the costly and elegant opera house go." He could not get close enough to see the "rear building" where his workroom and library were. He remembered that "the calamity was so general and so overwhelming that individual losses seemed insignificant in comparison...." Engraving from *Harper's Weekly*, October 28, 1871 (ICHi-02911, Chicago Historical Society).

out and had brought them home. He was going back and Root could go with him. "I think you'll be in time to see your place go," he told Root. Coming within a mile of the fire, they saw avenues lined with household goods guarded by terrified and panic-stricken owners. Coming closer, "dust, cinders and smoke, whirled by the frightful tornado which the flames created, grew blinding and tormenting beyond description." Root saw "limestone burned and crumbled, iron melted, brick walls crushed." "Delicate looking tongues of flame" shot across an open space twenty or thirty feet wide; a marble building "dissolved." On the north side of Chicago people moved their belongings again and again to keep ahead of the fire. There was no way to move them far enough. Some people who placed their belongings on the lakeshore watched them burn and had to go into the water to save themselves. Fire engines and equipment were destroyed before they could begin to work. Hoses curled and shriveled like paper. Root arrived in time to watch the fire envelope the "costly and elegant" Crosby's Opera House and to "bid good bye to the pleasant and convenient business house we had perfected." He could not get close enough to see the back of the building where his workroom and library were. He was particularly concerned about a green box he called "an old paper affair" in which he kept his "daily work" and all his unpublished manuscripts. The men who worked at Root & Cady had often laughed about his saying "If there's a fire, save that green box." Only a few months before the fire, the company had built a large brick vault in the cellar of the "rear building" to hold the printing plates for their large catalogue of books and sheet music. Each night the porter put Root's green box in the vault "with the other valuables." On the night of the fire the porter missed the box. James R. Murray's brother Robert, "hastily looking about just before the fire reached there, saw it." He remembered Root's request and saved the box.[43]

Root's son Charles, a salesman in the Root & Cady store, described the scene as a "hurricane of wind and fire" with a "rain of glowing cinders, clouds of dust and smoke, pillars of flame for lightning, and miles of crashing walls for thunder." People threw mirrors and glazed pictures from high windows and handled bedding with "gingerly care." One woman filled a tray with china and glassware, emptied it over a railing and went back inside to drag an old chair to a safer place. One man elbowed his way through the crowded street carrying a worn-out hoop skirt. Another hugged pieces of old stovepipe and a third clung to an empty peach bas-

An 1871 stereograph image of the ruins of Crosby's Opera House. For days after the fire, people waited anxiously to find out whether the safes and the brick vault had preserved the printing plates and account books. Root kept his "daily work" and his unpublished manuscripts in an old green paper box. Each night the porter was supposed to put the box in the vault. On the night of the fire he overlooked it but Robert Murray saw the box and saved it (ICHi-02767, Chicago Historical Society).

ket. One man, "surprised by the fire, bolted with his tooth-brush and a clean shirt, leaving almost all the money he had in the world to burn up in his bureau drawer." Charles Root was helping to carry the furnishings out of a house in the path of the fire when he accidentally stepped on a small mirror. The mirror belonged to an elderly woman who "with her few belongings, had camped out on the sidewalk." She demanded that Charles pay her for the mirror immediately. He thought how, less than an hour earlier, the walls had "crushed out of existence our little all." It occurred to him suddenly that "the public debt would be paid long before we could raise fifteen cents."[44]

Theodore Thomas's unrivaled orchestra was scheduled to play at Crosby's Opera House that night. When the flames "enveloped the beautiful building," Root thought of their fine instruments, some of which were left there. His mind also "ran over a list" of the valuable things that were being consumed: Root & Cady's expensive counters and desks, sheet music on long rows of shelves, "cords of books in the basement," hundreds of instruments — pianos and organs, fine violins, guitars and band instruments; the printing office and presses, and the pleasant room where his son Frederick, James R. Murray, and Root himself had done "so much pleasant and successful" work. All these were gone in a few minutes. It was sad, but the calamity was "so general and so overwhelming" that a loss like that of Root & Cady, even though it was a quarter of a million dollars, seemed "insignificant in comparison" with the total.[45] Just days earlier Root & Cady's new show-rooms for musical instruments had been "the brilliant scene" of their first "musical evening" of the season. Now Root told readers of the *Song Messenger,* "all is gone, my musical library and the thousand useful things that I have gathered about me in so many busy years, swept away in a moment."[46]

In the business part of the city, people could not tell where the streets were. Places that two days earlier had been as familiar as the rooms of one's own house were now "a strange, wild desolation." Root remembered the days immediately following the fire as a time of anxious waiting to find out whether the company's vault and safes had protected their printing plates and account books. Finally the vault and safes cooled enough to be opened. The contents were secure, although some of the papers were scorched.[47]

After the fire the city was totally dark. Root remembered long nights filled with foreboding. Each night residents patrolled the streets to prevent looting and vandalism. All the men were expected to take part in these patrols.[48] They watched the houses, guns in hand, in "gasless" darkness. One man fired two shots at his own shadow "and then ran several consecutive miles" before stopping to give the alarm, Charles wrote. "We might chill the reader's blood with some of our own hair-breadth escapes from trees, gate-posts and other ghastly and dangerous objects which were continually attacking us on our lonely beat."[49]

The principals in the firm of Root & Cady tried to keep the business going. Soon after the fire, mail delivery resumed and with it, orders for music merchandise. At first the orders were passed on to other companies, but as Root remembered, "It was not long before we had a large dwelling house on Michigan Avenue fitted up and stocked, and business went on.... We had lost all our stock, but the plates and copyrights remained."[50]

"I commence again with hope and energy," Root reported to readers of *The Song Messenger* very soon after the fire.[51] C. M. Cady and Towner Root planned to collect the insurance and pay the debts of the company in full, then continue in business. Their insurance paid less than half the expected amount. George Root agreed to give up some unencumbered real

My dear Sir;

Some months ago my sister Mrs Burnham sent me a letter from you requesting a copy of my father's autograph — Geo. F. Root. I was about leaving the city for a time & your letter, which I intended to answer promptly, got tucked away in a corner from which I have but just now rescued it. I have not at the moment an autograph signature to send you — I may discover one later; but I enclose a scrap of his music MS, a bit that passed through the great fire in '71 and though in a brick vault, was scorched somewhat. Very truly yours,

Frederic W. Root.

In response to a request for his father's autograph, Frederic Woodman Root sent this letter. In it he wrote "I enclose a scrap of his music MS, a bit that passed through the great fire in '71 and though in a brick vault, was scorched somewhat." Purchased from Hanzel Galleries, Chicago.

estate he owned, and two firms were formed. Towner Root, C. M. Cady, and William Lewis continued under the name of Root & Cady. They would sell pianos, organs, and the imported goods that were Lewis's department. The other firm was called George F. Root and Sons. Its principals were George, his sons Frederick and Charles, and his brother William.

George Root made it clear that he was to be "free to resume" his "professional life" as a teacher, "untrammeled by business cares." William and Charles were to manage the business.⁵²

The firm that had retained the name of Root & Cady sold the sheet music copyrights to S. Brainard's Sons of Cleveland on November 18, 1871, and the book catalog, plates and copyrights to John Church & Company of Cincinnati on February 23, 1872.⁵³ These sales totaled approximately $130,000, according to George Root's memory. "When the hard times that followed the fire came on," they could not "meet the great liabilities they had assumed," he wrote. The reorganized Root & Cady had to resort to bankruptcy, and the firm of George F. Root & Sons bought their stock "with the assistance of a wealthy friend." C. M. Cady left Chicago,⁵⁴ as did James R. Murray. Towner Root and William Lewis began again in 1873 as a firm called Root & Lewis.⁵⁵

After 1873 George F. Root & Sons continued in what Root called "a general music business" and published what he called "our works" jointly with John Church & Company. "It was a time of great business depression," he wrote, "but we had a 'tower of strength' in the Cincinnati house" and "we still published the *Song Messenger.*"⁵⁶

Early in 1875 Root & Lewis merged with Chandler & Curtiss and George F. Root & Sons to form Root & Sons Music Company.⁵⁷ Towner Root withdrew from this firm in 1880 to start a firm with his sons Frank and Walter called E. T. Root & Sons.⁵⁸ In 1876 the *Song Messenger* was merged into *The Musical Visitor,* which in Root's words "became our medium of communication with the musical public" from that time.⁵⁹

Almost immediately after the fire Root sent a piece called "Songs of the Olden Days"⁶⁰ to William A. Pond Company in New York. On the cover the publisher printed Root's message and reproduced his signature. "Dear Sirs. This song was on my desk at the time of the fire and was burnt, but I have rewritten it, and as we have no way of printing it here, will you please get it up for me? And obldige [sic] yours very truly, Geo. F. Root." The song was a musical hodgepodge, a form that was popular in those years. Bits of familiar songs were held together with a few measures of original melody. Listeners heard fragments of "Auld Lang Syne," "Coming Through the Rye," "The Last Rose of Summer," and "Home Sweet Home."

Hardly more than two weeks after the fire Root & Cady announced

Root's home in Chicago before the fire of 1871. *New England Magazine*, January 1896.

publication of three new songs with words and music by George Root. The announcement appeared in *The Chicago Magazine of Fashion, Music and Home Reading*. The songs were published in sheet music form with the imprint of Root & Cady and dated 1871. "Passing Through the Fire" pictured the destruction Root had seen. "Ye Have Done It Unto Me" was a message of appreciation "Inscribed to All who have helped us while we've been 'Passing Through the Fire.'" "From the Ruins Our City Shall Rise" voiced optimism and confidence.

S. Brainard's Sons in Cleveland published a song with words and

The interior of Root's Chicago home in later years. *New England Magazine,* January 1896.

music by George Root called "Lost and Saved." In addition to Brainard's name on the cover there was the name of the new company, Geo. F. Root & Sons. "Lost and Saved" described a family returning from an evening church service to find their house in flames. A child was missing; the first chorus ended "Lost in the fire!" Miraculously the child appeared in the doorway. The family "knew the angels saved her."

"The papers have told you of the burning of Chicago," a new magazine called *Church's Musical Visitor* [61] said, and "every music store in the city was burned." The actor Joseph Jefferson, who inspired Root's "Little Church Around the Corner," was in Chicago, ready to give performances for a week to benefit Chicago's actors.

For Chicago's musicians and music businesses, the fire meant that money must now be diverted from the arts to pay for "brick and mortar" and for new merchandise to sell, the *Musical World* commented. Many musicians had left the city "to seek not only shelter but work elsewhere."[62] Like so many others, George Root faced the challenge of beginning again.

8

Music for the People
1871–1895

"From the re-adjustment after the fire," Root recalled, "I was in my old life again — the Normal in the summer, conventions at various times and in various places, and at my desk making books and songs the rest of the time." From the 1870s into the 1890s he taught Normal classes and musical conventions from Maine to the Midwest. In 1872 Chicago University conferred on Root an honorary doctorate in music.[1]

Writing for his *Song Messenger* readers, Root claimed that each town where he conducted a musical convention had what he called a "specialty." At Scranton, Pennsylvania, he saw coal mines and iron furnaces. At Glastonbury, Connecticut, he saw sleighbells being made. At Richmond, Virginia, he saw tobacco "manufactories." Bridgeton, New Jersey, was memorable for nails: Orange County, New York, for butter; Vermont for marble and Akron, New York, a village near Buffalo, for the limestone used in making cement. He was particularly amused by the suggestion of a Bangor, Maine, resident that since Root spent so much time in the nearby sawmills they might move the musical convention to a sawmill and seat the class on logs.[2]

In addition to his teaching in Normal Musical Institutes and Musical Conventions, Root served as president of Chicago Musical College from 1872 to 1876. Originally called the Chicago Academy of Music, it was founded in 1865 by Florenz Ziegfeld, father of the man who later created the Ziegfeld Follies. William A. Root was business manager of the college from 1870 to 1872 and Charles T. Root was treasurer from 1872 to 1876.[3] In 1954, Chicago Musical College merged with Roosevelt University.[4]

As Root said, when he wasn't traveling and teaching, he was at his desk compiling books and writing songs. In the years 1871–1890 he produced more than twenty books for a wide variety of singers. *First Years in Song-Land* was intended for "day schools and juvenile singing classes." *The Welcome* was a Sunday School collection for children in the Swedenborgian Church, which Root and his family had joined in 1863. *The National School Singer* focused on those times in the schoolroom when "music would be appropriate and helpful." *The Triumph* was designed for singing schools, musical conventions and choirs, and was evidently Root's best-selling book of its kind. His 1872 *Normal Musical Handbook* offered his methods of teaching. It was a product of years of thinking about how people learn and how best to teach them. Although it was fairly technical, Root's down-to-earth approach crept in. "Practice every new lesson you teach," he advised, "every tone, every word, every motion." Practice alone, he urged. "It will not be the first time that chairs, bureau and washstand, or bare walls, have been the only audience of a first lesson on some new subject, or in some new way of treating an old one." In a chapter called "Mental Health," Root warned teachers against "poisons of the mind," which were "wrong desires and motives"; envy, "unkindness to those who prevent our gratification," and "disregard of the rights of others."[5] Five sections were crowded into the book: one on note reading, two on teaching vocal music, one on teaching harmony and composition, and a combination dictionary and index.

Through the years Root had become a voice for what Lincoln called public sentiment. In 1874 his *Trumpet of Reform* conveyed what many reform-minded people were thinking. When it was published, almost half the people in the United States lived on farms. Root had grown up on a farm that was threatened in a financial panic in the 1830s; this book voiced the protests of farmers threatened by monopolies and falling prices. As far back as the spring of 1863 the carpenters and joiners of Chicago had announced that they were forming a "Protective Union." In 1865 there had been a "Sewing Women's Protective Union" in the city.[6] The Chicago *Tribune* had warned in 1866 that after slavery "the next great problem for the American people" would be monopolies.[7] In the same year leaders formed the National Labor Union, one of the first attempts to create a nationwide labor organization, and Root & Cady published a song called "Our Protective Union."[8]

According to its title page, *The Trumpet of Reform* was intended for "the Grange, the Club and All Industrial and Reform Organizations." Farmers organized the National Grange in 1867 when railroads were taking control of agricultural land and threatening to monopolize the handling and shipping of farm products to market. Prices for farm products fell. The farmers' position grew weaker; railroads and middlemen gained strength. As 1874 began the Grange had more than ten thousand members.[9]

"The Hand That Holds the Bread" documents its moment in history in much the same way the Civil War songs document theirs. Root dedicated this song, words and music, "To the Farmers of America." The melody was dignified and martial. The words began "Brothers of the plow!" and urged action against oppression by monopolies. The chorus claimed "heaven gives the power to the hand that holds the bread."

Mrs. S. M. Smith wrote strong, colorful protest poems about farmers' problems. George Root set to music her "New Farmers' Song" called "Hear! Hear the Shout! or, The People's Army" and included it in *The Trumpet of Reform*. Her words pointed out the danger of losing the products of a farm, or even the farm itself. She suggested that former soldiers might have to fight again, this time for their own rights, and with votes as their weapons.

With songs like "The Laborer on Election Day," Root's setting of a poem by John Greenleaf Whittier, *The Trumpet of Reform* could serve the Grange's purpose: to rally the farm vote. Root's "Tramp, Tramp, Tramp" became "Tramp, Tramp, Tramp, the Grange is Marching" with words by Mrs. S. M. Smith, ending with the assurance of a coming day that would "set free the latest slave in freedom's land." Root's "Battle Cry of Freedom" became a "Battle Cry of Labor." The new words by Mrs. Smith proclaimed, "We're mustering for victory, a million voters strong, shouting the battle cry of freemen!" Powerful industrialists formed "rings" to control their own areas of trade, such as shipping freight or selling merchandise. Rings were the subject of a poem from a magazine called *The Industrial Age*. The poem supported the idea of crushing monopolies and described rings "in selling school books, in telegraphic news, in planters and in reapers and in everything we use."

The temperance movement came back into prominence and gained strength. Since the publication of Root's *Musical Fountain* in 1866, Temperance organizations had not had as much impact as they hoped. In 1869 a Prohibition Party had been organized. By 1888 some people advocated controlling the sale of alcohol with a system of licensing laws. The Prohibition Party opposed the licensing system. Starting in 1872, Prohibition candidates ran for president in each election. In 1888 the party got about 250,000 votes.[10] In the same year Root voiced the opinions of the Prohibitionists in a collection of songs called *The Glorious Cause*. It was clearly a campaign tool for legislation to prohibit the sale of alcoholic beverages; one of the songs was titled "Fight the Battle at the Polls." In the Preface Root argued for "a total suppression of the liquor traffic," which he called "a fearful cause of crime, pauperism and insanity."[11] He tried to influence public opinion with a song titled "Don't Wait Till the Drunkard Is Made."[12] A song titled "May We Ask You, Christian Brother" asked sternly, "Do you pray one way and vote another?"[13] A Prohibition version of Root's "Battle Cry of Freedom" began "Yes, we'll rally for the right, friends, we'll rally once again, this time for total Prohibition." The chorus proclaimed: "United forever! Hurrah, all, hurrah! Down now and ever the still and the bar." Root's new words for "Tramp, Tramp, Tramp" conveyed a mother's concern for her sons and her ardent opposition to legislation that would permit "a licensed hell."

Between 1871 and 1895 Root produced far fewer songs for publication as sheet music than in earlier years, while he composed at least twenty-five cantatas. He called these "cantatas for the people," the same kind of music as his "songs for the people." He categorized his cantatas as juvenile, scriptural or secular and gave as examples *The Flower Queen, Daniel,* and *The Haymakers*.[14] Root and his daughter Clara Louise Burnham, a successful novelist, wrote cantatas for Easter and Christmas from 1878 through 1890. Many of these later cantatas were lighthearted, designed to charm and entertain. Among their titles were *Catching Kris Kringle, Santa Claus' Mistake*, and *Judge Santa Claus*. Into the mid–1890s Root and Burnham wrote cantatas for other occasions as well, among them *Phyllis, the Farmer's Daughter* and *The Festival of the Flowers*.

Years before Walt Disney made cultural history with the film *Snow White*, Root and his daughter Clara Louise Burnham wrote an operetta based on the same story.[15] The play opened with a chorus of forest children singing to the "most beautiful" creature, Princess Snow White, on her sixteenth birthday. According to the printed "Directions" the queen, costumed in "a trailing gown, the more gorgeous the better," sang a song called "Magic Mirror," and demanded to be recognized as the most beautiful of women. A "voice outside" answered that Snow White was far lovelier. The queen ordered a huntsman to take Snow White into the woods and bring back only her heart and her eyes. The huntsman left Snow White in the woods alive. A prince, costumed in tights, velvet trunks, a doublet and a plumed hat, met the huntsman in the woods. In a duet they sang "O jealousy, how pitiless." Snow White found the home of the dwarfs who, costumed in brown and wearing pointed hoods, bushy beards and mustaches, sang "O we are the seven dwarfs, crusty and old." The evil queen found Snow White and killed her. When the grieving prince lifted her up, she came back to life as the chorus sang "She lives!"

Root had wanted for a long time to see England again. He sailed July 17, 1886, on the steamship *Ethiopia*. He went first to Glasgow, Scotland, to talk with the publishers Bailey and Ferguson about writing a cantata for them. In England the publisher J. Spencer Curwen entertained him. On the morning of his sixty-sixth birthday Root heard the sound of a boys' choir singing a serenade under his window.[16] Visiting Westminster Abbey, he was "much attracted by a new marble bust of Longfellow." After considerable difficulty he arranged to visit a session of Parliament, "one day too late to hear Mr. Gladstone" but he felt the other speakers were "well worth hearing."[17]

Curwen gave a garden party at which teachers and conductors greeted Root "as an old friend." These men had used his books in teaching and had conducted his compositions; one of them told him they "had been brought up" on his works.[18]

On a particular Sunday Curwen and Root went to the Chapel Royal, St. James's Palace, which Root called "the worshiping place of royalty and nobility when in London." It was "a small chapel, long and narrow, but rich and elaborate in decorations," particularly the section reserved for the royal family. One of the "gentlemen of the chapel royal" surprised Root by revealing that he had given *The Haymakers* seventeen times.[19]

In London Root found a number of his works in the catalog of the national library. "Let my reader see this picture," he wrote later. He was in "the largest reading-room in the world," a "vast rotunda" where hundreds of people could read and study. His works covered twenty-three pages in the handwritten catalog with four to six entries per page. For "Just Before the Battle, Mother" there were twelve editions, vocal and instrumental, by six different publishers.[20]

Root called his *Flower Queen* "the first American cantata printed in England." He observed that most American cantatas had appeared there soon after their publication in the United States. This proved, according to Root, "not that we are better composers than the English, but that we are nearer and more in sympathy with those for whom we write."[21]

The London Sunday School Union published their own edition of Root's cantata, *Under the Palms,* and volunteered to pay royalty on it, which legally they did not have to do. Root explained that "All American compositions were as free to them as theirs were to us"[22] at the time. The English publisher of Root's cantata *David the Shepherd Boy* had the accompaniment arranged for a large orchestra. Attending a Swedenborgian Church conference in Lancashire, Root made contacts that led to his writing several more cantatas.

"On the steamship *City of Rome* coming home" there was a concert for the benefit of a "seamen's charitable association," Root reported. He sang a solo titled "The Sea." Someone recognized him as the composer of "The Battle Cry of Freedom" and "Tramp, Tramp, Tramp"; Americans on board "gave three ringing cheers." Root found it pleasant "to find, after all, that a 'prophet' might have some 'honor in his own country.'"[23]

On March 8, 1889, Root was honored with a celebration of his work. Two hundred students and teachers and two hundred guests attended the event in the Hyde Park section of Chicago where he lived. Chicago papers described the scene: flags and banners on the walls, tablets with the names of his best-known songs. On the platform army muskets stood in stacks of three. Birds' nests, symbolizing a united and peaceful country, "rested" in the "cradles formed by the bayonets." An army tent with "a miniature campfire" stood on one side. Root's portrait, "draped in national colors," hung over the platform. Root listened as letters from distinguished people were read. The tributes reflected the mixture of nostalgia and respect with which the public looked back on the Civil War. The governor of Illinois, J. W. Fifer, wrote about those years when "more than a million voices joined in the chorus, 'The Union Forever.'" He predicted that history would place Root's name beside those of "our great generals." Samuel Francis Smith, author of the words of "America" ("My country, 'tis of thee), wrote, "There is no greater honor or privilege than to have attuned the harp of the nation to words and tunes of patriotic zeal." The poet James Russell Lowell recalled Root's war songs and "how vividly our hearts beat in tune to them." Col. Fred Grant, son of Ulysses S Grant, wrote "His songs were a great comfort to the soldiers during the war, and helped to lighten the fatigues of many a weary march. Tell Dr. Root that I am grateful for the service he rendered."

Dr. H. H. Belfield, principal of the Chicago Manual Training School, had been a prisoner of war July 31, 1864, in Newnan, Georgia. He recalled that the prisoners sang Union war songs. He admitted that when they sang "Rally round the flag, boys, down with the *traitor*" he expected some kind of retribution; instead, a growing audience of their captors wanted to hear more.[24] He went on to describe imprisonment in late summer 1864 near Charleston, South Carolina. He and his fellow prisoners were horrified by the condition of other prisoners arriving from Andersonville. The Charleston prisoners shared their scant food with the newcomers, then sang for them "long into the night." Their final song was "Tramp, Tramp, Tramp," the words of which encouraged the hope of freedom.[25]

In a letter written in August, 1891, Lydia Avery Coonley described Root as a "gentleman of the old school." He was past the age of seventy; she said he stood tall and straight and his hair was white. He had a kind face and "gentle" eyes. She called his voice "a deep bass, full and round" and said she enjoyed seeing him sit at the piano, play his own accompaniments and sing his favorite songs: "Rocked in the Cradle of the Deep"; Henry Russell's "Ivy Green"; and Schubert's "Wanderer." [26]

"Time has changed the terrible realism of the march and the battle-field into tender and hallowed memories," Root observed in his autobiography. "The songs that were then sung have come back with redoubled interest." On "all patriotic occasions" they were brought out again. Root felt that "the most deeply stirred and enthusiastic audiences" of the time were those at the "war-song

George F. Root about 1890. *New England Magazine*, January 1896.

concerts." He remembered with special pleasure a concert given by the Apollo Club of Chicago. Root conducted his song of a lifetime; Jules Lumbard sang it "as he had in the 1860s." The huge crowd stood and joined with the band and chorus, singing "Yes, we'll rally round the flag, boys." The sound was "never to be forgotten."[27] Soon after that concert Root was elected a member of the Military Order of the Loyal Legion of the United States. At his initiation, he was asked to sing his most famous song. The Loyal Legion was founded in 1865 for officers and former officers of the United States Army. As years went by the honor of eligibility was extended to the eldest sons of veteran officers. A third group of eligible men were those who "rendered important service" during the war.[28]

Finishing his autobiography in 1891, Root claimed that he could not imagine "a pleasanter life for myself than the one I now live." When he was not traveling and teaching normals or conventions, he worked at home. His workroom was "at the top of the house," as far from "the parlor and the piano" as possible. The view from his windows was worth the climb to the top floor. He could look "east over the ever-changing waters of the lake" or north over "one of its bays" to the center of the city, only seven miles away. Each weekday he went to his "pleasant quarters" at the Chicago branch of John Church Company, his publishers, "in case any one wishes to see me." About fifty trains passed each way every day. Root thought "the lovely ride by the lake" could not be equaled anywhere in the world. He had begun the autobiography on October 1, 1888, when his family gathered to celebrate the fiftieth anniversary of his leaving home, as he said, "to commence my musical life." Most of the autobiography was written in 1889 and first published serially in *Church's Musical Visitor*. He apologized for "the appearance of self-praise" created by "certain sayings and events" in his account. "I hope the reader will see that my story would not be complete without them, and on that ground excuse the apparent egotism."[29] The reader who expected a detailed personal account would be disappointed. Root's diary had been destroyed in the Chicago fire.

A review reprinted from *The New York Examiner* said *The Story of a Musical Life* brought to mind the once-familiar saying that if a man were permitted to write all the songs of a country he need not care who made its laws. Popular songs had a serious effect on people's character, the paper claimed. "The favorite songs of the season are an index of the average culture of the people who enjoy them." Music could "make the people either better or worse"—it would either elevate or degrade taste. The *Examiner's* reviewer described Root's autobiography as "the story of a typical American life," its "struggles and triumphs" leading to the success that came with "perseverance."[30]

At the age of 71, Root hadn't changed his mind about music for "the people." Some critics and professional musicians denounced the illustrious Madame Patti's singing "Home, Sweet Home" and "The Last Rose of Summer" in her concerts. Root gave his strong opinion of their criticism in an article written for *Church's Musical Visitor* and picked up by *Music* magazine. People could benefit musically "only by music that they like," he wrote. A single concert performance was no place, nor was it an appropriate time, to educate people in music they did not understand. Listeners must enjoy music in order for it to have emotional or aesthetic value for them. Root warned critics not to assume that their judgments were expressions of public opinion; and, he insisted, "as in other matters of education, you must begin where the people are."[31] In a similar article about "Jenny Lind and the Old Songs," he praised Theodore Thomas's orchestra concerts where people gradually learned to appreciate better music through repeated hearings.[32]

In 1893 Chicago hosted the World's Columbian Exposition; Root was vice-chairman of the "Committee on Musical Congresses." While Chicago prepared for the "Columbian" fair, Root composed the music for a cantata, *Columbus, the Hero of Faith*.

On a winter night in 1895, the last year of Root's life, the stage of the Chicago Auditorium was decorated for a War Song Concert with tents to make it resemble an army camp of thirty years earlier. In the audience was Lydia Avery Coonley, who described the event in a magazine article. Seventy-five-year-old George Root sang the verses of his "Battle Cry"; an audience estimated at five thousand answered with the chorus. As the song was coming to a close Robert Lincoln, son of the assassinated president, was the first to stand. Men shouted "Hurrah!" and "Bravo!" Women waved their handkerchiefs. Finally, far up in the balcony someone led three cheers for George Root.[33]

In the summer of 1895 Root and his wife Mary Olive went to their summer home on Bailey Island, Maine, earlier than usual to prepare for their fiftieth wedding anniversary. Root enjoyed his summer's work. He was writing two cantatas.[34] Appropriately for the composer of "Rally Round the Flag," one of them was *Our Flag with the Stars and Stripes*. This cantata was a historical sketch of the United States from the Revolution to the Civil War. Columbia, Uncle Sam and Father Time were among the characters. Most of the music was new, but in a Civil War scene "The Battle Cry of Freedom" and "Tramp, Tramp, Tramp" were included. The cantata ended with a "Song of Peace" and the full chorus waving flags and singing "Hail to the Red, White and Blue!"

A flagpole stood beside Root's summer home, which was called The Mooring. Every day he raised and lowered an eighteen-foot flag there, his daughter wrote.[35] On August 6, 1895, Root worked all morning at his desk as usual. He seemed in good health apart from an occasional pain in his chest, "which was considered neuralgic," his daughter said. His brief attacks were "the only cloud over this happy summer of '95" and they were infrequent. He had had a brief attack of pain the day before, but "this morning he felt well." He helped one of his sisters choose the material for building shelves. He lifted boxes and boards "with as much vigor and interest as ever." After that he went to his desk and worked all morning. He took off his spectacles and laid them on his manuscript, then rose from his chair, gave his arm to his wife, and they went to their son's house next door for the noon meal. "He was in the best spirits, enjoyed the meal, and accepted an invitation from my brother to go sailing," Clara recalled. He went home, perhaps to change clothes, and "when he reached his room, was suddenly attacked by the pain in his chest." Through an open window he spoke with his son, telling him that he "was ill and could not go." He went to bed immediately. At 1:30 his family sent for a doctor who applied "palliatives" but "in half an hour he was unconscious" and at 2:30 he was dead.[36] His death certificate gave his age as "74 years, 11 mos. 7 days."

Family members had come to Bailey Island to celebrate the fiftieth wedding anniversary. Root's wife, his children, and his oldest sister were with him when he died. Someone lowered to half-staff the flag he had raised that morning. Clara believed her father had died the way he would have wished, with no "season of infirmity" when he could not write. He had gone "into that world where he implicitly believed he would be permitted still to be useful," she wrote. The funeral was held at home, in a room "full of sunshine and flowers."

The Reverend William Worcester conducted the funeral service August 9. "God is our refuge and strength, a very present help in trouble," he began. He spoke of Root's empathy with "the life of the people" and said Root gave expression to that life "in songs which were the voice of the people."[37] More than forty relatives sang the one piece Root wanted sung on this occasion, the Doxology: "Praise God from whom all blessings flow."[38] Early the next morning Root's sons Frederick and Charles took the casket in a "plain wagon" to the wharf, his daughter Clara recalled. A white boat carried it away. In the cemetery at North Reading, Massachusetts, his body, wrapped in the flag, was buried beside his parents. Chicago's music businesses were closed on the afternoon of August 9 in observance of Root's funeral. John Church Company closed its businesses in Cincinnati, New York, and Boston all day on the 9th.[39]

"Apparently, no one who once saw him ever forgot him," Root's grandson Ralph wrote. Ralph had traveled extensively in the Midwest some years earlier. Wherever he went, it seemed, he met elderly people who had attended Root's musical conventions. These people spoke "endlessly" of "what a wonderful man he was," Ralph recalled. "I was standing on the railroad platform in Galena, Kansas, one day in 1902 when a little old man walked up to me and asked 'Was George F. Root your grandfather?' When I said 'Yes,' he replied, 'If I had a grandfather like that, I'd be the happiest man alive,' and walked quickly away." Ralph gave his personal impressions of his grandfather, calling him "a deeply religious man, a total abstainer all his life from everything one is supposed to abstain from. He was the personification of gentleness, self-abnegation and conscientiousness." The conscientiousness caused him to spend many hours in prayer. His "wickedest thought," in grandson Ralph's opinion, "was that the sermon might have been ten minutes shorter" and his most dreaded temptation was "to say damn when he hit his thumb with a hammer."

George Root's family remembered how his gentle nature served him well in one of the early Chautauqua sessions. Hastily built barracks housed the participants. Thin partitions separated the bedrooms. One night two women "chattered" loudly in the next room. Root finally spoke out in his deep, resonant voice. "Excuse me, ladies, but will you kindly speak a little louder? I didn't quite catch what Fannie said to Wilbur."[40]

At Root's grave in Harmony Vale Cemetery stands a four-sided monument. On one side are the words "Poet" "Teacher" "Singer" and "Patriot." "He loved God and Man and was beloved of both" is chiseled on another side and on a third, "His gentle memory is the heritage of his kindred."

In 1895 the John Church Company published a "Requiem March for Piano or Organ by George F. Root." His picture was on the cover. A "Note" described the circumstances. "This March was written at the publishers' request, for a special occasion, but was never printed. An unlooked-for special occasion presented itself August 6, 1895, in the death of Dr. Root himself, and the March now appears in memoriam of its author."

On July 4, 1896, a crowd estimated at ten thousand people assembled at the Coliseum in Chicago for a War Song Festival to benefit the George F. Root monument fund. "It was a great day for the 'Battle Cry of Freedom," one observer wrote. The song seemed to take on a "newborn power as Chicago's greatest singers took the solos" and a thousand children sang the choruses. Jules Lumbard, the "white-haired veteran" who "was first to sing that famous battle hymn thirty-five years before,"[41] sang it on this occasion.

Root had earned a place in the country's history. When he died the Chicago *Tribune* called him the "musician of the people." He had become a spokesman for the public, giving voice to their feelings, their experiences and their concerns through music. He had still not written great classical works in the tradition of the European composers.

Root found himself giving his own assessment of his musical career unexpectedly in 1876. Honored to be asked to give the welcoming address at the initial meeting of the Music Teachers' National Association, Root suggested that attendees hear the presentations given at this meeting with open minds, "each more determined to find the truth than to find himself right."[42] One of the presentations, however, was a verbal attack on popular music and those who wrote it. Twenty-two year-old George W. Chadwick delivered a speech in which he called popular music "trash" and described it as "dishonest, inartistic, miserable stuff." He questioned the right of songwriters to "debase" music "simply to earn bread and butter." Chadwick was on his way to becoming an influential teacher, composer, conductor, pianist, and organist. Root was the most successful composer of popular music present.[43] He had faced criticism many times, but this was in a professional gathering of seventy-five colleagues.

What Root said first in reply to Chadwick cannot be known because the reporter assigned to record the meeting, presumably in shorthand, was late. Arguing his case, Root summarized what he had written and why. He explained that the publisher Nathan Richardson had derided his six popular songs and then paid him $3,000 in royalties for one of them. He admitted that friends had asked, "Why don't you write better music?" To appease his sense of duty, he had tried writing in a classical style. His attempts at composing in that style went unsung. At first he was ashamed to put his name on his popular songs. Now he was ashamed that he had used a pseudonym. He ended strongly: "What have musicians of our class done? We have made this, if not the most, one of the most musical countries upon the face of the earth." Then, in case that sounded immodest, he added, "If it is not now it soon will be."[44]

Root studied what he called "the musical culture of the people"[45] from the perspectives of songwriter, teacher, and publisher. In his lifetime the whole country sang his songs. Thousands attended his music classes, hundreds of thousands bought and used his books. His self-assessment appeared in his autobiography: "I am simply one who, from such resources as he finds within himself, makes music for the people, having always a particular need in view. This, it seems to me, is a thing that a person may do with some success, without being either a genius or a great composer."[46] The Chicago *Tribune* concluded, "His life and work are part of the history of the American people."[47]

Appendix: Songs

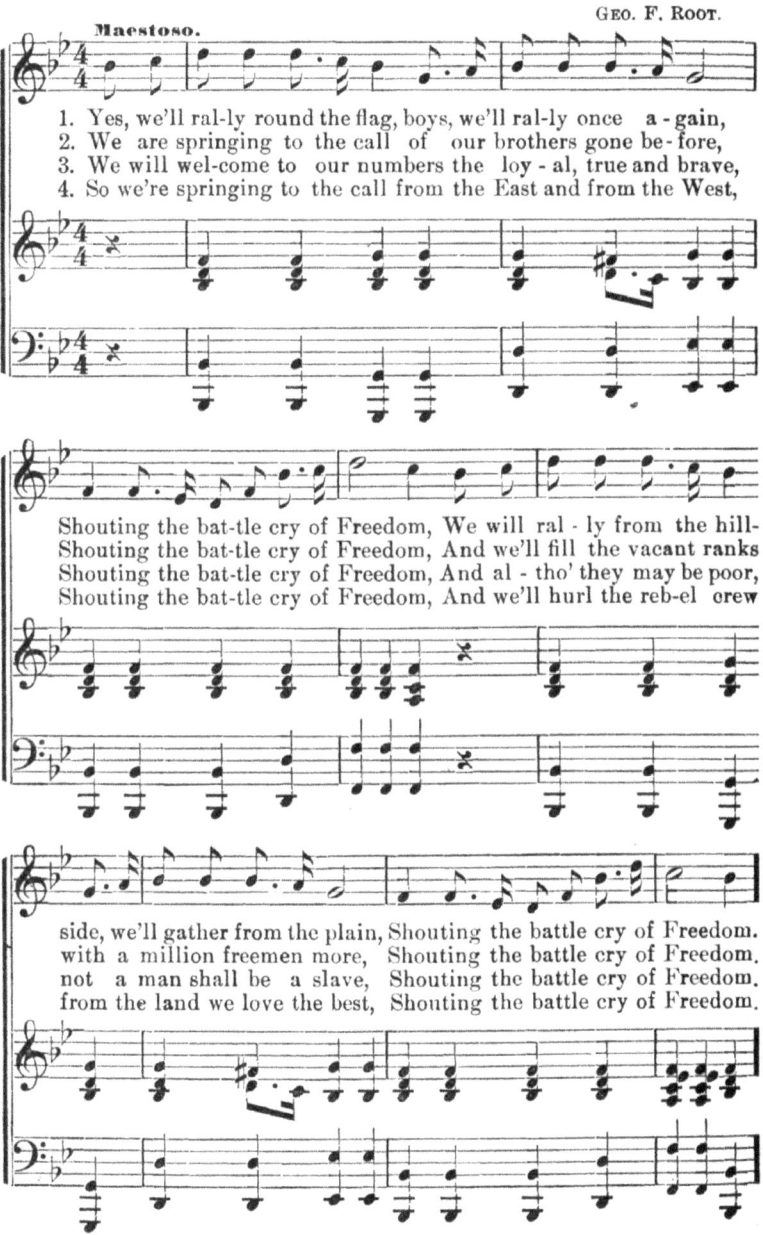

THE BATTLE CRY OF FREEDOM. Continued.

THE BATTLE CRY OF FREEDOM. Concluded.

TRAMP! TRAMP! TRAMP! Continued.

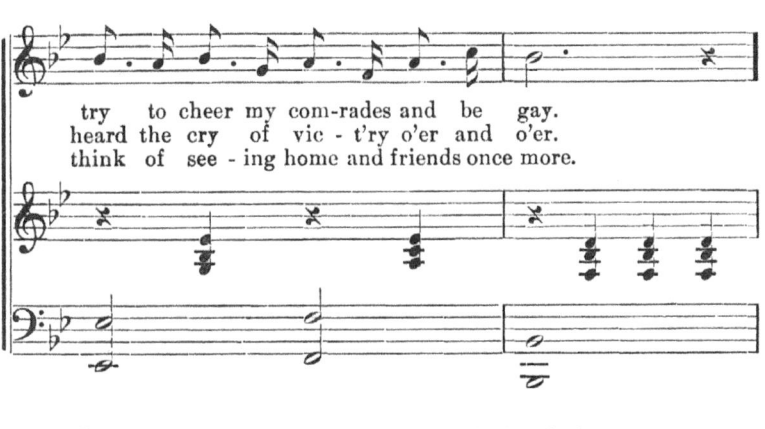

try to cheer my com-rades and be gay.
heard the cry of vic - t'ry o'er and o'er.
think of see - ing home and friends once more.

When the chorus is sung, this may be omitted after the first verse.

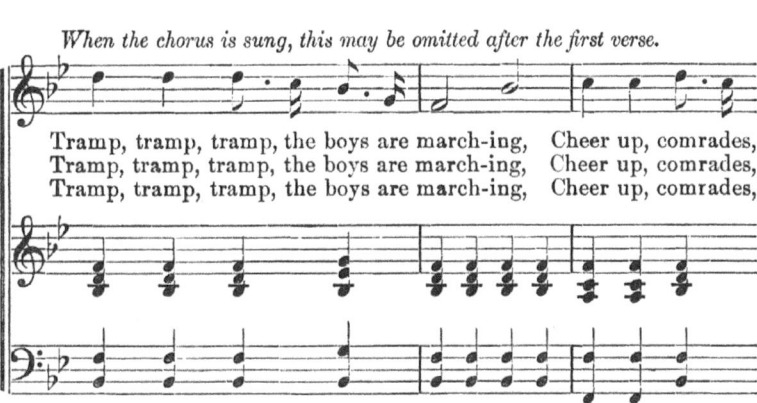

Tramp, tramp, tramp, the boys are march-ing, Cheer up, comrades,
Tramp, tramp, tramp, the boys are march-ing, Cheer up, comrades,
Tramp, tramp, tramp, the boys are march-ing, Cheer up, comrades,

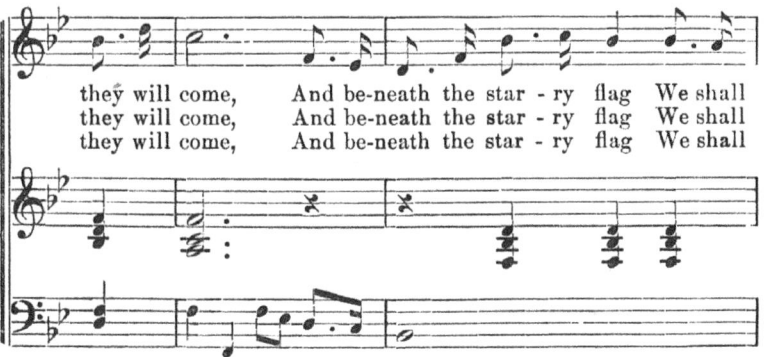

they will come, And be-neath the star - ry flag We shall
they will come, And be-neath the star - ry flag We shall
they will come, And be-neath the star - ry flag We shall

TRAMP! TRAMP! TRAMP! Concluded.

Appendix: Songs 207

The Vacant Chair.

ANDANTINO.

1. We shall meet, but we shall miss him, There will be one vacant chair; We shall linger to ca-
2. At our fire-side sad and lonely, Often will the bosom swell At remembrance of the
3. True they tell us wreaths of glory Ev-er-more will deck his brow, But this soothes the anguish

FINE.

ress him While we breathe our evening prayer. When a year ago we gathered, Joy was
sto - ry How our noble Willie fell: How he strove to bear our banner Thro' the
on - ly Sweeping o'er our heart-strings now. Sleep to - day, O ear - ly fall - en, In thy

For Chorus sing 1st verse in D. C.

in his mild blue eye, But a golden cord is severed, And our hopes in ru - in lie.
thickest of the fight, And up - hold our country's honor, In the strength of manhood's might.
green and narrow bed, Dirges from the pine and cypress Mingle with the tears we shed.

THE HAZEL DELL. Continued.

THE HAZEL DELL. Concluded.

2. In the Ha-zel Dell my Nel-ly's sleep-ing, Where the flow-ers wave, And the si-lent stars are nightly weep-ing O'er poor Nel-ly's grave; Hopes that once my bosom fondly cherished Smile no more on me; Ev'ry dream of joy, a-las, has perish'd, Nelly dear, with thee.

3. Now I'm wea-ry, friendless and for-sak-en, Watching here a-lone Nelly, thou no more will fondly cheer me With thy lov-ing tone; Yet for-ev-er shall thy gentle im-age In my mem-'ry dwell; And my tears thy lonely grave shall moisten, Nelly dear, fare-well.

Chapter Notes

Introduction

1. Leonard Grover, "Lincoln's Interest in the Theater." Privately printed, n.p., n.d., unpaginated.
2. Kenneth A. Bernard, *Lincoln and the Music of the Civil War* (Caldwell, Idaho, 1966), p. 84.
3. F. Lauriston Bullard, *Tad and His Father* (Boston, 1915), p. 65.
4. George F. Root, *The Story of A Musical Life: An Autobiography* (Cincinnati, 1891), p. 83. Cited hereafter as Root, *Story*.
5. Root, *Story*, p. 136.
6. *Chicago Tribune*, August 8, 1895.

Chapter 1

1. Mary F. Root Peck, *A Little History of a Large Family, Memoir of Sarah Flint Root by Her Daughter*. Typescript, 1891–1892, p. 18.
2. Samuel Eliot Morison, *Harvard in the Seventeenth Century, Part II* (Cambridge, 1936), p. 115.
3. Peck, *A Little History*, p. 18.
4. *Genealogical Register of the Descendants of Thomas Flint, of Salem....* Compiled by John Flint and John H. Stone. Andover, Massachusetts, 1860, p. 40.
5. Peck, *A Little History*, p. 11, N.P. Willis grew up to become an influential writer.
6. Peck, *A Little History*, p. 14.
7. Lydia Avery Coonley, "George F. Root and His Songs." *New England Magazine* (January, 1896), p. 557.
8. Peck, *A Little History*, pp. 9–10, 12.
9. Peck, *A Little History*, p. 16–17.
10. *North Reading, Massachusetts: A Guide to its Places and People*. Written and Compiled by the Federal Writers' Project of the Works Progress Administration for Massachusetts. Frederick W. Cook, Secretary of the Commonwealth, Cooperating Sponsor. (Boston and Cambridge, 1937), p. 432.
11. Peck, *A Little History*, p. 9.
12. Peck, *A Little History*, p. 19. Both George Frederick Root and Ebenezer Towner Root were baptized September 8, 1822, by the Reverend James Bradford in the Congregational Church in Sheffield. Source: Records of the Congregational Church, Sheffield, Massachusetts. Sheffield Historical Society, Mark Dewey Research Center.
13. Peck, *A Little History*, pp. 22, 24. Leo J. Murphy, compiler. "North Reading and the Ephraim Pratts, Colonial Soldiers and Tanners." *North Reading Review: Annals and Reminiscences*. December, 1964, p. 79. Frederick F. Root sold the property to his father-in-law, Daniel Flint, in 1837. When Daniel died in 1838 his will gave her use of the farm for her lifetime. Source: Digest of court records by Mary Rubenstein, North Reading, Massachusetts.
14. Peck, *A Little History*, pp. 23–25.
15. Murphy, "North Reading," p. 81. Peck, *A Little History*, p. 28.
16. Peck, *A Little History*, p. 26; Murphy, "North Reading," p. 80.

17. Peck, *A Little History*, p. 27. Root, *Story*, p. 3.
18. Peck, *A Little History*, p. 27.
19. Peck, *A Little History*, p. 34.
20. Peck, *A Little History*, p. 54.
21. George F. Root to Frederick Ferdinand Root, April 19, 1838. Copy loaned by the late Charles Woodman Root, a great-grandson of George F. Root.
22. Root, *Story*, p. 3–4. Americans had mixed feelings about the theater and its music. From the eighteenth century onward there was a popular music business, and many of the popular songs came from the theater or were adapted from operas. The theater was looked down upon by the most respectable citizens because actors may have been lowlifes; because a lady did not present herself to the public to be looked at in a theatrical setting; because theater essentially dealt with drama, which was by nature fiction and therefore distasteful to a truth-seeking religious public.
23. Root, *Story*, p. 6.
24. Root, *Story*, pp. 3–4, 7. Peck, *A Little History*, p. 39.
25. Root, *Story*, p. 8.
26. Root, *Story*, pp. 8, 10–11, 13. Among the new tunes Root was learning to play at this time were "Ward," "Hamburg," "Boylston," and "Hebron." The words of "Hebron" began "Thus far the Lord hath led me on." Hymn tunes had names that were independent of the words that could be sung with them. Theoretically, any set of hymn words with a certain number of lines and a certain number of syllables per line could be sung with a hymn tune that had the same structure.
27. Root, *Story*, pp. 13–14.
28. Root, *Story*, pp. 9, 15.
29. Root, *Story*, p. 17.
30. Root, *Story*, pp. 16–17.
31. Charles Hamm, *Yesterdays: Popular Song in America* (New York, 1979), p. 178.
32. Root, *Story*, pp. 18–20.
33. Root, *Story*, pp. 9–10.
34. Root, *Story*, pp. 14–15.
35. Root, *Story*, p. 20.
36. Root, *Story*, pp. 25–26.
37. Root, *Story*, pp. 26–27.
38. Frederick F. Root to George F. Root, March 15, 1839.
39. Root, *Story*, p. 27.
40. Peck, *A Little History*, pp. 39–41, 45.
41. Peck, *A Little History*, p. 42.
42. Root, *Story*, pp. 24–25.
43. Root, *Story*, pp. 22–23.
44. Root, *Story*, p. 30, pp. 32–33.
45. Root, *Story*, pp. 24–25
46. Root, *Story*, pp. 30–31.
47. Root, *Story*, pp. 31–32.
48. In his autobiography Root referred to this as the Winter Street church. Its formal name was Central Congregational Church, according to the *Boston Musical Gazette*, April 26, 1847.
49. Root, *Story*, pp. 33–35.
50. Root, *Story*, pp. 35–36.

Chapter 2

1. Root, *Story*, pp. 37–39.
2. Root, *Story*, p. 38. Also known as "The Church of the Strangers," this was a Presbyterian church.
3. Root, *Story*, pp. 37–38.
4. Rutgers Female Institute commencement programs and annual circulars, 1847–1864. New York Historical Society Library.
5. Peck, *A Little History*, p. 54.
6. Frederick F. Root, unpublished journal, November 8–30, 1845.
7. Root, *Story*, p. 27.
8. Peck, *A Little History*, p. 48.
9. Sarah M. Reilay to Major Weyant, June 6, 1928. Kate Chase file, New York Historical Society.
10. *New York Musical Review & Choral Advocate*, May 1853, p. 72. Cited hereafter as *Review*. Published from 1850 to 1873, the magazine went through several changes of its title: *New York Musical Review and Choral Advocate*, *New York Musical Review and Gazette*, *Musical Review and Musical World*, *New York Weekly Review of Music, Literature, Fine Arts, and Society*, and *New York Weekly Review*.
11. Root, *Story*, pp. 39, 53.
12. Root, *Story*, pp. 46–48.
13. Root, *Story*, p. 43.
14. George F. Root to Sarah Flint Root, June 23, 1845.
15. James Pierce Root. *Root Genealogical Records, 1600–1870*. New York, 1870, p. 486.
16. Peck, *A Little History*, pp. 47–48.
17. George Woodman to Mary Olive Woodman, March 3, 1845.
18. Frederick Ferdinand Root to George F. Root, March 15, 1839.

19. Peck, *A Little History*, p. 55.
20. Peck, *A Little History*, p. 60.
21. Root, *Story*, p. 41.
22. Root, *Story*, p. 52. Evidently one of his Boston hymn tunes was "Rosedale." In a later book it is dated 1843.
23. "See the Sky Is Darkling." (G. P. Reed, Boston, 1845.) The words were written by "H. D.," whose identity was not explained.
24. Root, *Story*, 52–53. *The Young Ladies Choir* was published in 1846 by Leavitt, Trow and Company of New York.
25. What Root called "the first book that I had anything to do with that sought a publisher" was *Root and Sweetser's Collection of Church Music; Comprising Many of the Most Popular and Useful Tunes in Common Use, together with a Great Variety of New and Original Psalm and Hymn Tunes, Sentences, Motets, Anthems, Chants, Etc. Designed for the Use of Choirs, Congregations, Singing Schools, and Societies*. New York: John Wiley, 1849. In retrospect, Root decided the *Collection* "could not be excelled" for "scientific but uninteresting exercises," and he explained, "I did not then realize what people in elementary musical states needed" (*Story*, p. 54). A note in *Root and Sweetser's Collection* referred users to *The Singer's Manual for Teachers, Pupils, and Private Students* by Frederick A. Adams, A. M., G. F. Root, and J. E. Sweetser (New York, 1849) for "a scientific exhibition of the principles and methods of vocal culture."
26. William Flint Root was born January 8 and died December 21, 1848. Genealogical research by Mary Rubenstein of North Reading, Massachusetts, indicated that he was called Willie.
27. Root, James P. *Root Genealogical Records*, p. 486.
28. Root, *Story*, p. 40
29. Peck, *A Little History*, p. 58.
30. *Boston Musical Gazette*, November 23, 1846.
31. Root, *Story*, pp. 41–43. In 1847 Eisfeld wrote a piece called "A Voice from the Lake" for Root's quartet. Root had it printed in *The Story of a Musical Life* (1891), pp. 229–231.
32. *Boston Musical Gazette*, September 28, 1846.
33. Root, *Story*, p. 49.
34. Root, *Story*, p. 50.
35. "The Voice of Love (Gently, Ah, Gently)." Words by W. L. Rede. G. P. Reed, Boston, 1848.
36. *The Columbian Lady's and Gentleman's Magazine, Embracing Literature in Every Department, Embellished with Steel Line and Mezzotint Engravings, Music and Fashions*. Edited by Stephen M. Chester. March 1848, pp. 142–143.
37. Root, *Story*, 55–56.
38. *Boston Musical Gazette*, October 1, 1850, p. 232.
39. *Musical Review and Choral Advocate*, December 1850, pp. 97, 106. Prior to Root's departure for Europe, the paper announced that he would be their Paris correspondent while he was there. The issues for 1851, which would have contained his letters, have not been located.
40. *Choral Advocate*, December 1850, pp. 106–107.
41. Van Alstyne, Fanny (Crosby), *Memories*, p. 81. The farewell song is also mentioned in her *Life-Story*, p. 81.
42. Root, *Story*, pp. 59–60.
43. Root, *Story*, pp. 65–66.
44. Root, *Story*, p. 63.
45. Root, *Story*, pp. 65–68.
46. Root, *Story*, pp. 63–70
47. Root, *Story*, pp. 75–78.
48. Root, *Story*, pp. 78–80.
49. *The Flower Queen; or the Coronation of the Rose*. By George F. Root (Mason Brothers, 1852).
50. Frances Jane (Fanny) Crosby (1820–1915) became blind when she was six weeks old and wrote her first hymn at the age of eight years. Over a span of eighty years she wrote the words of several thousand hymns. She taught at the New York Institute for the Blind from September 1847 to March 1 1858, according to newspaper clippings in a Fanny Crosby scrapbook at New York Public Library, Lincoln Center. In the course of her career she taught English grammar, rhetoric, and Greek, Roman and American history.
51. Root, *Story*, pp. 81–82.
52. *Review*, April 5, 1856, p. 97.

Chapter 3

1. Root, *Story*, p. 83.
2. *Boston Musical Gazette*, September 28, 1846.
3. Ronald L. Davis, *A History of Music in American Life*, Volume I (Malabar, Florida), 1982, p. 106.
4. Root, *Story*, p. 91.
5. Julius Mattfeld, ed. *Variety Music Cav-*

alcade 1620–1961: A Chronology of Vocal and Instrumental Music Popular in the United States (Englewood Cliffs, New Jersey), 1952, p. 90.

6. Root, *Story*, p. 89.

7. "The Hazel Dell" (William Hall & Son, New York, 1852). Root signed the first editions of "Hazel Dell" with his pseudonym, Wurzel. Later editions named both Wurzel and Geo. F. Root.

8. Quinn and O'Neill, eds. *The Complete Poems and Stories of Edgar Allan Poe*, Volume II (New York, 1973), p. 982.

9. Jon W. Finson, in *The Voices That Are Gone*, discussed the circumstances that surrounded these songs. At that time most deaths occurred in the home; family or friends prepared the body for burial; the body remained in the home until the funeral; people sometimes surrounded the face of the deceased with fresh flowers in the casket.

10. "Pictures of Memory." To John P. Crosby, Esq. Words by Alice Carey (William Hall & Son, New York, 1852). The usual spelling of her name is Cary.

11. *Review*, June 1, 1852, p. 89.

12. Root, *Story*, 95–96. "Gently, Ah, Gently (The Voice of Love)" was published four years before "Pictures of Memory" and his first hit song, "The Hazel Dell."

13. Root, *Story*, p. 83.

14. "Fare Thee Well, Kitty Dear" (William Hall & Son, New York, 1852). On many songs of this period no lyricist is named and no source is given for the words.

15. Crosby, Fanny (Frances J. Van Alstyne). *Memories of Eighty Years* (Boston, 1906), pp. 111–112.

16. *Review*, December 1, 1852, 185.

17. "Mary of the Glen." Words by Charles G. Eastman, Esq., (Wm. Hall & Son, New York, 1852).

18. "The Reaper on the Plain." Words by C. G. Eastman. Dedicated "To Charles T. White Esq." (William Hall & Son, New York, 1852).

19. " The Old Folks Are Gone." Words and Music by G. Friedrich Wurzel (William Hall & Son, New York, 1852).

20. "Early Lost, Early Saved." Words by the Rev. Dr. Bethune (William Hall & Son, New York, 1852).

21. *Review*, July 1, 1852, p. 106.

22. "They Sleep in the Dust" (William Hall and Son, New York, 1852).

23. *Musical Review*, May 1, 1852, p. 73.

24. "Gently, Gently Wake the Song" (William Hall & Son, New York, 1852). Root, *Story*, pp, 28, 91; Epstein, *Music Publishing*, 21.

25. " Mother, Sweet Mother, Why Linger Away?" Words by Miss Frances Jane Crosby (William Hall & Son, New York, 1852).

26. "The Father's Coming." Words by Mary Howitt, music by George F. Root (William Hall & Son, New York, 1852). "The Father's Coming" was dedicated to C. M. Cady, who later became a principal in the music firm of Root & Cady. Chauncey Marvin Cady (1824–1889) attended Oberlin College for one year and then studied at the University of Michigan, where he was awarded the Bachelor of Arts degree. A notice in the *Musical Review and Choral Advocate* for January 1, 1852, announced that Cady had become a dealer in sheet music and instruments and would ship orders to all parts of the country. Epstein, *Music Publishing*, pp. 23–24. In November 1852 the *Review* announced that Cady would have "editorial charge" of the magazine.

27. *Review*, May 1, 1852, pp. 72–73.

28. "The Topsy Polka" (William Hall & Son, New York, 1852).

29. Harry Birdoff, *The World's Greatest Hit— Uncle Tom's Cabin* (New York, 1947), p. 79.

30. David McCullough, "The Unexpected Mrs. Stowe" in *Brave Companions: Portraits in History* (New York, 1992), p. 43.

31. George Root's sister Helen married the Rev. George Adams on December 30, 1851. Source: Genealogical chart by Mary Rubenstein, North Reading, Massachusetts.

32. Charles Hamm, *Yesterdays: Popular Song in America* (New York and London: W. W. Norton and Company, 1979), p. 84.

33. "Poor Robin's Growing Old. Song and Chorus As Sung by Wood's Minstrels." Written by G. Friedrich Wurzel (William Hall & Son, New York, 1853). No lyricist was credited for the words.

34. *New York Clipper*, September 3, 1853.

35. *Review*, February, 1853, p. 32.

36. "The Greenwood Bell." Words by Frances Jane Crosby (William Hall & Son, New York, 1853). Root dedicated this song to his brother-in-law J. C. Woodman, one of the teachers in the initial session of the New York Normal Musical Institute. Woodman's hymn, "State Street," appeared in Bradbury and Root's book *The Shawm*.

37. "Green-Wood Cemetery," <www.greenwood.com/brooklynsgwc.asp> (Summer, 2001).

38. *Review,* January 19, 1854, p. 31.
39. "They've Sold Me Down the River (The Negro Father's Lament)." By G. Friedrich Wurzel (William Hall & Son, New York, 1853).
40. Root, *Story,* p. 89.
41. Root and Mason conducted a musical convention in August 1853 that closed with a performance of the cantata *Daniel* by three hundred singers. *Review,* January 5, 1854, p. 11.
42. Root, *Story,* p. 89. Like similar books of the time, *The Shawm* had a title that could function as an introduction and perhaps as an advertisement: *The Shawm; A Library of Church Music; Embracing About One Thousand Pieces, Consisting of Psalm and Hymn Tunes Adapted to Every Meter in Use, Anthems, Chants, and Set Pieces; To Which is Added an Original Cantata, Entitled DANIEL; OR, THE CAPTIVITY AND RESTORATION. Including also, The Singing Class; an Entirely New and Practical Arrangement of the Elements of Music, Interspersed with Social Part-Songs for Practice. By William B. Bradbury and George F. Root, Assisted by Thomas Hastings and T. B. Mason.* The publisher was Mason Brothers. *Shawm* was historically the name of a wind instrument, a predecessor of the clarinet.
43. *Review,* October 1855, p. 155.
44. *Review,* March 1853, p. 43.
45. *Review,* April 1853, pp. 57, 59.
46. Root, *Story,* pp. 89–90.
47. Murphy, "North Reading," p. 83.
48. Research papers compiled by Mary Rubenstein, North Reading, Massachusetts.
49. *Review,* March 1853, p. 40.
50. *Review,* May 1853, p. 71.
51. Root, *Story,* pp. 84–87.
52. *Review,* March 1, 1852, p. 42 and April 1, 1852, p. 55.
53. Root, *Story,* p. 88.
54. *Review,* August 1853, pp. 118–119.
55. *Review,* February 2, 1854, pp. 34, 81.
56. *Review,* September 14, 1854, p. 324; October 26, 1854, p. 373; November 9, 1854, p. 389; November 23, 1854, p. 403.
57. Root, *Story,* p. 98. "There's Music in the Air" appeared in the December 15 issue of the *Review* as a quartet. In 1857 a new arrangement of it appeared in sheet music. In 1864 J. W. Davies and Sons of Richmond, Virginia, published their own edition of the song. *Variety Music Cavalcade* listed it as one of the most popular songs in America in 1854.
58. George C. D. O'Dell, *Annals of the New York Stage* (New York, 1927–1949). Volume VI, p. 327.
59. "Old Josey." Song and Chorus by Wurzel (William Hall & Son, New York, 1854).
60. *Review,* May 25, 1854, p. 190.
61. Nancy A., Walker, *Fanny Fern* (New York, 1993), pp. 13, 17.
62. Root, *Story,* p. 59.
63. Peck, *A Little History,* p. 11.
64. *Review,* May 19, 1855, p. 169.
65. "Little Daisy. Ballad. The Subject from Ruth Hall." Music by G. F. Wurzel (Firth Pond & Co., New York, 1855).
66. *The Pilgrim Fathers.* Words by Miss Frances Jane Crosby (New York: Mason Brothers, 1854).
67. George F. Root to Helen Adams, July 31, 1854
68. *Review,* September 14, 1854, p. 324.
69. *Review,* April 26, 1855, pp. 138–139.
70. *Review,* January 18, 1855, pp. 30–31.
71. *Review,* January 18, 1855, p. 1.
72. *Richmond Daily Dispatch,* March 13, 1855, pp. 19, 20.
73. Olson, Ivan Walter Jr. "The Roots and Development of Public School Music in Richmond, Virginia 1782–1907." Unpublished doctoral dissertation, University of Michigan, 1964, pp. 26–28.
74. *Review,* March 29, 1855, p. 107.
75. *Review,* April 26, 1855, pp. 140, 141.
76. "Come to Me Quickly." By Wurzel (William Hall & Son, New York, 1855).
77. "My Weary Heart Is All Alone." Song and Chorus by G. F. Wurzel. Dedicated to Francis H. Brown. One edition dated 1855 was published by S. Brainard's Sons, Cleveland, probably after 1855.
78. *Review,* September 8, 1855, p. 311.
79. *Variety Music Cavalcade.* "Rosalie, the Prairie Flower." By Wurzel (Geo. F. Root.) Russell & Richardson, Boston, 1855). The song still appeared occasionally in song collections almost a century after it was written. These later collections dropped the third verse, about the death of a lovely child. By then that theme was no longer popular.
80. Julius Mattfeld, *Variety Music Cavalcade* (Englewood Cliffs, New Jersey, 1962).
82. Root, *Story,* 110–111. $3,000 in royalties indicated that more than 125,000 copies had been sold according to Russell Sanjek, *American Popular Music,* Vol. II, p. 120. The six songs in the "Rosalie" group have a collective cover titled "Six Songs by Wurzel" with "Geo. F. Root" in smaller letters and a list of the original six titles below. The original six were "Glad to Get Home," "The Honeysuckle

Glen," "Rosalie, the Prairie Flower," "The Church Within the Wood," "All Together Again," and "Proud World, Good bye! I'm Going Home."
  82. Root, *Story*, pp. 95, 97.
  83. Root, *Story*, p. 91.
  84. This comment appeared in the *Review* May 31, 1856, p. 166. The August 3, 1854 issue of the *Review* noted that Root had just taught a class in Beemersville, Sussex County, New Jersey.
  85. *Review*, July 14, 1855, p. 231.
  86. Story, 101.
  87. Root, Story, p. 104. *Review*, July 14, 1855, p. 225.

Chapter 4

  1. Root, *Story*, pp. 19–20.
  2. Among his songs for a particular year (1857) were "Departed Days," "Grieve Not the Heart That Loves Thee" and "Home's Sweet Harmony." In the same year (according to *Variety Music Cavalcade*) his arrangement of "Flee As a Bird" (with words by Mary S. B. Dana) was among the most popular songs in the country, as was J. P. Webster's "Lorena."
  3. Root, *Story*, p. 101.
  4. *Review*, August 8, 1857, p. 247.
  5. Root, *Story*, p. 101.
  6. He would be absent from the musical convention scene part of the time, but he would not be out of touch. During the summer, people could address mail to Willow Farm, North Reading, Massachusetts. After that he could be reached through his publishers: Mason Brothers, William Hall & Son, Firth Pond & Company, all in New York, and Oliver Ditson and George P. Reed & Company in Boston. *Review*, July 14, 1855, p. 237.
  7. *Review*, September 22, 1855, p. 321.
  8. Root was scheduled to teach in Deckertown (Sussex County), New Jersey, for the first week of September; Chester (Orange County), New York, for the second week and Glastonbury, Connecticut, for the third and fourth weeks. *Review*, September 8, 1855, p. 309. He would be in Westport, Connecticut, for the first week of October; Le Roy (Genesee County), New York, for the second week (a seven-day convention) and Perry (Wyoming County), New York, for seven days beginning October 18. *Review*, October 6, 1855, p. 340. For the first three weeks of November he planned to teach evening classes in Reading, Massachusetts, a few miles from his home. He would be in Sag Harbor, Long Island, for the fourth week of November. *Review*, November 17, 1855, p. 389.
  9. Olson, "Public School Music in Richmond, Virginia 1782–1907," p. 30.
  10. Richmond *Daily Dispatch* Wednesday, December 5, 1855.
  11. Richmond *Dispatch*, December 17, 1855.
  12. Richmond *Enquirer*, December 28, 1855.
  13. Root, *Story*, p. 103.
  14. Richmond *Enquirer*, Tuesday Morning, December 25, 1855.
  15. *Review*, February 9, p. 40.
  16. *Review*, March 8, p. 72.
  17. *Review*, April 19, p. 119. Readers could follow the prominent musical convention teachers—Mason, Bradbury, Woodbury, Cady, Root and others—through the *Review's* "Special Notices" announcing their schedules by the month, and through occasional reports by participants or observers, sometimes by the teachers themselves. In addition to listing Root's musical conventions and their locations, the *Review* published a series of his articles on vocal training in 1856.
  18. *Review*, March 22, 1856, p. 86.
  19. *Review*, February 9, 1856, p. 40; March 8, p. 72; March 22, p. 86; April 19, p. 119; May 31, p. 166.
  20. *Review*, November 15, 1856, pp. 358–359.
  21. Root, *Story*, 112.
  22. Root, *Story*, 99; Dena J. Epstein, compiler, Root & Cady Publishing Company Archives, The Newberry Library.
  23. Root *Story*, p. 107.
  24. The students came from Georgia, Alabama, Virginia, Tennessee, Ohio, Iowa, Michigan, Illinois, Wisconsin, New Jersey, Pennsylvania, Connecticut, New York, Maine, New Hampshire, Vermont and Massachusetts.
  25. Root, *Story*, p. 107.
  26. *Review* [1856] June 14, p. 182; June 28, p. 197; July 12, p. 214; July 14, p. 182; August 9, p. 247.
  27. Root, *Story*, p. 108.
  28. *Review*, October 4, 1856, p. 306.
  29. *Review*, October 4, 1856, p. 306.
  30. *Review*, September 6, 1856, p. 279.
  31. *Review*, November 29, 1856, pp. 377, 375.
  32. *Review*, February 7, 1857, p. 37.
  33. *Review*, March 21, 1857, p. 89.
  34. From the opera *Amilie*, by Rooke. *Review*, May 6, 1857, pp. 149–150.
  35. Root, *Story*, p. 114.

36. *Review,* August 22, 1857, p. 262.
37. *Review,* February 7, 1857, p. 35.
38. Root, *Story,* pp. 114–115.
39. *Review,* April 5, 1856, p. 97.
40. Gilbert Chase, "America's Music, the First Century." *The American Music Teacher,* September/October 1976, p. 18.
41. Painters and composers represented farm life and rural scenes in their works. William Sidney Mount idealized rural life in paintings such as "Long Island Farm House," "Farmers Nooning," and "Dance of the Haymakers." William Henry Fry composed a symphony called "A Day in the Country."
42. Root, *Story,* p. 113.
43. *Review,* October 4, 1856, pp. 308, 315.
44. *Review,* June 13, 1857, p. 192.
45. Root, *Story,* p. 113. When *The Haymakers* was printed in the back of *The Festival Glee Book,* the role of Snipkins was omitted. When the cantata was issued as a separate publication, Snipkins's solos were grouped in an appendix and labeled to show where in the performance each of them belonged. If the cantata was to be sung "book in hand, without costume and action," the part of Snipkins was to be omitted, since its successful performance depended on "appropriate action," according to the "Explanations and Directions" in the separate edition.
46. Root, *Story,* pp. 113–114.
47. *Review,* June 25, 1857, p. 199.
48. Epstein, *Music Publishing,* p. 35.
49. Lowell Mason to W. W. Killip, February 26, 1860. Lowell Mason Papers, MSS 33. Irving S. Gilmore Music Library, Yale University.
50. Root, *Story,* p. 98. Performances of *The Haymakers* were still sung in the 1870s. The last known publication of the work was dated 1904. In 1984 A-R editions republished *The Haymakers,* edited by Dennis R. Martin. In 1978 New World Records released a recording of part two of *The Haymakers* with liner notes by Dena J. Epstein. In 1998 the recording was re-released as a compact disc.
51. *Review,* July 25, 1857, p. 230.
52. *Dwight's Journal of Music,* July 4, 1857, pp. 111–112.
53. *Dwight's Journal of Music,* July 25, 1857, pp. 133–134.
54. *Review,* September 5, 1857, pp. 278–279.
55. Root, *Story,* 109–110. Root's account of this visit and W. W. Killip's account were both written years after the incident took place, and they differed in some of the details.
56. *Review,* August 8, 1857, p. 246.
57. *Review,* September 5, 1857, 278–279.
58. *Review,* September 6, 1856, p. 281 and September 20, p. 289.
59. *Review,* August 22, 1857, p. 264.
60. *Review,* January 24, 1857, p. 24.
61. *Review,* January 10, 1857, pp. 5–6.
62. Root, *Story,* p. 132.
63. In Noah Webster's 1855 *Dictionary of the English Language* (New York: Harper & Brothers), *glee* was defined as "a composition for voices in three or more parts."
64. *Review,* November 28, 1857, p. 370.
65. *Review,* December 26, 1857, p. 402.
66. *Review,* October 17, 1857, p. 325.
67. *Review,* November 14, 1857, p. 362.
68. *Review,* October 31, 1857, p. 344–345. Planning for the coming year, Root explained that he did not organize musical conventions, but only "made arrangements" with associations that were already organized. His "terms" were "about fifty dollars a day—the variation from this price depending upon the number of days required, amount of traveling, and other expenses."
69. *Review,* December 12, 1857, p. 389.
70. *Review,* December 26, 1857, p. 406.
71. More than a hundred singers attended the four-day Morristown convention, which began December 1. *Review,* December 12, 1857, p. 386.
72. *Review,* December 26, 1857, p. 406.
73. These conventions were scheduled for Danbury, Connecticut, beginning February 17, 1858; Florida, (Orange County) New York, February 23; Afton, New York, March 2; Troy, Pennsylvania, March 9; and Niagara Falls March 15. *Review,* February 20, 1858, p. 57.
74. *Review,* March 20, 1858, p. 81. At the first concert Root's cantata *Daniel* was performed. The second program consisted of glees, quartets and solos.
75. *Review* April 3, 1858, p. 102.
76. *Review* March 6, 1858, p. 69.
77. Review May 18, 1858, p. 151.
78. Mary Olive and Charles Root to Frederick Woodman Root, May 7, 1858.
79. *Review,* Aug 21, 1858 p. 259.
80. *Review,* July 24, 1858, pp. 229–230.
81. *Review,* August 7, 1858, p. 245.
82. *Review,* August 21, 1858, p. 261.
83. *Review,* September 4, 1858, p. 274.
84. *Review,* April 3, 1858, p. 105.
85. *Review,* July 10, 1858, p. 210.

86. *Review,* September 4, 1858, p. 281.
87. Root, *Story,* p. 122.
88. Epstein, *Music Publishing,* p. 33, and Epstein, Root & Cady Publishing Company Archives, The Newberry Library.
89. *Tribune,* March 3, 1859.
90. Cady attended Union Theological Seminary from 1851 to 1853. George Root taught there in 1852–55.
91. Undated circular, Root & Cady, Chicago History Museum library.
92. Root, *Story,* p. 122.
93. Root, *Story,* pp. 126–127.
94. Root, *Story,* pp. 127–128.
95. *Review,* December 11, 1858, p. 389.
96. Root, *Story,* p. 129.
97. *Review,* February 19, 1859 p. 54.
98. "Mercantile Record," 1859–60. Epstein, Root & Cady Publishing Company Archives, The Newberry Library.
99. Epstein, *Music Publishing,* p. 35.
100. Epstein, *Music Publishing,* p. 37.
101. Helen Call Root was born April 30, 1856. At this time George and Mary Olive had two sons and two daughters. Their oldest son, Frederick, would soon be ten years old.
102. Root, *Story,* p. 121.
103. *Review,* November 26, 1859, p. 368.
104. *Review,* November 13, 1858, pp. 353–354.
105. *Review,* February 5, 1859, p. 38.
106. *Review,* February 19, 1859, p. 49.
107. *Review,* April 10, 1859, p. 120.
108. Carol Pemberton, *Lowell Mason: His Life and Work* (Ann Arbor, Michigan, 1985), p. 159.
109. *Review,* August 6, 1859, p. 246.
110. *Review,* September 4, 1858, p. 278.
111. *Review,* April 30, 1859, p. 129.
112. *Review,* August 6, 1859, p. 246.
113. Lowell Mason to W. W. Killip, February 21, 1859. Lowell Mason Papers, MSS 33. Irving S. Gilmore Music Library, Yale University.
114. Lowell Mason to W. W. Killip, February 26, 1860. Lowell Mason Papers, MSS 33. Irving S. Gilmore Music Library, Yale University.
115. Pemberton, Carol, pp. 157, 159–160. Killip, born in 1832, was an organist and choir director in Geneseo, New York, until 1857.
116. *Review,* August 20, 1859, p. 263.
117. *Review,* October 15, 1859, p. 325.
118. *Tribune,* October 15, 1859.
119. *Review,* December 10, 1859, p. 391.
120. *Review,* February 19, 1859, pp. 53, 57 and March 5, 1859, p. 69.
121. *Review,* March 19, 1859, pp. 81, 85.
122. *Dwight's Journal of Music,* March, 1859 quoted in Epstein, Dena J., liner notes for New World Records CD, *The Haymakers* by George F. Root.
123. *Review,* April 2, 1859, p. 102.
124. *Review,* June 11, 1859 p. 182.
125. *Review,* October 29, 1859, p. 336.
126. *Review,* December 10, 1859, p. 390.
127. *Review,* February 18, 1860, p. 57.
128. *Review,* March 3, 1860, p. 73.
129. The word "Diapason" meant, among other things, an organ stop that produced the instrument's characteristic tone quality. On the cover of the book there was an image of a pipe organ with a full pedal board.
130. Apparently when this collection was announced would-be contributors sent their compositions to the author-compiler. In the Preface to *The Diapason,* Root thanked Mason and Bradbury especially "for valuable assistance and contributions" and said other friends had given him aid. He said "much really excellent music that was sent for publication did not find a place in this work simply because there was of that particular meter or style more than he could print."
131. *Review,* June 9, 1860, p. 192.
132. *Review,* December 8, 1860, p. 359.
133. *Review,* September 15, 1860, p. 287.
134. *Review,* April 14, 1860, p. 115.
135. *Review,* May 12, 1860, p. 153.
136. *Review,* April 14, 1860, p. 120.
137. *Review,* April 14, 1860, p. 115.
138. *Review,* July 21, 1860, p. 231.
139. *Review,* October 13, 1860, p. 305.
140. *Review,* June 23, 1860, p. 200.
141. Root, *Story,* pp. 204–205.
142. George P. Upton, *Musical Memories: My Recollections of Celebrities of the Half Century 1850–1900* (Chicago, 1908), p. 272.
143. *Tribune,* December 3, 1860.
144. Root, *Story,* p. 123.
145. Epstein, *Music Publishing,* p. 34. *Tribune,* July 21, 1860.
146. *Tribune,* January 23, 1861.
147. *Tribune,* January 1, 1860.
148. *Tribune,* January 4, 1860.
149. *Tribune,* February 6, 1861.
150. Long, *Civil War Day by Day,* p. 31.
151. *Tribune,* April 3, 1861.
152. Sanjek, *American Popular Music,* pp. 371–372.
153. *Tribune,* February 23, 1861.
154. "Rock Me to Sleep, Mother" (G. D.

Russell and Company, Boston, 1861).
155. *Tribune,* March 14, 1861.
156. Upton, *Musical Memories,* p. 272.
157. Guyer, *History of Chicago; Its Commerce and Manufacturing Interests and Industry* (Chicago, 1862), p. 179.
158. *Tribune,* April 12, 1861.
159. Sanjek, *American Popular Music* II, p. 225; Irwin Silber, *Songs of the Civil War* (New York, 1960), p. 4.
160. Hamm, *Yesterdays,* p. 230.

Chapter 5

1. Root, *Story,* pp. 130–131.
2. *Chicago Tribune,* April 15, 1861.
3. "The First Gun Is Fired" (Root & Cady, Chicago, 1861).
4. Root, *Story,* p. 132.
5. Epstein, *Music Publishing,* p. 43.
6. *Tribune,* April 16, 1861.
7. *Tribune,* April 19, 1861.
8. *Tribune,* May 3, 1861.
9. *Tribune,* April 22, 1861.
10. "Public sentiment is everything," Lincoln said in his first debate with Stephen A. Douglas. "With public sentiment, nothing can fail; without it, nothing can succeed." Consequently, one who "moulds public sentiment" goes farther than one makes laws or hands down decisions. He "makes statutes and decisions possible or impossible to be executed." Abraham Lincoln, *Political Debates Between Abraham Lincoln and Stephen A. Douglas in the Celebrated Campaign of 1858 in Illinois; including the preceding speeches of each at Chicago, Springfield, etc. ALSO, The Two Great Speeches of Abraham Lincoln in Ohio in 1859, and a Complete Index to the Whole.* O. S. Hubbell & Company, 1895, p. 125.
11. Hamm, *Yesterdays,* p. 230.
12. "God Bless Our Brave Young Volunteers" (Root & Cady, Chicago, 1861).
13. *Tribune,* May 23, 1861.
14. "Forward, Boys, Forward!" (Root & Cady, Chicago, 1861).
15. *Tribune,* June 3, 1861.
16. *Tribune,* July 15, 1861.
17. Published by Root & Cady, 1861.
18. *Review,* November 23, 1861, p. 281.
19. "Love Thy Mother, Little One. Cradle Song" (Oliver Ditson & Company, Boston, 1861).
20. *Tribune,* September 9, 1861.
21. *Tribune,* February 3, 1862; *Tribune,* April 1, 1862.
22. *Tribune,* August 11, 1861.
23. Root, *Story,* p. 139.
24. *Tribune,* September 26, 1861.
25. Worcester *Sunday Telegram,* April 4, 1948, p. 21.
26. *Tribune,* October 22, 1861.
27. *Tribune,* October 24, 25, 1861. Stephen B. Oates, *With Malice Toward None: The Life of Abraham Lincoln* (New York, 1977), p. 263.
28. *Tribune,* October 28, 1861.
29. Worcester *Telegram,* May 28, 1939.
30. Worcester *Daily Spy,* October 31, 1861.
31. He was head of the Washburn and Moen Company, reportedly the largest manufacturer of wire in the country at that time. Washburn served one year in the Massachusetts House of Representatives and one year in the state senate. From "An Intimate Reminder of 'The Vacant Chair'" by Frank J. Metcalf in the *Worcester Telegram,* May 28, 1939.
32. Root, *Story,* p. 137.
33. *Tribune* November 2, 1861.
34. *Tribune* October 31, 1861.
35. Root, *Story,* p. 137. "Stand Up For Uncle Sam, My Boys!" Words unattributed (Root & Cady, Chicago, 1861). Root dedicated this song to Dr. H. D. Train.
36. *Tribune* October 23, 1861.
37. *Tribune,* November 28, 1861.
38. *Tribune,* December 31, 1862.
39. *Review,* January 4, 1862, p. 7.
40. "Circular. The Tenth Annual Morris County Musical Convention" Morristown, New Jersey, December 30, 1861. In The Joint Free Public Library of Morristown and Morris Township, Morristown, New Jersey.
41. *Review,* February 15, 1862, p. 44.
42. *Review,* March 1, 1862, p. 54.
43. *Review,* March 29, 1862, p. 79.
44. *Review,* April 12, 1862, p. 90.
45. *Tribune,* January 6; January 13, 1862.
46. The song began "We wait beneath the furnace-blast the pangs of transformation. Not painlessly doth God recast and mould anew the nation."
47. *Tribune,* January 27, 1862.
48. *Tribune,* February 1, 1862.
49. *Tribune,* February 17, 1862.
50. Carol Brink, *Harps in the Wind: The Story of the Singing Hutchinsons* (New York, 1947), pp. 207–211. More recent research has raised questions about Lincoln's actual statement. See Alan Lewis, *Heralds of Freedom: The Hutchinson Family Singers,* Volume I, chapter 5, pp. 1–3. <http://www.geocities.com/

unclesamsfarm/hutchinsons.htm>
51. *Tribune*, March 20, 1862.
52. *Tribune*, March 27, 1862.
53. *Tribune*, April 15, 1862.
54. *Tribune*, April 28, 1862.
55. Guyer, *History of Chicago*, pp. 179–180.
56. Root, *Story*, pp. 144–145.
57. *Tribune*, April 19, 1862.
58. *Tribune*, April 22, 1862.
59. *Tribune*, May 2, 1862.
60. Root, *Story*, 137–138.
61. Bertram G. Work, compiler, *Songs of Henry Clay Work* (New York, n.p., n.d.).
62. *Tribune*, May 2, 1862; May 8, 1862.
63. *Tribune*, June 13, 1862.
64. *Tribune*, July 16, 1862.
65. *Tribune*, July 16, 1862.
66. *Tribune*, July 4, 1862.
67. *Tribune*, July 17, 1862.
68. *Tribune*, July 19, 1862.
69. *Tribune*, July 21, 1862.
70. Root, *Story*, pp. 132–133. Root & Cady was in the "Larmon Block," a four-story building on Courthouse Square, according to Cook, *Bygone Days*, 175.
71. *Tribune*, July 28, 1862.
72. *Tribune*, July 25, 1862.
73. Root, *Story*, p. 10.
74. Root, *Story*, pp. 141–142.
75. Dena J. Epstein, "The Battle Cry of Freedom." *A Quarterly Journal of Studies in Civil War History* IV, 3 (September, 1958), p. 311.
76. *Tribune*, August 2, 1862.
77. Ishbel Ross, *Angel of the Battlefield: The Life of Clara Barton*. (New York, 1956), p. 53.
78. Lucien B. Crocker, "Episodes and Characters in an Illinois Regiment." Military Order of the Loyal Legion of the U.S.—Illinois Commandery, *Military Essays and Recollections* (Chicago, 1891), cited in Epstein, "Battle Cry," p. 315.
79. Benjamin P. Thomas, Editor. *Three Years with Grant as Recalled by War Correspondent Sylvanus Cadwallader* (New York, 1955), pp. 96–97.
80. Jesse R. Young, *What a Boy Saw in the Army* (NewYork, 1894), pp. 275–276.
81. Epstein, "Battle Cry," p. 315.
82. Nicholas Smith, "The Battle Hymns of Nations." Wisconsin Commandery War papers, Vol. 3, pp. 485–486. Quoted in Epstein, Root & Cady Publishing Company Archives, The Newberry Library.
83. George P. Upton, *Musical Memories: My Recollections of Celebrities of the Half Century 1850–1900* (Chicago, 1908), pp. 302–303.
84. Epstein, "Battle Cry," p. 313.
85. Gottschalk, Louis Moreau. *Notes of a Pianist* Jeanne Behrend, Ed. (New York, 1864), pp. 181–182.
86. Root, *Story*, p. 133. Root did not mention the name of the president or give any further information about this testimony. Several writers have assumed that Root referred to Lincoln. In an article on "Patriotic Music" in *The New Grove's Dictionary of American Music* (1986), J. J. Fuld wrote: "President Lincoln wrote to Root: 'You have done more than a hundred generals and a thousand orators.'" When he was asked, Mr. Fuld was not able to give a source for this statement. Colonel Nicholas Smith wrote: "The late Charles A. Dana ... assistant secretary of war during the rebellion, said a short time before his death in 1897 that George F. Root 'did more to preserve the Union than a great many brigadier generals, and quite as much as some brigades.'" This statement appeared in Smith's book, *Stories of Great National Songs* (1899), and in his article, "The Battle Hymns of Nations" published in *War Papers* "Read Before the Commandery of the State of Wisconsin, Military Order of the Loyal Legion of the United States." Published by the Commandery (Milwaukee, 1903), Vol. 3. Charles Woodman Root, a great-grandson of George Root, wrote that the family had many discussions about the question of a communication between Root and Lincoln. There were no details and it became a family legend. Charles Woodman Root to P. H. Carder, October 11, 1968.
87. Root, *Story*, p. 202.
88. Root, *Story*, pp. 133–135.
89. *Tribune*, January 13, 1862; September 1, 1862.
90. "De Day Ob Liberty's Comin!" Words & Music by G. F. Wurzel (Root & Cady, Chicago, 1862).
91. Willard A. and Porter W. Heaps, *The Singing Sixties* (Norman, Oklahoma, 1960), p. 89.
92. James M. McPherson, *Battle Cry of Freedom* (New York, 1988), p. 504.
93. *Tribune*, September 4, 1862.
94. *Tribune*, September 23, 1862.
95. *Tribune*, September 26, 1862.
96. *Tribune*, September 29, 1862.
97. *Tribune*, September 29, 1862.
98. *Tribune*, July 4, 1862.
99. *Tribune*, September 24, 1862.
100. Epstein, *Music Publishing*, pp. 48, 50.

The Silver Lute continued in print for some years. A later edition has the 1862 copyright date and an advertisement on the back for an 1882 book by George Root.
101. *Tribune*, November 6, 1862.
102. *Tribune*, December 31, 1862.
103. *Tribune*, December 25, 1862.
104. "Oh, Haste on the Battle." Words by R. Tompkins (Root & Cady, Chicago, 1862).
105. "Call 'Em Names, Jeff." Words by R. Tompkins, music by Wurzel (Root & Cady, Chicago, 1862).
106. *Tribune*, December 31, 1862.
107. *Tribune*, January 13, 1863.
108. *Tribune*, January 8, 1863. Lists of Chicago area men killed, wounded or missing in the battle of Stone's River at Murfreesboro were in the *Tribune* January 14, 17, and 23.
109. *Tribune*, January 15, 1863.
110. "Who'll Save the Left. A Battle Scene." Words by R. Tompkins (Root & Cady, Chicago, 1863).
111. *Tribune*, Thursday, January 15, 1863, and Monday, January 26, 1863.
112. Root, *Story*, pp. 139–140.
113. *Tribune*, April 2, 1863.
114. George Root's father, Frederick F. Root, died June 6, 1866, at Willow Farm. After that his mother, Sarah Flint Root, lived for periods of time with each of her sons and daughters. In her last years she lived with Helen and George Adams, her daughter and son-in-law, in Orange, New Jersey, where she died September 30, 1881.
115. Root, *Story*, p. 140.
116. "My department now demanded nearly all the time I could spare from writing, and to attend to that properly I must give up conventions, and consequently, Willow Farm as home. So in 1863 I moved my family to Chicago." Their oldest son Frederick Woodman Root had studied piano with B. C. Blodgett and William Mason. In Chicago "F. W." found work as an organist and divided his time between organ practice and work at Root & Cady. When the younger son Charles finished school in Chicago, both boys went to Europe to study music and languages. F. W. made music teaching his profession and Charles joined Root & Cady. Root, *Story*, pp. 143–144.
117. *Song Messenger*, June, 1863.
118. A song called "Clear the Way" and subtitled "Song of the Pacific Railroad" was published as sheet music in 1856 by its composer, Stephen C. Massett. This song had only one verse, the words of which were identical with the first verse of the one in the *Song Messenger*. The melody was different.
119. *Tribune*, April 9, 1863, and April 10, 1863.
120. *Tribune*, April 21, 1863.
121. *New York Times*, April 21, 1863.

Chapter 6

1. *Tribune*, April 30, 1863.
2. *Song Messenger*, May, 1863.
3. "Brave boys are they! Gone at their country's call. And yet, and yet, we cannot forget, that many brave boys must fall."
4. "O Jimmy farewell! your brothers fell, way down in Alabarmy; I thought they would spare a lone widder's heir, but they grafted him into the army."
5. Root, *Story*, pp. 138–139.
6. This session was advertised originally as a class for teachers. In a later ad "all who wanted to study music or to "improve themselves in this delightful art" were urged to attend. *Tribune*, June 1, 1863.
7. *Tribune*, June 16, 1863.
8. *Tribune*, July 1, 1863.
9. *Tribune*, July 4, 1863.
10. *Tribune*, July 11, 1863.
11. "Within the Sound of the Enemy's Guns." Words by the Rev. T. Newton Jones (Root & Cady, Chicago, 1863). Dedication: "In Remembrance of Gettysburg."
12. *Tribune*, July 14, 1863.
13. *Tribune*, July 17, 1863.
14. *Tribune*, August 25, 1863.
15. This was presumably the same T. Newton Jones who wrote the poem "Within the Sound of the Enemy's Guns."
16. The concert was part of a Sunday school celebration at Iowa Wesleyan University.
17. *Song Messenger*, August 1863.
18. *Song Messenger*, August 1863, p. 78.
19. *Review*, September 26, 1863, p. 234 (1860–1864 name for the *Review* was *Musical Review* and *Musical World*).
20. *Song Messenger*, September 1863.
21. *Review*, September 26, 1863, p. 234.
22. *Tribune*, Friday, July 17, 1863.
23. *Eye of the Storm*. Written and illustrated by Private Robert Knox Sneden, ed. Charles F. Bryan, Jr., and Nelson D. Lankford (New York, 2000), p. 168.
24. Sneden, *Eye of the Storm*, p. 171.
25. No sheet music copy of "On the Field

of Battle, Mother" has been found. The only version found is the single verse in the *Song Messenger,* August 1863. "On the Field of Battle, Mother" was filed for copyright July 25, 1863. The printing plate number, used by the publisher to identify and collate the printing plates, was 328. Some months later "Just Before the Battle, Mother" appeared with the same plate number.

26. "Just Before the Battle, Mother." Words and music by Geo. F. Root (Root & Cady, Chicago, 1863).
27. *Tribune,* September 30, 1863.
28. *Tribune,* October 16, 1863.
29. *Tribune,* November 1, 1863.
30. *Tribune,* November 18, 1863, cited in Epstein, *Music Publishing,* p. 51.
31. *Tribune,* July 28, 1863.
32. *Song Messenger,* November 1863.
33. *Tribune,* December 3, 1863.
34. *Tribune,* December 4, 1863.
35. *Tribune,* December 8, 1863.
36. "Will You Come to Meet Me Darling?" Words by Frances A. Baker (Root & Cady, Chicago), 1863.
37. *Song Messenger,* December 1863, p. 137.
38. *Tribune,* December 5, 1863.
39. *Tribune,* December 17, 1863.
40. *Song Messenger,* December 1863.
41 *Song Messenger,* February 1864.
42. *Song Messenger,* September 1863.
43. *Song Messenger,* March 1864, p. 190.
44. "Brother Tell Me of the Battle." Words by Thomas Manahan (Root & Cady, Chicago, 1864). "Comrades Hasten to the Battle." Words by Thomas Manahan (Henry Tolman & Co., Boston, 1864). "Oh, Will My Mother Never Come?" Song and Chorus. Words by M. Sullivan (Henry Tolman & Co., Boston, 1864).
45. *Tribune,* May 10, 1864.
46. *Tribune,* April 16, 1864.
47. "Just After the Battle" (Root & Cady, Chicago, 1864).
48. Sanjek, *American Popular Music* II, p. 227.
49. *Army Songster.* Richmond, Virginia. George L. Bidgood, 1864. Confederate Imprints (Microfilm) 3252.
50. Angle, Paul M., ed. *Three Years in the Army of the Cumberland,* pp. 300–302.
51. *Tribune,* February 8, 1864.
52. *Tribune,* February 16, 1864.
53. *Tribune,* February 23, 1864.
54. *Tribune,* May 20, 1864.
55. *Tribune,* April 17, 1864.
56. Epstein, *Music Publishing,* p. 52.
57. Furgurson, Ernest B. *Freedom Rising* (New York, 2004), pp. 233–234.
58. Norton, Army Letters, 196. Cited in the Epstein, Research Collection.
59. *Tribune,* November 12, 1863.
60. *Tribune,* March 22, 1864.
61. *Tribune,* June 4, 1864.
62. *Tribune,* August 8, 1864.
63. *Tribune,* August 16, 1864.
64. Thomas, "Colored Troops," 777–778. Henry Goddard Thomas was a Colonel in the 19th. U.S. Colored Infantry.
65. Root, *Story,* 137.
66. Karamanski, *Rally 'Round the Flag,* pp. 77–78.
67. *Tribune,* June 16, 1862.
68. *Tribune,* July 30, 1864.
69. *Tribune,* September 24, 1861.
70. For Kernstown: *Official Records of the War of the Rebellion* Vol. I, Serial no. 37, Part 1, pp. 315–319. For Mulligan's Death: *Chicago Tribune,* July 30, 1864. "Our Latest Disaster and Disgrace," *Tribune,* Sept 24, 1861. "Camp Mulligan—The Irish Brigade" (including their daily in-camp schedule), *Tribune,* July 8, 1861. For the surrender in Missouri: *Supplement to the Official Records of the Union and Confederate Armies,* ed. Janet B. Hewett, Part II, Vol. 38, Serial No. 50, pp. 103–104. General descriptions: A. T. Andreas, *History of Chicago,* Vol. II. New York, 1975, pp. 191–195; "The Siege of Lexington, Mo." By Colonel James A. Mulligan, in *Battles and Leaders of the Civil War,* ed. Robert Underwood Johnson and Clarence Clough Buel. New York, 1887, Vol. I, pp. 307–313.
71. *Tribune,* August 3, 1864.
72. *Tribune,* May 14, 1864.
73. *Tribune,* May 14, 1864.
74. "Kiss Me Mother, Kiss Your Darling." Words by Letta C. Lord (Root & Cady, Chicago), 1864.
75. "Can the Soldier Forget?" Words by Charles Boynton (Root & Cady, Chicago), 1864.
76. *Tribune,* May 10, 1864.
77. *Tribune,* July 26, 1864.
78. *Tribune,* May 26, 1864.
79. *Tribune,* May 13, 1864.
80. Long, *Day by Day,* p. 537.
81. *Tribune,* July 12, 1864.
82. Buffum, *Memorial,* pp. 311–312.
83. *Tribune,* June 10, 1864.
84. *Tribune,* July 13, 1864.
85. From The *Republican Campaign*

Songster for 1864. Words by Enos B. Reed. Quoted in Irwin Silber, *Songs America Voted By* (Mechanicsburg, PA, 1971), p. 93.
86. *Tribune,* September 2, 1864.
87. "Rally 'Round the Cause, Boys." Words by E. Mason, Jr. In Silber, *Songs America Voted By,* p. 92.
88. *Tribune,* September 7 and September 22, 1864. No copy of the song sheet has been found.
89. Epstein, *Root & Cady,* p. 47.
90. The words of the chorus (by Theodore J. Elmore) boasted "We have conquered, fairly conquered, conquered at the *ballot box,* and we'll ne'er be ruled by traitors like Vallandigham and Cox." *Tribune,* November 10, 1864.
91. *Tribune,* December 17, 1864.
92. *Song Messenger,* January 1864, p. 159.
93. Epstein, *Music Publishing,* p. 52.
94. Root & Cady, 1864. In the preface, Root gave credit to Dr. C. C. Miller of Marengo Ill., "from whom I have received much and important aid."
95. *Song Messenger Extra,* New Year's 1865, quoting a letter by Root in the November *Song Messenger.*
96. *Tribune,* September 23, 1864.
97. Sneden, *Eye of the Storm,* p. 178.
98. Sneden, *Eye of the Storm,* pp. 237–239.
99. *Tribune,* November 4, 1864.
100. *Tribune,* May 12, 1864.
101. *Tribune,* December 16, 1864.
102. *Tribune,* June 12, 1864.
103. Root, *Story,* 140–141.
104. Presumably George's brother, William Azariah Root.
105. Letter to Philo A. Otis signed John M. Hubbard, October 14, 1912. In Chicago Historical Society.
106. *Tribune,* January 14, 1865.
107. Root, *Story,* pp. 151–152.
108. *Tribune,* January 11, 1865.
109. "So we sang the chorus from Atlanta to the sea, while we were marching through Georgia."
110. *Tribune,* February 23, 1865.
111. *Song Messenger Extra,* New Year's 1865.
112. *Song Messenger,* March 1865.
113. Epstein, *Music Publishing,* p. 57.
114. *Tribune,* March 22 and 23, 1865.
115. Epstein, *Music Publishing,* p. 98.
116. *Tribune,* April 4, 1865.
117. *Tribune,* April 8, 1865.
118. *Tribune,* April 10, 1865.
119. *Tribune,* April 10, 1865.
120. *Tribune,* April 11, 1865.
121. *Tribune,* April 21, 1865.
122. Lossing, *Civil War,* III, 465.
123. "I Have Supped Full on Horrors," pp. 60–65, 96–101.
124. *Tribune,* April 15, 1865.
125. *Tribune,* April 19, 1865. On July 3, 1864 George and Mary Olive Root joined the Chicago Society of the New Jerusalem, which was also called the Swedenborgian Church (Epstein, *Music Publishing,* p. 20.) Emanuel Swedenborg (1688–1772), a remarkably successful scientist, taught followers that charity and serving others were as essential to the Christian life as faith. The Liturgy of the New Church was based on the Anglican Book of Common Prayer. The Newberry Library in Chicago owns a copy of an 1870 book, *An Order of Services for Morning and Evening Worship with Psalter, Selections, and Hymns, for the Use of the New Church.* On the title page "G. F. Root" is written in pencil. One of his associates said Root was strongly attracted to the "cheerful optimistic habit of mind" that characterized Swedenborgianism (Mathews, "George F. Root," *Music,* p. 508.) George James Webb introduced Root to the Swedenborgian church years earlier, while he was Root's voice teacher in Boston. He gave Root a book called *The Doctrines of the New Dispensation.* Years later in Chicago Root had a personal religious crisis. After a lecture by the Rev. John R. Hibbard in the New Jerusalem temple he discussed religious questions with the Rev. Hibbard. This led to his affiliating with the Swedenborgian church ("The New-Church Magazine," November 1895, pp. 486–489).
126. *Tribune,* April 22, 1865.
127. Root, *Story,* p. 137.
128. "Comrade, All Around Is Brightness." Words by Thomas Manahan (Root & Cady, Chicago), 1865.
129. *Tribune,* May 2, 1865.
130. *Tribune,* May 5, 1865.
131. Bernard, *Lincoln,* 308–309.
132. *Tribune,* May 4, 1865.
133. Bernard, *Lincoln,* 310.
134. *Tribune,* May 18, 1865.
135. *Tribune,* October 2 and October 30, 1864.
136. Root, *Story,* p. 141.
137. *Tribune,* May 31, 1865.
138. Root, *Story,* p. 103.
139. Root, *Story,* p. 137. "Starved in Prison"

was published by Root & Cady in 1865.

140. "They Have Broken Up Their Camps." Words by Major John B. Jewell (Root & Cady, Chicago), 1865.

141. Words by L. J. Bates (Root & Cady, Chicago), 1865.

142. Words by Beulah Wynne.

143. Words by Eben E. Rexford, music by G. Wurzel (Root & Cady, Chicago, 1865).

144. *Tribune,* June 29, 1865.

145. *Tribune* July 21, 1865.

146. Published by Root & Cady, 1865.

147. *Tribune,* October 5, 1865.

148. *Tribune,* November 7, 1865.

149. *Song Messenger,* September 1865. This popular quote was attributed to Andrew Fletcher: "I knew a very wise man that believed that, if a man were permitted to make all the ballads, he need not care who should make the laws of a nation." In addition to the mention of this quote in the *Song Messenger,* there were references to it in reviews of Root's autobiography and in the obituary article about Root in the New-Church magazine for November 1895.

150. *Song Messenger,* November 1865.

151. "Away on the Prairie Alone." Words by Sara Cottew (Root & Cady, Chicago, 1865).

152. *Tribune,* December 27–29, 1865.

153. *Variety Music Cavalcade,* p. 98.

154. *Variety Music Cavalcade,* p. 98.

155. Hanby died of tuberculosis in 1867 at the age of 33. Sources: brochure from The Hanby House, Westerville, Ohio, and Root, *Story,* p. 142.

156. Root, *Story,* p. 136.

Chapter 7

1. *Tribune,* December 21, 1865.

2. *Tribune,* April 11, 1866.

3. *Tribune* April 11, 1866. The first edition was dated 1866 and published by Root & Cady. The enlarged edition was dated 1867 and included "the odes of the good templars." An 1894 edition was published by the John Church Company of Cincinnati, and another edition by Church was dated 1895.

4. Words by M. B. C. Slade.

5. "Mabel" (Root & Cady, Chicago, 1868).

6. Words by Ellen H. Flagg (Root & Cady, Chicago, 1866).

7. Words and music by Geo. F. Root (Root & Cady, Chicago, 1866).

8. (Root & Cady, Chicago, 1867.) Root was "assisted in the preparation of the words by 'Paulina.'"

9. (S. Brainard's Sons, Cleveland, 1871.) Mrs. L. M. Morehead, author of the words, dedicated them to John G. Whittier.

10. "Honor to Sheridan." (Root & Cady, Chicago, 1867.) Words by Paulina.

11. Root & Cady, Chicago, 1867

12. *Tribune,* May 31, 1866.

13. *Song Messenger,* January 1868.

14. *Song Messenger,* February 1868.

15. Root, *Story,* p. 141.

16. Epstein, *Music Publishing,* p. 60.

17. Root, *Story,* p. 148–150.

18. *Song Messenger,* June 1868 *Extra.*

19. Root, *Story,* p. 145.

20. *Song Messenger,* October 1868, p. 153; *Song Messenger Extra,* October 1868, p. 2.

21. The *Chicago Tribune* on December 19, 1868, reported sales of 27,000 copies of *The Triumph* in its first three months. At four months sales had reached 50,000. In his autobiography Root reported that 90,000 copies were sold in the first year with a profit to Root & Cady of $30,000.

22. *Song Messenger Extra,* June 1868.

23. In *Pacific Glee Book,* ed. Frederic W. Root and James R. Murray (Chicago: Root & Cady, 1869). There was no specific credit for the words.

24. "Somewhere" (Root & Cady, Chicago, 1869). In writing the words Root was assisted by Mrs. M. B. C. Slade.

25. Stuart, Suzette G. "Illustrated Guide Book," Church of the Transfiguration, New York, 1963. "The Little Church Around the Corner," undated brochure. The song was published by Root & Cady in 1871.

26. *Song Messenger,* March 1871, p. 42.

27. "Poverty Flat, or Her Letter" (Root & Cady, Chicago, 1870).

28. "Banner of the Fatherland" (Root & Cady, Chicago, 1870).

29. On the cover he stated the reason for writing the song: "Americans! France is exhausted by this terrible war. Many of her people are starving and utterly destitute. Let us not forget her early recognition of American Independence and the prompt and generous aid she then rendered to our struggling Republic, and let us now share with her from our abundance in this hour of her need."

30. *Song Messenger,* April 1870, and Root, *Story,* pp. 145–146.
31. *Song Messenger,* April 1870.
32. *Tribune,* April 11, 1866.
33. *Song Messenger,* June 1871.
34. *Song Messenger,* January 1871.
35. *Song Messenger,* February 1871.
36. *Song Messenger,* August 1868.
37. *Song Messenger,* October 1868.
38. Supplement to the *Song Messenger,* January 1871.
39. Reprinted in *The Song Messenger,* August 1871. Quoted in Epstein, *Music Publishing,* p. 79.
40. Root, *Story,* p. 152.
41. Kogan and Cromie, *The Great Fire,* p. 9.
42. George Root's account of the fire appeared in two sources: *The Story of a Musical Life,* pp. 152–158, and *The Song Messenger,* October 1871. Charles Root's account appeared in *The Song Messenger,* October 1871.
43. Root, *Story,* p. 154.
44. *Song Messenger,* October 1871, p. 164.
45. Root, *Story,* p. 155.
46. *Song Messenger,* October 1871, p. 163.
47. Root, *Story,* pp. 154–155.
48. Root, *Story,* p. 156.
49. *Song Messenger,* October 1871, p. 164.
50. Root, *Story,* pp. 155–156. The plates for Root's *Musical Curriculum* were in the printing office and were destroyed. He revised *The Musical Curriculum* before new plates were made.
51. *Song Messenger,* October 1871, p. 163.
52. Root, *Story,* pp. 156–157.
53. Epstein, *Music Publishing,* p. 81.
54. Root, *Story,* p. 157.
55. Epstein, *Music Publishing,* p. 22.
56. Root, *Story,* p. 160.
57. Epstein, *Music Publishing,* 22.
58. Epstein, *Music Publishing,* p. 22.
59. Root, *Story,* pp. 161–162.
60. "Songs of the Olden Days." Words by Kate Cameron (William A. Pond & Company, New York, 1872).
61. November 1871.
62. *Musical World,* December 1871, p. 232.

Chapter 8

1. Root, *Story,* p. 158. This University of Chicago was not the one known by that name today. The old university closed in 1886; then in 1890 it was designated the "Old University of Chicago" to make the name "University of Chicago" available for a new school that was just being organized. Source: "Old University of Chicago Records 1856–1886," Typescript, Roosevelt University.
2. *Song Messenger,* April 1874.
3. "Notes of Dr. Felix Ganz." Typescript, Roosevelt University.
4. "Highlights of Chicago Musical College's First One Hundred Years," in "Centennial Bulletin of The Chicago Musical College Undergraduate and Graduate Divisions 1967–68, p. ix. Roosevelt University."
5. *Normal Musical Handbook,* pp. 55, 61.
6. *Tribune,* October 16, 1865.
7. *Tribune,* December 7, 1866.
8. Words by the Rev. William O. Cushing, music by George F. Root (Root & Cady, Chicago, 1866.)
9. Martin, Edward Winslow. History of the *Grange Movement* (Chicago: National Publishing Company, 1874), p. 407.
10. Silber, *Songs America Voted By,* 218.
11. Root, *Glorious Cause,* Preface.
12. Root's words for "Don't Wait Till the Drunkard Is Made" asked "Will temp'rance workers now in doubt about the thing to do / Allow a word in song to trace the course we should pursue?" The chorus suggested that "prevention is better than cure" and that "a government willing to aid is what we must work to secure."
13. Words and music were attributed to George Root.
14. Root, *Story,* p. 201.
15. Root, *Story,* pp. 200–201.
16. Root, *Story,* p. 198.
17. Root, *Story,* p. 191.
18. Root, *Story,* p. 192.
19. Root, *Story,* p. 186.
20. Root, *Story,* p. 194.
21. Root, *Story,* p. 174.
22. Root, *Story,* p. 168.
23. Root, *Story,* p. 199.
24. Finally, claiming that they were tired and hungry, the Union prisoners requested food. Belfield thanked Root for the much-needed food, still "gratefully remembered" after so many years. Root, *Story,* pp. 213–214.
25. Root, *Story,* pp. 214–215.
26. Lydia Avery Coonley Ward, cited in Waldo R. Browne, *Chronicles of An American Home*. Privately Printed. Copyright by John Stuart Coonley. Printed by Little and Ives Company, 1930, p. 81.
27. Root, *Story,* p. 202.
28. James R. Murray, "The Loyal Legion

and Dr. Root." Quoted in Root, *Story*, pp. 201–203.

29. Root, *Story*, Preface, n.p.

30. *Musical Visitor*, October 1891.

31. George F. Root, "Madame Patti and the Old Songs." From Advance Sheets of *Church's Musical Visitor*. In *Music* Magazine, March 1892, pp. 428–430.

32. George F. Root, "Jenny Lind and the Old Songs." *Music* Magazine, May, 1892, pp. 15–20.

33. Lydia Avery Coonley, "George F. Root and His Songs." *New England Magazine*, January, 1896.

34. The unfinished *Star of Light* told the story of the Birth of Christ. John Stuart Bogg wrote the words and Frederic W. Root, George's son, "contributed the last four numbers." John Church Company, 1896.

35. The source of most of the details of Root's death is his daughter Clara Louise Burnham's eleven-page pamphlet, "The Last Days of George F. Root."

36. The cause of death was probably angina pectoris, according to John Presland in *The New-Church Magazine*, November 1895.

37. A typescript of the funeral sermon is owned by a Root descendent.

38. Lydia Avery Coonley wrote: "It is a habit of the family to sing the Doxology at all their gatherings. It is a part of Christmas reunions; it is sung standing as a grace before Thanksgiving dinners; and at his request the circle of more than forty relatives sang, with the voice of their leader for the first time silent: 'Praise God from whom all blessings flow'; and though the voices faltered, they did not fail, but carried the harmony on to the great Amen." In "George F. Root and His Songs." *New England Magazine* (January, 1896), p. 570. Mrs. Coonley (1845–1924) was the mother of John Stuart Coonley, who married Root's granddaughter Louise.

39. *Musical Visitor*, September 1895.

40. Ralph Root to Mrs. H. E. Vaughan, January 18, 1943. Root & Cady Publishing Company Archives, The Newberry Library.

41. Smith, *National Songs*, p. 106.

42. Proceedings of the Music Teachers National Association, Delaware, Ohio, 1876. Published under the Auspices of the MTNA by George H. Thomson, Job Printer, 1877, n.p. Reported phonographically by John Collins. Delaware. Ohio.

43. Yellin, Victor Fell. *Chadwick, Yankee Composer*. Washington: Smithsonian Institution Press, 1990, pp. 23–25.

44. MTNA *Proceedings*, 1876.

45. Root, *Story*, pp. 19.

46. Root, *Story*, p. 98.

47. *Chicago Tribune*, August 8, 1895.

Bibliography

Brainard's Musical World, 1871–1875.
Chicago Tribune, 1858–1895.
Choral Advocate and Singing-Class Journal. Later titles: *Musical Review and Choral Advocate*, 1852–1853; *New York Musical Review and Choral Advocate*, 1854–1855; *New York Musical Review and Gazette* 1855–60; *Musical Review and Musical World* 1860–1864. The later titles are cited as *Review.*
Church's Musical Visitor, 1871–1895.
Song Messenger of the Northwest, 1863–1875. Changed to *The Song Messenger*, 1870.

Books and Articles

Alexander, J. Heywood. "Brainard's (Western) Musical World." *Notes: The Quarterly Journal of the Music Library Association.* March, 1980.

Andreas, Alfred Theodore. *History of Chicago,* Volume II. [Reprint] New York: Arno Press, 1975.

Angle, Paul M., ed. *Three Years in the Army of the Cumberland: The Letters and Diary of Major James A. Connolly.* Bloomington: Indiana University Press, 1959.

Army Songster. Richmond, VA: George L. Bidgood, 1864. Confederate Imprints (microfilm) 3252.

The Athenaeum: Journal of Literature, Science, the Fine Arts, Music, and the Drama. Number 3538, August 17, 1895.

Bernard, Kenneth A. *Lincoln and the Music of the Civil War.* Caldwell, Idaho: The Caxton Printers, Ltd., 1966.

Birdoff, Harry. *The World's Greatest Hit— Uncle Tom's Cabin.* New York: S. F. Vanni, 1947.

"Boston Academy of Music's Teachers' Institute (Continued.)" *Boston Musical Gazette,* April 26, 1847.

Brink, Carol. *Harps in the Wind.* New York: The Macmillan Company, 1947.

Brown, William Wells, M.D. *The Negro in the American Rebellion: His Heroism and His Fidelity,* New Edition. Miami, Florida: Mnemosyne Publishing Inc., 1969. Originally published in 1880 by A. G. Brown & Co., Boston.

Browne, Waldo R. *Chronicles of an American Home.* Copyright by John Stuart Coonley. Privately printed by Little and Ives Co., 1930.

Buffum, F. H. *A Memorial of The Great Rebellion: Being a History of The Fourteenth Regiment New-Hampshire Volunteers, Covering Its Three Years of Service, With Original Sketches of Army Life, 1862–1865.* Issued by the Committee of Publication. Boston: Franklin Press: Rand, Avery, & Company. 1882.

Bullard, F. Lauriston. *Tad and His Father.* Boston: Little, Brown, and Company, 1915.

Cary, Alice and Phoebe. *The Poetical Works of Alice and Phoebe Cary. Household Edition with Illustrations.* Boston and New York: Houghton, Mifflin and Co., The Riverside Press, Cambridge. 1882 (1865, 1867, 1873, 1876).

Chase, Gilbert. "America's Music, the First Century." *American Music Teacher,* September/October, 1976.

Cook, F. F. *Bygone Days in Chicago.* Chicago: A. C. McClurg, 1910.

Coonley, Lydia Avery. "George F. Root and His Songs." *New England Magazine* XIII (January 1896).

Crocker, Lucien B. "Episodes and Characters In An Illinois Regiment." In *Military Essays and Recollections.* Military Order of the Loyal Legion of the U. S.—Illinois Commandery, Chicago, 1891. Cited in Epstein, "Battle Cry." In *Quarterly Journal of Studies in Civil War History,* September, 1958.

Crosby, Fanny. (Frances J. Van Alstyne). *Fanny Crosby's Life-Story, by Herself.* New York: Every Where Publishing Company, 1903.

_____. *Memories of Eighty Years.* Boston: James H. Earle and Company, 1906.

Davis, Ronald L. *A History of Music in American Life,* Volume I. Malabar, Florida: Robert Krieger Publishing Company, 1982.

"A Day at North Reading, Massachusetts." Unsigned article. *Dwight's Journal of Music,* July 4, 1857, pp. 111–112.

"A Day in Providence." *Boston Musical Gazette,* November 23, 1846.

Epstein, Dena J. "The Battle Cry of Freedom." *A Quarterly Journal of Studies in Civil War History* IV, 3 (September, 1958), pp. 307–318.

_____. *Music Publishing in Chicago Before 1871: The Firm of Root & Cady, 1858–1871.* Detroit Studies in Music Bibliography 14. Detroit: Information Coordinators, Inc., 1969.

Federal Writers' Project of the Works Progress Administration for Massachusetts. *North Reading, Massachusetts: A Guide to its Places and People.* Frederick W. Cook, Secretary of the Commonwealth, Cooperating Sponsor. Boston: Houghton Mifflin Co.; Cambridge: The Riverside Press, 1937.

Fern, Fanny. *Ruth Hall and Other Writings.* Edited and with an Introduction by Joyce W. Warren. New Brunswick, New Jersey: Rutgers University Press, 1986.

Finson, Jon. W. *The Voices That Are Gone: Themes in Nineteenth-Century American Song.* New York: Oxford University Press, 1994.

Flint, John and John H. Stone, compilers. *Genealogical Register of the Descendants of Thomas Flint, of Salem, Massachusetts.* Andover, MA: Printed by Warren F. Draper, 1860.

Furgurson, Ernest B. *Freedom Rising.* New York: Alfred A. Knopf, 2004.

Gac, Scott. *Singing For Freedom: The Hutchinson Family Singers and the Nineteenth-Century Culture of Reform.* New Haven and London: Yale University Press, 2007.

Gossett, Thomas F. *Uncle Tom's Cabin and American Culture.* Dallas: Southern Methodist University Press, 1985.

Gottschalk, Louis Moreau. *Notes of a Pianist.* Edited by Jeanne Behrend. New York: Alfred A. Knopf, 1964.

The Grant Songster: A Collection of Campaign Songs for 1868. Chicago: Root & Cady, 67 Washington St.

Grover, Leonard. "Lincoln's Interest in the Theater." Privately printed, n.p., n.d.
Guyer, Isaac D. *History of Chicago: Its Commerce and Manufacturing Interests and Industry.* Chicago: Church, Goodman and Cushing, 1862.
Hamm, Charles. *Yesterdays: Popular Song in America.* New York and London: W. W. Norton and Company, 1979.
Heaps, Willard A. and Porter W. Heaps. *The Singing Sixties.* Norman, Oklahoma: 1960.
Johnson, Patricia Carley, ed. "I Have Supped Full on Horrors." *American Heritage,* October, 1959.
Jones, F. O., ed. *A Handbook of American Music and Musicians Containing Biographies of American Musicians and Histories of the Principal Musical Institutions, Firms and Societies.* Canaseraga, N.Y.: 1886 (published by the author). Reprint: Da Capo Press, New York, 1971.
Karamanski, Theodore J. *Rally 'Round the Flag: Chicago and the Civil War.* Chicago: Nelson- Hall Publishers, 1993.
Kogan, Herman and Robert Cromie. *The Great Fire: Chicago 1871.* New York: G. P. Putnam's Sons, 1971.
Lane, David. *A Soldier's Diary: The Story of a Volunteer, 1862-1865.* N.P., 1905.
Long, E. B. with Barbara Long. *The Civil War Day by Day: An Almanac 1861-1865.* New York: Da Capo Press, 1971.
Lossing, Benson J. *The Civil War in the United States of America*, Vol. III. Hartford: T. Belknap, 1868.
Martin, Edward Winslow. *History of the Grange Movement; or, the Farmer's War Against Monopolies: Being a Full and Authentic Account of the Struggles of the American Farmers Against the Extortions of the Railroad Companies. With A History of the Rise and Progress of the Order of Patrons of Husbandry, Its Objects, Present Condition and Prospects. To Which Is Added Sketches of the Leading Grangers.* Chicago: National Publishing Company, 1874.
Mathews, William S. B. "George F. Root, Mus. Doc." *Music* (September 1895).
Mattfeld, Julius, ed. *Variety Music Cavalcade 1620-1961: A Chronology of Vocal and Instrumental Music Popular in the United States.* Englewood Cliffs, New Jersey: Prentice-Hall, Inc., 1952.
Matthews, Brander. "The Songs of the War." *Century Magazine,* August 1887.
McCullough, David. "The Unexpected Mrs. Stowe" in *Brave Companions: Portraits in History.* New York: Prentice Hall Press, 1992.
McPherson, James M. *Battle Cry of Freedom: The Civil War Era.* New York: Ballantine Books (Oxford University Press), 1988.
Metcalf, Frank J. "An Intimate Reminder of 'The Vacant Chair.'" *Worcester Telegram,* May 28, 1939.
Morison, Samuel Eliot. *Harvard in the Seventeenth Century,* Part II. Cambridge, MA, 1936.
Mulligan, Colonel James A. "The Siege of Lexington, Missouri." In *Battles and Leaders of the Civil War,* Volume I. New York: The Century Company, 1887.
Murphy, Leo J., compiler. "North Reading and the Ephraim Pratts, Colonial Soldiers and Tanners." *North Reading Review: Annals and Reminiscences,* No. 17, December 1964.
Murray, James R., ed. "Memorial Number in Honor of Dr. George F. Root." *Church's Musical Visitor* XXIV, 9 (September 1895).
"Music Teachers' Institute and Musical Convention, Nunda, Livingston County, New York." *Boston Musical Gazette,* October 1, 1850.

Music Teachers National Association. *Proceedings.* Delaware, Ohio, 1876. Published under the Auspices of the MTNA by George H. Thomson, Job Printer, 1877.
North Reading, Massachusetts: A Guide to Its Places and People. Federal Writers' Project of the Works Progress Administration for Massachusetts. Frederick W. Cook, Secretary of the Commonwealth, Cooperating Sponsor. Boston: Houghton Mifflin Company; Cambridge: The Riverside Press, 1937.
Oates, Stephen B. *With Malice Toward None: The Life of Abraham Lincoln.* New York: Harper and Rowe, 1977.
Odell, George C. D. *Annals of the New York Stage,* 15 Vols. New York: Columbia University Press, 1927–1949.
An Order of Services for Morning and Evening Worship with Psalter, Selections, and Hymns, for the Use of the New Church. Brooklyn, New York, 1870.
Pemberton, Carol. *Lowell Mason: His Life and Work.* Ann Arbor, Michigan: 1985.
Perry, Mark. *Conceived in Liberty: Joshua Chamberlain, William Oates, and the American Civil War.* New York: Viking Penguin, 1997.
Pierce, Bessie L. *A History of Chicago,* 3 Vols. New York: Alfred A. Knopf, 1940.
Pleasants, Henry Jr. and George H. Straley. *Inferno at Petersburg.* Philadelphia and New York: Chilton Book Company, 1961.
Poe, Edgar Allan. *The Complete Poems and Stories of Edgar Allan Poe with Selections from His Critical Writings.* With an introduction and explanatory notes by Arthur Hobson Quinn. Texts established, with bibliographical notes, by Edward H. O'Neill. Illustrated by E. McKnight Kauffer. Volume II. New York: Alfred A. Knopf, 1973.
Political Debates Between Abraham Lincoln and Stephen A Douglas In the Celebrated Campaign of 1858 in Illinois; Including the Preceding Speeches of Each at Chicago, Springfield, etc. ALSO, The Two Great Speeches of Abraham Lincoln in Ohio in 1859, and A Complete Index to the Whole. Cleveland, Ohio. O. S. Hubbell & Co., 1895.
Presland, John. "George Frederick Root." *The New-Church Magazine,* November 1895.
Redkey, Edwin S., ed. *A Grand Army of Black Men: Letters from African-American Soldiers in the Union Army, 1861–1865.* Cambridge: Cambridge University Press, 1992.
Root, George F. "Jenny Lind and the Old Songs." *Music* Magazine, May 1892.
———. "Madame Patti and the Old Songs." From the Advance Sheets of *Church's Musical Visitor.* In *Music: A Monthly Magazine Devoted to the Art, Science, Technic, and Literature of Music.* March 1892.
———. *The Story of a Musical Life: An Autobiography.* Cincinnati: The John Church Company, 1891.
Root, James Pierce. *Root Genealogical Records, 1600–1870.* New York: Anthony and Company, 1870.
Ross, Ishbel. *Angel of the Battlefield: The Life of Clara Barton.* New York: Harper and Bros., 1956.
Sanjek, Russell. *American Popular Music and Its Business: The First Four Hundred Years,* Volume II: From 1790 to 1909. New York: Oxford University Press, 1988.
Scheips, Paul J. "Hold the Fort! The Story of a Song from the Sawdust Trail to the Picket Line." *Smithsonian Studies in History and Technology* Number 9. City of Washington: Smithsonian Institution Press, 1971.
Silber, Irwin. *Songs America Voted By.* Mechanicsburg, Pennsylvania: Stackpole Books, 1971.
———. *Songs of the Civil War.* New York: Columbia University Press, 1960.
Smith, Col. Nicholas. *Stories of Great National Songs.* Milwaukee: The Young Churchman Co., 1899.

Smith, Nicholas. "The Battle Hymns of Nations." Military Order of the Loyal Legion of the United States, Wisconsin Commandery. *War Papers,* Volume 3. Quoted in Epstein, Root & Cady Publishing Company Archives, The Newberry Library.

Sneden, Robert Knox. *Eye of the Storm: A Civil War Odyssey.* Written and illustrated by Robert Knox Sneden. Edited by Charles F. Bryan, Jr., and Nelson D. Lankford. New York: The Free Press, 2000.

Songs for The Grange. Set to Music and Dedicated to the Order of Patrons of Husbandry in the United States. Philadelphia: J. A. Wagenseller, Printer. 1874.

Stowe, Harriet Beecher. *Uncle Tom's Cabin or, Life Among the Lowly.* New York: Vintage Books, 1991.

_____. *Uncle Tom's Cabin or, Life Among the Lowly.* Notes and Chronology by Kathryn Kish Sklar. New York: Vintage Books, 1991.

"Teachers' Class of the Boston Academy of Music." *Boston Musical Gazette,* August 28, 1848.

Thayer, Alexander W. "The Normal Music School at North Reading." *Dwight's Journal of Music,* July 25, 1857.

Thomas, Benjamin P., ed. *Three Years with Grant as Recalled by War Correspondent Sylvanus Cadwallader.* New York: Alfred A. Knopf, 1955.

Thomas, Henry Goddard. "The Colored Troops at Petersburg." *Century Magazine,* September 1887.

Thompson, Harold W., ed. *A Pioneer Songster: Texts from the Stevens-Douglass Manuscript of Western New York 1841–1856.* Ithaca, New York: Cornell University Press, 1958.

Trudeau, Noah Andre. *Like Men of War: Black Troops in the Civil War 1862–1865.* Boston: Little, Brown and Company, 1998.

Trulock, Alice Rains. *In the Hands of Providence: Joshua Lawrence Chamberlain and the American Civil War.* Chapel Hill, North Carolina: The University of North Carolina Press, 1992.

Upton, George P. "The Chicago Musical College — An Historical Sketch." In *Catalogue of the Chicago Musical College.* Chicago, 1907.

_____. *Musical Memories: My Recollections of Celebrities of the Half Century 1850–1900.* Chicago: A. C. McClurg and Company, 1908.

Walker, Nancy A. *Fanny Fern.* New York: Twayne Publishers, 1993.

Whittle, D. W., Editor. *Memoirs of Philip P. Bliss.* Contributions by the Rev. E. P. Goodwin, Ira D. Sankey, and Geo. F. Root. Introduction by D. L. Moody. New York: A. S. Barnes and Company, 1877.

Work, Bertram G., compiler. *Songs of Henry Clay Work.* Printed by J. J. Little and Ives Company, New York, n.d.

Yellin, Victor Fell. *Chadwick, Yankee Composer.* Washington: Smithsonian Institution Press, 1990.

Young, Jesse B. *What a Boy Saw in the Army.* New York: Hunt and Eaton, 1894.

Unpublished Materials

Burnham, Clara Louise. "The Last Days of George F. Root." Eleven-page pamphlet, privately printed, n.d.

Ganz, Felix. "Notes of Dr. Felix Ganz." Typescript, Roosevelt University.

Hubbard, John M. Letter to Philo A. Otis, October 14, 1912. In Chicago History Museum Research Center.

Olson, Ivan Walter, Jr. "The Roots and Development of Public School Music in Richmond, VA 1782–1907." Unpublished doctoral dissertation, University of Michigan, 1964.

Peck, Mary F. Root. *A Little History of a Large Family: Memoir of Sarah Flint Root by Her Daughter.* Typescript, 1891–1892.
Reilay, Sarah M. Letter to Major Weyant, June 6, 1928. Kate Chase File, New York History Society Library.
Root, Frederick Ferdinand. Journal, November 8–30, 1844.
_____. Letter to George F. Root, March 15, 1839.
Root, George F. Letter to Frederick Ferdinand Root, April, 1838.
_____. Letter to Sarah F. Root, June 23, 1845.
Root, Mary Olive and Charles T. Letter to Frederick Woodman Root, May 7, 1858.
Root, Ralph. Letter to Mrs. H. E. Vaughan dated Jan. 18, 1943.
Rutgers Female Institute. Commencement Programs and Annual Circulars 1847– 1864. New York Historical Society Library.
"Tenth Annual Morris County Musical Convention." Morristown, New Jersey, December 30, 1861. Circular. Joint Free Public Library of Morristown and Morris Township, Morristown, New Jersey.

Archives

Epstein, Dena J., compiler. Root & Cady Publishing Company Archives, The Newberry Library.
Lowell Mason Papers, MSS 33, in the Irving S. Gilmore Music Library, Yale University.

Pamphlets, Brochures, Circulars, Bulletins

Church of the Transfiguration. "Illustrated Guide Book with Historical Sketch of the Church of the Transfiguration: The Little Church Around the Corner." New York City. New Edition. Revised and reset by Suzette G. Stuart, 1963.
Hanby House brochure, Westerville, Ohio, n.d.
"Highlights of Chicago Musical College's First One Hundred Years," in *Centennial Bulletin of the Chicago Musical College Undergraduate and Graduate Divisions 1967– 68*, Roosevelt University.
"The Little Church Around the Corner" (Church of the Transfiguration) One East 29th St. New York City, n.d.
"Old University of Chicago Records 1856–1886." Typescript, Roosevelt University.
Rutgers Female Institute Commencement Programs and Annual Circulars 1847–1864. New York Historical Society Library.

Official Publications

United States War Department. *War of the Rebellion: Official Records of the Union and Confederate Armies*, 128 Vols. Washington, D.C., 1880–1901.
_____. *Supplement to the Official Records of the Union and Confederate Armies*. Part II, Volume 38. Serial Number 50. Janet B. Hewett, ed.

Internet Sources

Green-Wood Cemetery. www.green-wood.com/brooklynsgwc.asp
Lewis, Alan. Heralds of Freedom: The Hutchinson Family Singers. www.geocities.com/unclesamsfarm/hutchinsons.htm.

Index

*Numbers in **bold italics** indicate pages with photographs.*

Abbott, Gorham D. 28, 30
Abbott, Jacob (father) 18
Abbott, Jacob (son) 18–19, 21, 22–23, 25, 31–32, 48
Abolition of slavery 68, 111
Academy Vocalist (book; GFR) 51, 54
Adams, Helen Root (sister) 59–60
Alary, Giulio 33
"All Together Again" (song; GFR) 80
Andersonville Prison 149, 152, 191
Andover Theological Seminary 71
Argentina 10, 11, 18
Arlington's Minstrels 140
Autobiography of George F. Root (*The Story of a Musical Life*) 25
"Away on the Prairie Alone" (song; GFR) 163

Bailey and Ferguson, publishers 189
Ball's Bluff, battle 107–109
Bands: in Chicago 137, 144; in the Union army 106–107
"Banner of the Fatherland" (song; GFR) 172
Barnum, P.T. 30
Bassini, Carlo 91
"Battle Cry of Freedom" (often called "Rally Round the Flag"; song, GFR) 1–2, 116–120, 127, 133–134, 135, 138, 140, 145, 146, 154–155, 161, 193, 196, 218*n*86; in Confederate "Army Songster" 140; Confederate edition (Schreiner) 139–140; political parodies 128, 147, 171; reportedly ordered sung on battlefields 133; Root's account of writing 116; score ***199–201***; sheet music cover ***117***; temperance parody 165–166; two versions in Root's *Bugle Call* 130; two versions: "Rallying Song" and "Battle Song" (GFR) 118
Beauty and the Beast (play) 97
Beecher, Henry Ward 69, 77–78, 155–156
Beethoven, Ludwig van 85, 112
Belle Isle prison 149
Belshazzar's Feast, cantata (GFR) 94
Berlioz, Hector 33
"Better music" 40, 65, 196
Blackwood's Magazine 37
Bliss, Philip P., and Root & Cady 130
Board of Music Trade 88, 161
Boston Academy of Music 13, 16, 19, 21, 25, 29, 30, 60
Boston Common 19
Boston Handel and Haydn Society 6, 14
Boston, Massachusetts 5, 6, 11, 12, 14
Boston Musical Gazette 25, 37
Bowdoin Street church 13, 20
Bradbury, William B. 28, 32, 35, 53, 55, 65–66, 71, 83, 86, 90, 91, 92, 95
Bradford, Margaret Flint 6, 7
Brainard *see* S. Brainard's Sons
Bross, Colonel John A. 142–143
"Brother, Tell Me of the Battle" (song; GFR) 139
Bugle Call (collection of songs; GFR) 129–130, 136
Burnham, Clara Louise Root 85, 194, 224*n*35
"Bye and Bye" (song; GFR) 62

Cady, C.M. (Chauncey Marvin) 49, 53, 86, 113, 122, 212*n*26; general manager and finance manager at Root & Cady 126; in

233

reorganization after the Chicago Fire 179–181
"Call 'Em Names, Jeff" (song; GFR) 124
"Can the Soldier Forget" (song; GFR) 145
Cantata, as defined in Root's lifetime 35–36
Catching Kriss Kringle (cantata; GFR) 188
Cedar Creek, battle of 146
Chadwick, George W. 196
Charlestown, Massachusetts 18, 27
Chase, Kate 24
Chicago 87, 88
Chicago Auditorium 193
Chicago Fire 3, 175–185
Chicago Musical College, Root as president 185
Chicago Musical Institute 86; see also Normal Musical Institute
Chicago Musical Review 86
Chicago Musical Union 86, 92, 96, 125
Chicago Society of the New Jerusalem (also called Swedenborgian Church) *see* New Jerusalem Church
Chicago *Tribune* 3
Choral Advocate and Singing-Class Journal 31, 32, 210*n*10; see also *Review*
Christy's Minstrels 37, 48, 52, 105, 112
Church, John & Company *see* John Church & Company
Church music 13, 15–16, 19; African-American 61
Church's Musical Visitor 193; Root's autobiography 192
"Clear Cold Water" (song; GFR) 49, 50
"Clear the Way" (song; GFR) 126
Columbian Lady's and Gentleman's Magazine 30
"Columbia's Call" (song; GFR) 167
Columbus, the Hero of Faith (cantata; GFR) 193
"Come to Me Quickly" (song; GFR) 62
"Comrade, All Around Is Brightness" (song; GFR) 158
"Comrade, I Will Guard Thy Mother" (song; GFR) 145
"Comrades, Hasten to the Battle" (song; GFR) 139
Confederate editions of Root's songs 134–135, 139–140
Coonley, Lydia Avery 9, 191, 193
Copperheads 110, 127, 140
Coronet (book; GFR) 162
Crater, battle 142
Creation (Franz Joseph Haydn) 14
Crosby, Fanny 25, 32, 35, 38, 45, 53, 211*n*50
Crosby's Opera House 159, 163; burned 176–177; engraving (fire) *176*; ruins *178*

"Crosby's Opera House Waltz" (Frederick Woodman Root) sheet music cover *160*
"Cultivation of the Voice" (lectures; GFR) 25, 29
Curwen, J. Spencer (publisher) 189

Daniel (cantata; GFR) 53, 56, 188
David, the Shepherd Boy (cantata; GFR, accompaniment arranged for orchestra) 190
"De Day Ob Liberty's Comin'" (song; GFR) 121
Death and mourning 52, 62
Death of a beautiful girl as theme in songs 38, 48, 212*n*9
Diapason (book; GFR) 94, 110, 216*n*129–130
Diary of George F. Root 25
Disney, Walt 188
Dodworth's (band) 128
"Don't You See Me Coming" (song; GFR) 89
Douglas Brigade Band (formed by Root & Cady) 107
Duprez & Green's New Orleans Minstrels and Brass Band 141
Dwight's Journal of Music 76, 93
"Dying Soldier" (song; GFR) 149

"Early Lost, Early Saved" (song; GFR) 48
Eisfeld, Theodore 23, 29, 61, 211*n*31
Elijah (oratorio; Mendelssohn) 34, 61, 138
Emancipation Proclamation 122, 123, 124, 136
E.T. Root & Sons 181
Exempts 132

"Fare Thee Well, Kitty Dear" (song; GFR) 44, 52, 212*n*14
"Farewell Father, Friend and Guardian" (song; GFR) 157–159; sheet music cover *157*
"Father Abraham's Reply to the 600,000" ("adapted and partly composed" by GFR) 121
"Father's Coming" (song; GFR) 49
Fern, Fanny 3, 57–59
Festival Glee Book (GFR) 79–80, 110
Festival of the Flowers (cantata; GFR) 188
"First Gun Is Fired" (song; GFR) 102–103, 104, 109; sheet music cover *102*
First Years in Song-Land (book; GFR) 186
Firth, Pond and Company 62
Flint, Daniel 6, 7, 10, 11, 12, 16

Flint, Priscilla (maternal grandmother) 6
Flint, Putnam (uncle) 8, 9, 10, 23
Flint, Sarah *see* Root, Sarah Flint
Flint, Warren (uncle) 23
Flower Queen (cantata; GFR) 35–36, 40, 50, 52–53, 68, 73–74, 188, 190
Flute 8, 11, 93
"Flying Home" (song; GFR) 80
Flynt, Josiah 5
"Foes and Friends" (song; GFR) 166
"For All and Forever, the Flag of the Free" (song; GFR) 167
Fort Sumter, South Carolina 96, 101
Forest Choir (book for "young people in Day Schools"; GFR) 167–168
"Forest Requiem" (song; GFR) 89
"Forward, Boys, Forward!" (song; GFR) 105
Foster, Stephen 37, 38, 40, 48, 52, 57, 62, 138
Fourth of July 76, 115
"From the Ruins Our City Shall Rise" (song; GFR) 182
Fry, William Henry 23

"Gently, Ah, Gently" (song; GFR) 40
"Gently, Gently, Wake the Song" (song; GFR) 48
George F. Root & Sons 180, 181
Gettysburg 132
Girac, Emile 23
Glasgow, Scotland 189
Glorious Cause (book; GFR) 188
"Glory! Glory! Or the Little Octoroon" (song; GFR) 166–167
"God Bless Our Brave Young Volunteers" (song; GFR) 104
"Gone to the War" (song; GFR) 126, **127**
"Good Bye Old Glory" (song; GFR) 161
Goodwin, Annette 11
Goodwin, Daniel 17
Gottschalk, Louis Moreau 33, 112, 119
Grant, Colonel Fred 190–191
"Grant Songster" (campaign publication; Root & Cady) 171
Great Western (band) 122, 149, 158
"Greenwood Bell" (song; GFR) 52
Grout, Lt. John William 107, 109
Guyer, Isaac D. (*History of Chicago*) 112–113

Hall, William *see* William Hall & Son
Hanby, B.R. (Benjamin Russell) 163, 222*n*155
Handel, George Frederick 6–7, 40, 85
Harmony Hall 11, 12, 13, 16, 18, 19
Harper's magazine 81
Harte, Bret 3, 172

Hastings, Thomas 55, 57
"Have Ye Sharpened Your Swords" (song; GFR) 106
"Have You Sold Your Matches, Tom?" song (GFR) 164
Haydn, Franz Joseph 14, 85
Haymakers, 74–76 (cantata) 78, 79, 84, 88, 92–93, 96, 188, 189, 215*n*50
"Hazel Dell" (song; GFR) 38, 40, 52, 80, 212*n*7; score **205–207**; sheet music cover **39**
"Hear the Cry That Comes Across the Sea" (song; GFR) 172, 222*n*29
"Higher" music 28
History of Chicago (Isaac D. Guyer) 112–113
Homer, Levi P. 34–35
"Honor to Sheridan" (song; GFR) 167
Hutchinson Family Singers 31, 100, 111, 112, 128, 217*n*50
Hymns 13, 17, 210*n*26

"If He Can" (song; GFR) 89
"In the Silent Midnight Watches" (song; GFR) 57
"I'se on de Way" ("Freedman's song arranged and composed" by Wurzel; GFR) 141–143
"It Is the Savior's Voice" (song; GFR) 57

"Jewels" (gospel song; GFR) 172
Jimmy's Wooing" (song; GFR) 105
John Church & Company 181, 192, 195
Johnson, A.N. 11, 12, 13, 16, 18, 19, 32
Jones, T. Newton 132, 219*n*15
Jubilee (book; William B. Bradbury) 92
Judge Santa Claus (cantata; GFR) 188
Jullien, Louis Antoine 51
"Just After the Battle" (song; GFR) 139
"Just Before the Battle, Mother" (song; GFR) 49, 139, 146, 162–163, 189; originally "On the Field of Battle, Mother" 134–135, 220*n*25; political parodies 148, 221*n*90
"Just Before Election, Andy" 171; sheet music cover **135**

Kelly and Leon's Minstrels 153, 163
Kernstown, second battle 143
Killip, W.W. 76, 77, 91, 215*n*55
"Kiss Me Mother, Kiss Your Darling" (song; GFR) 145
"Kitty Ryder" (song; GFR) 97, 105
Kreissman, August 73

"Last Days of George F. Root" 224*n*35

"Lay Me Down and Save the Flag" (song; GFR) 143–144
"Lay of the Wounded Heart" (song; GFR) 30
Leather industry 9, 23
Lewis, William 173, 180, 181
Libby Prison 134, 149, 150
Light Guard Band 105, 116, 117, 122, 143, 145, 147, 149
"Lilly Brook" (song; GFR) 89
Lincoln, Abraham 1–2, 24, 108, 112, 121, 129, 132, 144, 146–148, 159, 218n86; assassination 156; burial 158; enlistment of black men 141; first call for volunteers 101; second call for troops 116
Lincoln, Henry T. 27, 28, 29, 31
Lincoln, Robert 193
Lincoln, Tad 1–2
Lind, Jenny 30–31
"Little Daisy" (song based on Fanny Fern's novel, *Ruth Hall*; GFR) 59
London Sunday School Union 190
Longfellow, Henry Wadsworth 189
Loomis, George B. 73, 90
"Lost and Saved" (song; GFR) 183
"Love Thy Mother, Little One" (song; GFR) 106
Lowell, James Russell 190
Lumbard, Frank 116, 127, 145
Lumbard, Jules (J.G.) 96, 104, 109, 116, 137–138, 192, 196
Lumbard brothers 103, 116, 119, 122, 125

"Mabel" (song; GFR) 166
"Man the Ship" (song; GFR) 89
Mann, Horace 25
"Marseillaise" 33–34, 115, 116
"Mary of the Glen" (song; GFR) 45–46, 80
Mason, Lowell 13, 20, 21, 25, 26, 32, 37, 49, 51; and church music reform 16, 17; at musical convention in Richmond, Virginia 68; and New York Normal Musical Institute 55; in Normal Musical Institute at North Reading 71, 73, 78, 95; on "politics and chicanery" of musical conventions 91–92
Mason Brothers (publisher) 35, 55, 57
"May Moore" (song; GFR) 105
McVickers Theater 97, 112
Mendelssohn, Felix 28, 29, 40, 80, 112, 138
Mercer Street church 22, 32, 53, 60, 66
Message Bird 37–38
Messiah (George Frederick Handel) 14, 32, 56, 61, 71, 77, 81
Meyerbeer, Giacomo 112

Military Order of the Loyal Legion of the United States 192
Minstrel show companies and halls 137
Minstrel shows 30, 38
Miss Haines' School for Young Ladies 24
Moody, Dwight L. 130, 172
"Mother, Oh Sing to Me of Heaven" (song; GFR) 106
Mount Vernon 73
"Mourner, Why This Fruitless Sorrow?" song (GFR) 57
Mozart, Wolfgang A. 85
Mulligan, Colonel James A. 143–144
Murfreesboro, or Stone's River, battle 124
Murray, James R. 118, 133, 139, 164, 169, 174, 181
Music in the Civil War 99
Music magazine 193
Music Teachers' National Association 196
Musical conventions (GFR) 37, 59–61, 65–69, 72–73, 81–87, 90–92, 110–111, 162, 169, 185, 214nn6, 8, 17, 24, 215nn67, 68, 73
Musical Curriculum (book; GFR) 148–149, 174, 175
Musical Education Society 11, 16
Musical Fountain (book; GFR) 165–166, 188, 222n3
Musical taste 94, 138, 165, 173–174
Musical Visitor see *Church's Musical Visitor*
"My Beau That Went to Canada" (song; GFR) 161
"My Father's Bible" (song; GFR) 89
"My Heart Is Like a Silent Lute" (song; GFR) 109
"My Home Is on the Prairie" (song; GFR) 89
"My Mother She Is Sleeping" (song; GFR) 89
"My Weary Heart Is All Alone" (song; GFR) 62

National School Singer (book; GFR) 186
"Never Forget the Dear Ones" (song; GFR) 80
New Jerusalem Church (Swedenborgian) 156, 221n125
New Orleans 24
New York City 21–22, 27
New York Clipper 51
New York Musical Review and Choral Advocate 37, 49, 86
New York Normal Musical Institute see Normal Musical Institute
New York State Institution for the Blind 22, 24–25, 28, 32, 54

Nineteenth Illinois Infantry 124, 125, 137, 158; Band 107
"Noble Law of Maine" (song; GFR) 50
Normal Musical Handbook (GFR), 186
Normal Musical Institute 56, 66, 67, 76–77, 90, 95, 113, 169; in Chicago 78, 86, 95, 131; in North Reading, Massachusetts 71, 73, 85, 86, 90, 172–173
Normal schools 55
"North and South" (song; GFR) 161
North Reading, Massachusetts 5, 6, 7, 10–11, 68, 71–72, 209n13

"O Come and Buy My Hot Corn" (song; GFR) 57
"O Come You from the Indies" (later "O Come You from the Battlefield," song; GFR) 105–106
"Oh, Are Ye Sleeping, Maggie" (song arranged by GFR) 89
"Oh, Haste on the Battle" (song; GFR) 123, 125
"Oh, Will My Mother Never Come?" (song; GFR) 139
"Old Folks Are Gone" (song; GFR) 48, 52, 80
"Old Folks at Home" (Stephen Foster) 38, 48
"Old Friends" (song; GFR) 50
"Old Josie" (song; GFR) 57
"On, Boys, On" (song; GFR) 89
"On, On, On, the Boys Came Marching" (song; GFR) 161
"On the Field of Battle, Mother" *see* "Just Before the Battle, Mother"
"On the Red Field of Blood" (song; GFR) 144
"Only Waiting" (song; GFR) 89
Opera 32–33, 51, 57
Organ 18, 20
Our Flag with the Stars and Stripes (cantata; GFR) 193–194
"Our Pastor" (song; GFR) 80
Our Song Birds, "Juvenile Musical Quarterly" 163–164

"Pacific Railroad" (song; GFR) 171
Paris 32–34, 211n39
Park Street Church 6, 19, 20
"Passing Through the Fire" (song; GFR), 182
Peck, Mary F. Root (sister of GFR) 7, 8, 18, 23, 28
Perkins, Theodore 90, 91
Phyllis, the Farmer's Daughter (cantata; GFR) 188

Piano 12, 24
Piano music (GFR) 50
"Pictures of Memory" (song; GFR) 40–47, 212n10; sheet music *41–47*
Pilgrim Fathers (cantata; GFR) 56–57, 59–60
Poe, Edgar Allan 38
"Poor Robin's Growing Old" (song; GFR) 51–52
Popular music 15, 32, 37, 43, 51, 57, 61, 62, 141, 193, 196, 214n2
Potharst, Jacques 33
"Poverty Flat, or Her Letter" (song; GFR) 172
"Prairie" songs 62, 79
Pratt farm 7, 8
Prize for Our Sunday School (book; GFR) 172, 175
Public school music 16
"Public sentiment" 99, 186, 217n10

Quartet, GFR's family 29, 30, 53–54, 61, 78

"Rally Round the Flag" ("Battle Cry of Freedom," song; GFR) 125, 140, 141, 145, 146, 148, 149, 152, 156, 191, 192, 194
"Reaper on the Plain" (song; GFR) 46
Review (originally *Choral Advocate and Singing-Class Journal*) 50, 57, 60, 210n10
Richardson, Nathan 62–65, 196
"Ring the Bells of Heaven" (later words to a tune by GFR) 166
"Rock Me to Sleep, Mother" (song; GFR) 97, 98
Romanticism 36, 57, 215n41
Root, Azariah (grandfather) 7
Root, Charles Towner (son) 28, 29, 48–49, 56, 85, 173; description of Chicago Fire 177–178, 179; in reorganization after Chicago Fire 179–181; treasurer of Chicago Musical College 186
Root, Clara Louise (daughter; married Walter Burnham) 56, 85
Root, Cynthia (sister) 11, 23, 29, 61
Root, Ebenezer Towner (called Towner) 7, 9, 10, 11, 17, 24, 27, 51, 81–82, 96, 181
Root, Frances Amelia (sister) 11
Root, Frederick Ferdinand (father) 6, 7, 8, 9, 10, 17, 18, 23, 27, 29, 219n114
Root, Frederick Woodman (son) 28, 56, 85, 173
Root, George F. 1–3, 6, 7, 10, 11, 91, 122; autobiography, *The Story of a Musical Life* 192; autograph *63*; baptism 209n12; books (writing and compiling) 28,

93–94, 186–188, 211n25; Boston Academy of Music 21, 25; cantatas 188–189; death, funeral and burial 194, 195, 224nn36, 38; fiftieth wedding anniversary 193; flute 16; harmony 73; home in Chicago before the fire *182*; honorary doctorate 185; Illinois State Teachers' Association 163; interior of home in later years *183*; manager of publications, Root & Cady 126; married Mary Olive Woodman 26–27; monument fund 196; New York State Institution for the Blind 22; organ 18; photograph, 1860 *94;* photograph, 1868 *170;* photograph, c. 1870 *173*; piano 13; president of Chicago Musical College 185; private schools for young ladies 22–23, 24, 30; public schools 16; scrap of music manuscript that survived the Chicago Fire *180*; singing-school 16; study in Paris 32–34, 211n39
Root, George F. teaching 16, 21–25, 30, 54–57, 163 (*see also* musical conventions, normal musical institutes); Union Theological Seminary 24; voice class 21; writing music 27, 40, 48, 69, 78–79, 102–103
Root, Helen (sister; married George Adams) 11, 27, 29, 85
Root, Mary (sister; married James B. Peck) 11, 29
Root, Mary (daughter) 106
Root, Mary Olive Woodman (wife) **26–**27, 29, 32, 69, 85, 193–194
Root, Ralph (grandson) 195
Root, Sarah (sister) 11, 14
Root, Sarah Flint (mother) 5, 6, 11, 17, 25, 27, 29, 106, 219n114
Root, William A. (brother) 11, 27, 126, 153–154, 175; business manager, Chicago Musical College 185–186
Root, William Flint (son) 28, 211n26
Root & Cady 2, 86–87, 88, 96, 105, 122, 218n70; acquired sheet music plates of other publishers 169; began to publish sheet music 101; description of store and publishing operation 174–175; expansion in 1861 **98**; moved to Crosby's Opera House 159; outstanding newspaper advertisements 97; planned branch store 153–154; sales and manufacturing, reported 175
Root & Lewis (music company) 181
Root & Sons Music Company 181
Root, George F., & Sons *see* George F. Root & Sons
"Rosalie, the Prairie Flower" (song; GFR) 62, 80, 82, 213n82; sheet music cover *64*
Rossini, Gioacchino 85

Russell, Henry 14–15, 21, 48, 49, 57
Russell & Tolman 88
Rutgers Female Institute 23, 54
Rutgers Street church 23
Ruth Hall (novel; Fanny Fern) 57–59

S. Brainard's Sons, Cleveland 181, 183
Sabbath Bell (book; GFR) 69, 92
Santa Claus' Mistake (cantata; GFR) 188
Schubert, Franz 15, 21, 40, 137
Scott, Col. Joseph R. 125
Scott, Gen. Winfield 128
Secession 96, 115
"See, the Sky Is Darkling" (song; GFR) 27–28, 211n23
Sentiment 49
Seward, Fanny 156
Shawm (book; GFR and William B. Bradbury) 53, 213n42
"She Has Told It to the Winds" (song; GFR) 89
Sheet music 38, 188
Sheffield, Massachusetts 5, 6, 7, 8, 29
"Shining Shore" (song; GFR) 67, 106; score *70*
"Ship of Union" (song; GFR) 80
Silver Chime (book; GFR) 122
Silver Lute (book; GFR) 122–123, 136
Singing Schools 6, 16, 65
"Six Ballads by George Root" (Wurzel) 89
Slavery 111, 114, 121, 124
Smith, Samuel Francis 190
Smithsonian Institution, musical convention in 73, 90
Sneden, Robert Knox 134, 149
"Snipkins," character in Root's *Haymakers*, 74–75, 76, 215n45
Snow White (operetta; GFR) 188–189
"Softly She Faded" (song; GFR) 89
"Somewhere" (song; GFR) 171
Song Messenger of the Northwest (Root & Cady's periodical) 125–127, 174–175, 181
"Song of Spring" (song; GFR) 50
"Songs of the Olden Days" (song; GFR) 181
"Songs from Willow Farm" (six songs by GFR) 89
Spingler Institute 30, 54
"Stand Up for Uncle Sam, My Boys" (song; GFR) 129
Star of Light (cantata; GFR) 224n34
"Starved In Prison" (song; GFR) 159, 161
Steinway and Sons 136–137
Story of the Musical Life (autobiography; GFR) 25
Stowe, Calvin 50
Stowe, Harriet Beecher 3, 77–78

Index

"Summer's Farewell" (song; GFR) 57
Swedenborgian (New Jerusalem) Church 156, 186, 190

Tannery at Willow Farm 8, 10, 17
Temperance 28, 49, 79, 164, 165, 187–188
Thanksgiving Day 24, 84, 109
"That Little Church Around the Corner" (song; GFR) 171
Thayer, Alexander W. 77
Theater 32, 210 *n22*
"There's Music in the Air" (song; GFR) 57, 58, 213*n*57; sheet music cover **58**
"They Have Broken Up Their Camps" (song; GFR) 161
"They Sleep in the Dust" (song; GFR) 48, 80
"They've Sold Me Down the River" (song; GFR) 52
"Topsy Polka" for piano, Wurzel (GFR) 50, 52
Train, Hannah Flint 5, 19
Train, Samuel 5, 6, 10, 19, 23
"Tramp, Tramp, Tramp" (song; GFR) 149, 152–153, 155, 161, 175, 191, 194; broadside **150**; score **202–204**; sheet music cover **151**
Triumph (book of church music; GFR) 170, 175, 176, 222*n*21
Trumpet of Reform (book; GFR) 186–187
Twenty-Ninth U.S. Colored Volunteers 142

Uncle Tom's Cabin (Harriet Beecher Stowe) 38, 50–51, 52, 57, 77
Under the Palms (cantata; GFR) 190
Union Leagues 129
Union Theological Seminary 24, 53, 54, 86
University of Chicago 223*n*1
Upton, George P. 119

"Vacant Chair" (song; GFR) 99, 107–109; score **204**; sheet music cover **108**
Vass & Dean's (band) 122
Verdi, Giuseppe 112
"Voice of Love" (song; GFR) 30

War song concerts 191–192, 193

Washburn, Henry S. 109, 217*n*31
Webb, George James 13–14, 16, 21, 25, 71, 73
"Weeping, Sad and Lonely" ("When This Cruel War Is Over," song; Henry Tucker) 138
Weight lifting 169
Welcome (book; GFR) 186
"We'll Fight It Out Here on the Old Union Line" (song; GFR) 170–171
Western Musical Institute 56
Whittier, John Greenleaf 50, 187
"Who'll Save the Left?" (song; GFR) 125
"Will You Come to Meet Me, Darling?" (song; GFR) 137
William Hall & Son 38, 49, 52, 86
Willis, Nat (N.P.) 6, 58–59
Willis, R. Storrs 56
Willis, Sarah 58
Willow Farm 5, 8, **9**, **10**, 12, 13, 17, 24, 25, 29, 54, 74
Winner, Septimus (pseudonym Alice Hawthorne) 57
Winter Street church 20
"Within the Sound of the Enemy's Guns" (song; GFR) 132
Woodbury, I.B. 28, 32, 49
Woodman, Abby (sister of Mary Olive Woodman Root) 29
Woodman, George (brother of Mary Olive Woodman Root) 27, 29
Woodman, J.C. (brother of Mary Olive Woodman Root) 55–56, 212*n*36
Woodman, Mary Olive (wife of GFR) 26–27
Wood's Minstrels (and Henry Wood) 44, 52
Worcester, Massachusetts 11, 107, 109
Work, Henry Clay 113–115, 126, 130–131, 141
World's Columbian Exposition 193
Wurzel, G. Friederich (GFR pseudonym) 37, 45, 65, 142

"Ye Have Done It Unto Me" (song; GFR) 182
Young Ladies' Choir (book; GFR) 28

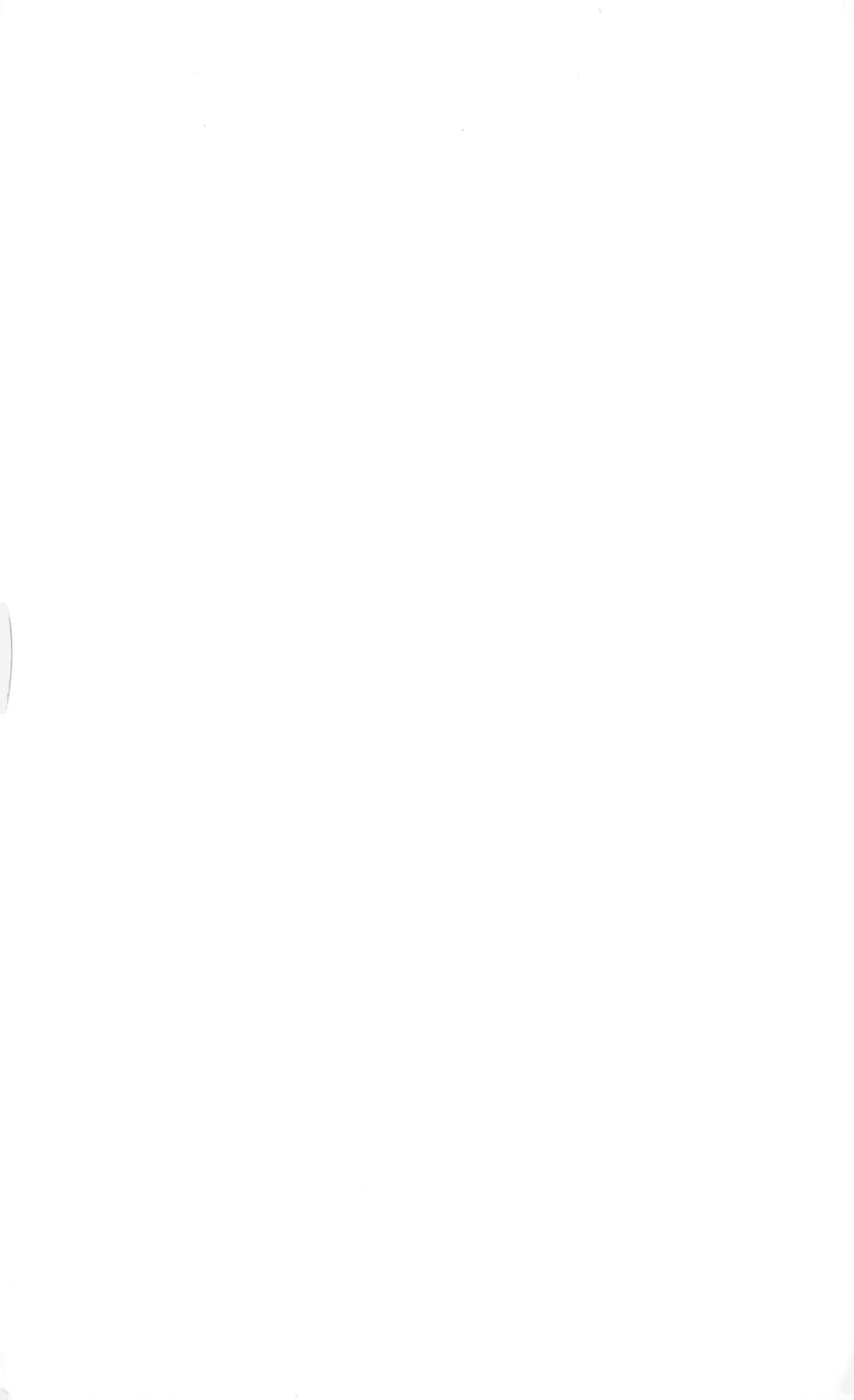